Third Solitudes

Tradition and Discontinuity in Jewish-Canadian Literature

MICHAEL GREENSTEIN

McGill-Queen's University Press
Kingston, Montreal, London

© McGill-Queen's University Press 1989
ISBN 0-7735-0675-6
Legal deposit first quarter 1989
Bibliothèque nationale du Québec

∞

Printed in Canada on acid-free paper

This book has been published with the help of
a grant from the Canadian Federation for the
Humanities, using funds provided by the Social
Sciences and Humanities Research Council of Canada.

Canadian Cataloguing in Publication Data

Greenstein, Michael
   Third Solitudes
   Includes index.
   Bibliography: p.
   ISBN 0–7735–0675–6
   1. Canadian literature — Jewish authors — History
and criticism. I. Title.
   PS8089.5.J5G74 1989   C810'.9'8924   C88–090470–4
   PR9187.2.J48G74 1989

PS
8089.5
.J4
G74
1989

Material reprinted from *The Collected Poems of Irving
Layton* by Irving Layton, and from *The Spice Box of the
Earth* and *Flowers for Hitler* by Leonard Cohen, used by
permission of the Canadian publishers McClelland and
Stewart, Toronto. Material by A.M. Klein reprinted by
permission of the A.M. Klein Estate. Portions of the
following have been reprinted by kind permission of
the authors: *The Tight Rope Walker* by Norman Levine;
Stony Plain and *Out of Place* by Eli Mandel; *Ordinary
Moving* by Phyllis Gotlieb; *Un Amour maladroit* and
Schabbat 70–77 by Monique Bosco; *Collected Poems* by
Miriam Waddington (Toronto: Oxford University
Press, 1986; copyright Miriam Waddington).

Contents

For my wife, Anita,
my children, Jordana and Daniel,
and my parents, with love

Acknowledgments

Portions of this book have been previously published in somewhat different form. I wish to thank George Woodcock and W.H. New for permission to reprint from *Canadian Literature* "Monique Bosco *en abyme*" and "History in *The Second Scroll*"; D.M.R. Bentley for permission to reprint "Canadian Poetry After Auschwitz" from *Canadian Poetry: Studies, Documents, Reviews*, No. 20; Alastair Niven for "Between Ottawa and St. Ives: Norman Levine's Tight-Rope Walkers" in *The Journal of Commonwealth Literature* Vol. XXIII, No. 1; ECW Press (Toronto) and the Canadian Literary Foundation (Toronto) for "Perspectives on the Holocaust in Henry Kreisel's *The Betrayal*" (*Essays on Canadian Writing* #23), and "Richler's Runners: Decentauring St. Urbain St." in *Perspectives on Mordecai Richler* ed. Michael Darling.

To my colleagues at the Université de Sherbrooke and the Université de Bordeaux, I owe much for my sense of Canadian literature. I am also indebted to Eli Mandel, an inspiring teacher, poet, and critic, and to Professors Seymour Mayne, Ira Nadel, Zailig Pollock, and Kenneth Sherman who have helped shape some of the ideas in this book. Professor D.H. Akenson's editorial comments proved invaluable during the process of revision. Also, Adam Quastel and Joan McGilvray at McGill-Queen's have assisted considerably in the final preparation of my manuscript. Finally, I owe my greatest appreciation to my wife Anita who has always been my closest reader and most patient critic.

Third Solitudes

Introduction

From his outpost on the shores of Lake Ontario, that curious American onlooker Leslie Fiedler observes that the Jewish writer in Canada inhabits a "No-man's-Land, the Demilitarized Zone" where he is "invisible from South of the Border as well as from the Other Side of the Atlantic."[1] While Fiedler singles out Leonard Cohen and Mordecai Richler, he overlooks the founder of Jewish-Canadian literature, Abraham Moses Klein — an ironic oversight since Fiedler's first novel, *The Second Stone*, appeared a decade after Klein's *The Second Scroll* first appeared in 1951. Other names need to be added to those mentioned by Fiedler, for in the relatively brief period since World War II when mid-century modernism shades into *fin-de-siècle* postmodernism, Jewish writers have contributed significantly to Canadian literature. Irving Layton and Leonard Cohen in Montreal, Phyllis Gotlieb in Toronto, and Miriam Waddington and Eli Mandel on the prairies have all paid homage to Klein in their poetry. And if Klein has influenced his fellow poets, so too in fiction are Jewish-Canadian authors indebted to him, for Klein's seminal short novel, *The Second Scroll*, acts as a point of departure for short stories and novels by Mordecai Richler, Henry Kreisel, Adele Wiseman, Jack Ludwig, Norman Levine, Naim Kattan, Monique Bosco, and Matt Cohen. At first glance, such a diverse group of writers appear to have little in common, but closer scrutiny reveals their recurrent attempts to mediate between tradition and modernism, home and exile, Jewish-Canadian particularism and universal significance. To understand better the ambiguities of this mediation in the works of Klein and those who follow him, it is necessary to look south of the border and across the Atlantic, for other voices in the Diaspora.

Although Klein published some poems in New York's *Menorah Journal* as early as 1927, and although Ludwig Lewisohn praised him as "the first contributor of authentic Jewish poetry to the English language," his relationship to his Jewish-American audience was as problematic as it was to his gentile Canadian readers.[2] If the New York Intellectuals, from Lionel Trilling (who originally published in the *Menorah Journal*) to Leslie Fiedler, generally disregarded Klein, his fellow poets at Montreal's *Preview* and *First Statement* — Patrick Anderson, Frank Scott, A.J.M. Smith, Leo Kennedy, and John Sutherland — occasionally found difficulties with his more "Jewish" themes. Doubly frustrated by this critical reception, Klein became ambivalent toward both readerships. Partial success and recognition in Canada were not enough for he had always sought an audience beyond Montreal: "The 'little magazine' reviews are good for one's immortal soul, but for one's mortal needs, give me a good spread in *Time* magazine, or a proper accolade in the *New York Times*. They set the tone, and all the bookstore registers echo their melody."[3] But when in 1944 American Jewish critics ignored *The Hitleriad*, he accused them of "dousing their Ellis Island smell with New England spice."[4] Without American registers, his mortal needs became more pressing and, combined with the knowledge of the Holocaust, led eventually to depression and an exile of silence that lasted from the mid-1950s until his death in 1972. It was then up to other Jewish-Canadian writers to pick up where he left off in the *avant-garde* of solitude.

If Klein's final silence or absence contributes to invisibility in a no-man's land, so too does the marginality of Montreal's ghetto where Mordecai Richler echoes Klein's melancholy about their lost tribe north of the border: "Looking down on the cultural life of New York from here, it appears to be a veritable yeshiva. I won't even go into the question of Broadway or television, but from *Commentary* by way of *Partisan Review* to the *Noble Savage*, from Knopf to Grove Press, the Jewish writers seem to call each to each, editing, praising, slamming one another's books, plays, and cultural conference appearances."[5] Despite the fact that Klein considered applying for the editorship of *Commentary* and that Knopf published *The Second Scroll*, despite the fact that two Canadian-born writers (Saul Bellow and Jack Ludwig) edited the *Noble Savage*, Montreal's hushed cosmopolitanism was barely audible beside Manhattan's hum and buzz of implication. Where Klein conducted a one-man show with internal conflicts that included ghost-writing, politics, and the law, the dialectic conflicts presented in *Partisan Review* were shared by many — a Jewish family of three generations. The New York Intellectuals' grand slamming (Rahv, Trilling, Kazin, Howe, Fiedler, Podhoretz) lent visibility and voice to Jewish-American writing: having interpreted modernism to

Americans, they helped pave the way for Bellow, Malamud, and Roth to enter the mainstream. Today, just as in Klein's time, New York's literary domination constitutes one of the poles against which the Jewish-Canadian identity defines itself.

While Jewish-American novelists and poets were well served by a host of Jewish critics who interpreted their work to a vast reading public, no similar critical mediation occurred in Canada where a diminished audience and belated cultural history created a relative vacuum for Klein's silence and invisibility. At Ellis Island, even before the turn of the century, huddled masses of immigrants were welcomed into the American melting pot by the words of Emma Lazarus. Later arrivals to the Port of Montreal, however, received no such welcome, having to wait for recognition in a conservative Canadian mosaic that did not force a quick abandoning of Yiddish roots. Abraham Cahan, editor of the *Jewish Daily Forward* from 1897 to 1951, author of *The Rise of David Levinsky* (1917), and forerunner to a rich Jewish-American literary culture, preceded Abraham Klein by at least a generation. With its head start, Jewish-American culture accommodated its writers by mid-century; in Canada, Klein was marginal in both time and place, and it remained for his successors in poetry and fiction to develop his voice and vision through the second half of this century. As the Jewish-American *alazon* ventures from New York to Chicago to the frontiers of a Hollywood future, the Jewish-Canadian *eiron* in Montreal and on the prairies returns to a vanishing European past.

Instead of embracing Whitman's America, Klein turned on the one hand to European, English, and Irish traditions, from Chaucer, Spenser, and Browning to the modern linguistic experiments of Joyce, and on the other, to Hebrew and Yiddish traditions from the Bible, Hassidism, Cabbala, and the poetry of Bialik. From Leopold Bloom's Dublin odyssey in *Ulysses*, Klein extrapolated polyglot silence, exile, and cunning to the immigrants' diaspora. Some of Klein's followers have also been influenced by Joyce's quest beyond modernism and have developed their own cunning responses to Kleinian silence and Canadian exile. For instance, Henry Kreisel's short story, "Chassidic Song," depicts a confrontation between a liberal Jew, travelling from Montreal to New York to give a paper on Leopold Bloom's Jewishness at a James Joyce conference, and an orthodox Jew, on his way to a Hassidic gathering. Montreal, New York, Dublin, and Hassidic Europe constitute some of the Jewish-Canadian polarities between past and present shared between the modern and traditional Jew. For even while remaining skeptical, secular Jewish-Canadian writers are drawn to a spiritual and mythical past where, in the words of Kreisel's Hassid, "melody is the pen of the soul."[6] So they take up their pens, sing in Yiddish and Hassidic rhythms, and invoke Buberesque dialogues and dances in an effort to overcome post-Holocaust absence. In the spirit and letter — not of the law but of Cabbala and fabled *aggadah* — their imaginations celebrate, with Leonard Cohen and Irving Layton dancing a *freilach*, awaking the miracle rabbis of Prague and Vilna in "Last Dance at the Four Penny." While Cohen links Kafka's Prague to Montreal, Eli Mandel extends the Diaspora's reach in "Snake Charmers" where he joins the magical circle with Klein, Layton, and Cohen, in an exotic marketplace, Djemma el Fna, connecting Paris, New York, Baghdad, and Jerusalem. Similarly, Phyllis Gotlieb, who has paid homage to Klein, writes sing-song verse of Hassidic traditions in Krasilevka, Anatevka, and the magical town of Chelm. Like oriental snake charmers, Jewish-Canadian poets try to lead the blind out of darkness through dazzling memorials and graceful songs that prevail over Klein's invisibility. Linking oriental and occidental ghettos, these poets give voice to the Diaspora's estranged yet familiar secular heritage.[7]

Layton also pays tribute in "Requiem for A.M. Klein" from *The Pole-Vaulter.* In the "Foreword" to this collection Layton proclaims Anne Frank as the prototype of all pole-vaulters who redeem the world. He concludes his volume with "I pole-vault / over my grave": a defiant gymnast of the spirit not only transcends the abyss, but leaps over history, revenging Nazi persecution and Klein's silence. After addressing Klein as a "medieval troubadour" and resolving to listen without irony to younger poets, Layton recalls his own apprenticeship under his teacher:

Though the reverent adolescent
Like the Virgil which fee-less you taught him
Would have taken your hand and led you out
Muttering the learned hexameters like a charm.[8]

Layton reverses the order of immortal bards from Virgil to Klein as he concludes with the latter's "fresh imperishable name." He learns from his precursors and lessons of history to mediate between blindness and vision, silence and voice, black and white, blanks and colours on the page, absence and a hidden Jewish presence — recurrent images in Jewish-Canadian poetry. By extension, in "Requiem for An Age" the poet laments the "muted fragment" of the modern world that silenced Klein. The "final wretchedness" consists of bowing to idols long decayed, old, and blind. In this grey world of uncertainties, "How shall we meet the burden of our times, / Or make profession of our tongue-tied faith / When all the lamps are gutted, one by one?"[9] Looking back through prophetic traditions, Layton transcends the silence and blindness of modernity with his moral vision. As did Klein, Layton meets not only "the burden of our times," but of the past as well.

In another tributary poem for Klein, "Breaking with Tradition," Miriam Waddington pictures "old masters" walking forward but speaking to their followers with backward glances.[10] This break with tradition is simultaneously and paradoxically a joining for Klein and his progeny, a continuity with painterly Dutch masters and Hassidim with fur hats and black greatcoats. In an imageless darkness, Klein's precursors and descendants gather, but their covenant is broken in order to be restored, each generation having to create anew. Tradition as discontinuity and adventure: just as Klein's dialectic both negates and incorporates earlier forms, so later Jewish-Canadian writers may rely on his example before parting company. Anticipating Waddington, Klein begins "A Psalm Touching Genealogy" with "Not sole was I born, but entire genesis" to demonstrate his continuity with centuries of forefathers and patriarchs. His poem ends "And there look generations through my eyes" not just to repeat the recurrence of precursors, but to prophesy the presence of Jewish-Canadian heirs who would touch on his example.[11] Klein's birth announcement incorporates earlier generations and later poets like Waddington, Gotlieb, Layton, Mandel, and Cohen who seek to revoke his silence and namelessness.

While Jewish-Canadian poetry shows a more direct Kleinian influence than corresponding fiction, some short stories and novels attest to his lingering presence. Most noteworthy is Henry Kreisel's paradigmatic "The Almost Meeting" which serves as a parable not just about Kreisel's missed encounter with an already reclusive Klein, but about all belated writers who quest for precursors. Klein's "representative" writes to his "follower": "I sense a bitterness in your hero because he cannot find his father. Let him not despair. An almost meeting is often more important than the meeting. The quest is all."[12] So much Jewish-Canadian fiction deals with the quests of anti-heroes, orphans, adolescents, and immigrants for their parents, their homeland, and a meaningful tradition. The story concludes with Klein's or Kreisel's final words to all exiled intermediaries: "It was impossible for me to see you ... You wanted to ask me things. I have no answers. But you are in my heart. Let me be in your heart also. We had an almost meeting. Perhaps that is not much. And yet it is something. Remember me."[13] This understatement invites invisibility yet underscores an entire theory about anxiety of influence, including Klein's own wrestling with British and biblical traditions which beg to be remembered. Within a Jewish context, direct encounter seems impossible, forbidden in the anti-representational second commandment and forestalled in *The Second Scroll* where Klein's messianic Uncle Melech Davidson exceeds the diasporic reach of his nameless nephew. In addition to this aniconic, temporal agon, there appears a Buberesque dialogue, heart-to-heart, if not face-to-face; forever asking, these writers have memory, desire, and metaphor if not ultimate answers. Klein, through his disappearing double in *The Second Scroll*, foreshadows absence and exile in Jewish-Canadian literature, a cultural mediation that remembers its tradition.

With their transatlantic vision and almost meetings, Klein, Kreisel, and other Jewish writers in Canada are heirs not only to Joyce's modernism and Buber's humanism, but also to the *Wissenschaft des Judentums* (Jewish Science), an intellectual movement that sought to combine Jewish and mainstream European philosophies of the Enlightenment.[14] While nineteenth-century Jewish philosophers attempted to ground their ideas in Hegelian dialectics, the twentieth century's Frankfurt School of Critical Theory demonstrated greater skepticism in its "negative dialectics" — a refusal to reconcile antitheses into a conclusive synthesis. Critical of totalizing authoritarian philosophies and their correspondent manifestation in political fascism, negative dialectics, like Keats's negative capability, seeks to prevent final doctrinaire positions in favour of a more open-ended and open-minded fluidity. A socialist but not a totalitarian communist, Klein, throughout his career, remained skeptical of dialectical modes of thought that could lead to political extremism. In his "Sestina on the Dialectic" (1946) he suspends belief: "But so it never will turn out, returning to rack within, without. And no thing's still."[15] Perhaps this negation is a semitic characteristic stemming from prohibitions in the Mosaic Code, especially the second commandment's anti-representational injunction which led scholars like Erich Auerbach to characterize the Old Testament as mysterious, obscure, "fraught with background" that constantly demands interpretation.[16] As well, it could derive from a form of rabbinic argument, the talmudic *pilpul*, which anticipates modern dialectics. Or, there may be continuities with Maimonides' twelfth-century *Guide for the Perplexed* which warns against interpreting the Bible literally and advocates a negative theology where God's attributes must be comprehended indirectly through negatives.

Whatever the explanations, this propensity for negation culminates in Kafka's enigmatic aphorism — "It is up to us to accomplish the negative. The positive is given" — where explanations immediately break down.[17] Disenchanted with absolutes of totalitarian authority, modern Jewish writers accomplish the negative, criticize, and subvert majorities from their own marginal positions. Some historians have argued both for the modern Jewish character of the Frankfurt School's negative dialectics and for its connection with current postmodern practices of deconstruction.[18] Indeed, the antithetical criticism of Jacques Derrida, Harold Bloom, and Geoffrey Hartman with its open-ended "heretic hermeneutics" has affinities with traditional rabbinic thought and with modern secular Jewish philosophy. Hartman describes Bloom's cabbalistic criticism in terms that would be equally applicable to Klein, Kafka, and Hartman himself: "Mythmaking, as Bloom conceives it, is by no means a synthesis, or redemptive iconography. It is a lyrical and apostrophic movement that never leaves the area of words or dialogic exchange. Like Buber's 'I-Thou,' fundamental words of desire, of an apostrophe that remains open because the desired 'Thou' is a relation and not an object and cannot be fixed or imaged."[19] Hence the quest at the heart of *The Second Scroll* is never fulfilled: another kind of negative, Uncle Melech's photograph is both a double and a multiple exposure, since overexposure to vicissitudes of the Diaspora denies fixed meetings. Without a final synthesis, negative dialectics creates its own third solitude, and Melech Davidson, a messianic figure, eagerly adopts it.

At the essence of its social theory, there is an unmistakable Jewish element in Critical Theory that is deeper than its explicit concern with anti-semitism.

The idea that dialectics is secularized hope, the translation of the desire for transcendence into history, and the identification with the suffering of past generations that are characteristic motifs of Critical Theory owe a great deal to the Jewish Messianic idea. The Messianic impulse, with its emphasis on redemption, utopia, and the radical negation of the existing order was, as Gershom Scholem points out, the "anarchic breeze" in Jewish orthodoxy. It is no less true that Critical Theory, with its similar emphasis, was the "anarchic breeze" in Marxist orthodoxy as well.[20]

When Jewish-Canadian writers from Klein to Richler, Cohen, Ludwig, Wiseman, and Gotlieb invoke Hassidic, cabbalistic, or messianic impulses from their European past, they may add an "anarchic breeze" of humour or irony to their socialist ideals. Their Jewish jokes, in conjunction with their critical skepticism and unorthodox hope, may overpower their powerlessness:

they can mock the exquisite *pilpul* of talmudic commentary while celebrating or reducing to absurdity, the wary ingenuity of the oppressed ... they share with Midrash its unusual habit of inventing dialogues of the most colloquial sort — dialogues that are intimate even in sacred contexts. Martin Buber's fundamental words, "I" and "Thou," that institute a relation of dialogue between God and man, or man and man, may grow out of this tradition.[21]

Buber's dialogue evolved from a childhood experience when he was taken from his parents' home in Vienna to the home of his paternal grandparents in Galicia where he was raised. After his mother's departure, a neighbouring child told him that she would never return, and in response to this trauma, the author of the "I-Thou" relationship "made up the word *Vergegnung* — 'mismeeting,' or 'miscounter' — to designate the failure of a real meeting between men."[22] In all probability, Kreisel was aware of Buber's Viennese autobiographical fragment, but, whatever the case, these almost meetings, Kafka's negative in need of accomplishment, and Klein's wandering away from home in "Autobiographical" serve to combine centres of the Diaspora from Montreal to Vienna and Prague. Moreover, their cabbalistic quests represent dialectical negations of purely rational thought, unearthing in their counter-history what had been hidden in the *Wissenschaft des Judentums*. That hidden subversive element from the first scroll to *The Second Scroll*, from the Freudian subconscious to Kafka's hermeneutic parables, remains in constant need of interpretation, for the final revelation never occurs. Klein's and Buber's pathos, then, is "that of the Jew who is not allowed voice or image except in the form of commentary and quotation, who is denied the image as a place of repose or as an icon blasted out of the past."[23] In part, this stiff-necked resistance to closure or synthesis is the result of a faceless "other" which faces centuries of anti-semitism and an endless waiting against the foreclosures of Christian *figura* where New Testament fulfils Old through Incarnation. Memories of wandering and the wandering of memory replace fixed images and positions. "The ambivalent projection of gentiles about Jews reveals the storied existence of the Jews as the *unresolved* primitive myth of Western civilization, a myth without a resolving ritual, a myth that is therefore acted out to the climax of self-destruction in the politics of the West."[24]

If Buber's "mismeeting" and the Frankfurt School's irresolute negative dialectics display Jewish characteristics, they are also forerunners of Derrida's deconstruction with its emphasis on open-ended free play in language and interpretation, its need to undo Hegelian synthesis. While Klein progressed from traditional forms to modernism and beyond, Derrida is firmly entrenched in post-modernism, and many of his poststructuralist theories may be applied to contemporary Jewish literature. Essential to the Derridean enterprise is a focus on marginal discourse and marginality, the reversal and displacement of such categories as centre and circumference. For Jewish thematics, Derrida's subversive strategy has a twofold consequence. On the one hand, instead of regarding the Jew as an outsider, we may now focus on that figure as central in the development of western culture. On the other, this process of reversal and displacement of hierarchies or established structures questions the relationship between Zion and Diaspora, making the latter predominant. Or, as Klein put it in one of his final, undelivered speeches, "In Praise of the Diaspora," "snatched from the centre, we learned circumference."[25] By its techniques of decentring, shifting margins, and raising the status of a diasporic no-man's land, deconstruction helps us learn the boundaries of Jewish writing in Canada.

Henry Kreisel intuitively deconstructs the notion of marginality in a letter to Roy Daniells in 1968, one year after the first appearance of Derrida's early essays:

If something is "marginal," then it must be marginal to something. So that if the point of reference is a specific *Canadian historical experience*, then clearly my own novels, for instance, are marginal to it. And so is Klein's *Second Scroll*. But what about his *Rocking Chair*? I have even more problems with the image if I remove it from the Canadian context, applying a test I learned from you, but applying it in reverse ... If you set Kafka beside Hasek, then Hasek is clearly more central to Czech experience, and Kafka is marginal. But what a margin! ... I realize that your conception of the margin makes some provision for accommodating writers like Kafka, but at the same time the image of the "margin" doesn't stand by itself. It has to be explained, and that weakens its impact. On the other hand, I grant you that it has the qualities of "teasing" us "out of thought."[26]

With their reversals, displacements, and thoughtful teasings Kreisel's marginal comments move in a Derridean direction or Kafkaesque trajectory that seeks a *via negativa*, foregrounding *The Second Scroll* and subsequent Jewish writing in Canada.

A Canadian Derridean, Robert Kroetsch, traces margins, mazes, dislocations, irresolution, blurred photographs, and genealogical quest patterns in Canadian writing: "A.M. Klein, in *The Second Scroll* (1951), anticipates all these quests (a kind of reverse migration) with a quest that is religious and political and formal in its implications."[27] Indeed, Kroetsch's postmodern quest differs from Northrop Frye's earlier observations comparing Jewish and Canadian histories: "I use a Jewish metaphor because there is something Hebraic about the Canadian tendency to read its conquest of a promised land, its Maccabean victories of 1812, its struggle for the central fortress on the hill at Quebec, as oracles of a future. It is doubtless only an accident that the theme of one of the most passionate and intense of all Canadian novels, A.M. Klein's *The Second Scroll*, is Zionism."[28] But for Jewish writers the promised land may lie elsewhere, the sense of loss may override victories, the central fortress may be replaced by a decentred diaspora — not as oracles of a future, but of a past to be regained. Alternating between dystopia and utopia, the Diaspora's labyrinth frustrates Zion. Frye's question about Canadian identity — where is here? — becomes compounded by a Jewish question — where was there? Klein's nameless narrator, a no-name man in no-man's land, mediates the transformations between old and new worlds, old and new languages, Zion and Diaspora. With a Hebrew alphabet, written from right to left, and an historical pull to eastern ancestries, Jewish writers reverse migrations and revert to origins. What Klein's double or multiple exposure captures are Fiedler's sense of Canada's invisibility, the first scroll's aniconic injunction, the irresolution of negatives, Kreisel's almost meeting, and Derrida's trace.

Another of Derrida's key linguistic and philosophic concepts is *différance*. The modern Jewish writer in Canada experiences *différance* not only with respect to a majority gentile culture, but also in relation to his own religion from which he is alienated. This "dissemination" of traditional meaning and authority places the writer in a "decentred" system affording unlimited freedom that must somehow be restrained through the formal act of writing. Jewish-Canadian writers find themselves decentred in several ways: they may look beyond the walls of their ghetto toward a Canadian vastness in nature or a gentile majority in society; they may look to the United States as a major centre of the Diaspora or they may look toward various European centres for their roots. To the Canadian sense of lonely long-distance runners probing a receding horizon, the Jewish perspective adds a belief that the answer to all quests and questions is always over the next horizon. But, there is never an answer. *Différance* is wandering — nomadic texts, mean(der)ings. Derrida also uses *différer* in the sense of "to defer." Just as spatial dimensions multiply and scatter, so time is deferred both through messianic rejection and backward through tracing of origins. Memory undermines the pragmatism of the present. In addition to spatial and temporal interference, religious and linguistic dissemination lead to a disorienting of identity, so that the marginal Jew fills absence with writing, revising a tradition from his own secular perspective. Mediation, displacement, deferment, exile, absence, equivocal meaning — these are the themes not only of Derridean interpretation, but of Jewish writing in Canada from Klein to the present.

Consider one of Derrida's autobiographical fragments from his Algerian childhood:

In Algeria, in the middle of a mosque that the colonists had changed into a synagogue, the Torah once out from *derrière les rideaux*, is carried about in the arms of a man or child ... Children who have watched the pomp of this celebration, especially those who were able to give a hand, perhaps dream of it long after, of arranging there all the bits of their life.

What am I doing here? Let us say that I work at the origin of literature by miming it. Between the two.[29]

This passage is fraught with instability and displacements: Algeria is both colony and part of the Diaspora; mosque has been transformed into synagogue; the Torah shifts from a veiled middle position towards other peripheries; the watching child is watched by adult memory; and the hint of a *rite de passage* between child and adult suggests an intermediary stage for rearranging origins through repetition. If this Algerian scene seems remote from Canada, one need only remember how Klein's narrator tours the Jewish section of North Africa and visits the synagogue in Safed in Israel where an old man and young boy probe the deepest mysteries of Torah. Or, closer to home, one may turn to Klein's description of his Montreal synagogue: "in the centre of the synagogue ... before the Ark of the Covenant, there was sound and exaltation. Wine had been drunk, and the Torah was being cherished with singing and dance ... Circular, too, was the dance, a scriptural gaiety, with wine rejoicing the heart, and Torah exalting it to heights that strong wine could not reach."[30] Klein, poet of Hassidic joy, transcends Klein, lawyer of Torah's laws, even as he distances himself from participating in the service. Insider and outsider interchange in a fluctuating state of "in-betweenness."

Leonard Cohen also shifts boundaries of the Diaspora in his departure from Klein's more central Torah, yet he too tries to capture its spirit in "Lines from my Grandfather's Journal":

Doubting everything that I was made to write. My dictionaries groaning with lies. Driven back to Genesis. Doubting where every word began. What saint had shifted a meaning to illustrate a parable. Even beyond Genesis, until I stood outside my community, like the man who took too many steps on Sabbath. Faced a desolation which was unheroic, unbiblical, no dramatic beasts.

The real deserts are outside tradition ...

Prayer makes speech a ceremony. To observe this ritual in the absence of arks, altars, a listening sky: this is a rich discipline.[31]

In his ritual of absence, Cohen's observant skepticism celebrates tradition and modern individual talent. Dictionaries lie because their definitions fail to capture metaphoric resonances of poetry, so Cohen traces language back to absent origins via parabolic drifts and shifting meanings. To revise family lines the Jewish secularist is driven back in memory even as he is driven forward through a modern Canadian landscape. Just as Kreisel's Hassid tells his secular counterpart to remember his grandfather, so Leonard Cohen — a postmodern Jew from Westmount — remembers his grandfather in strangely discontinuous songs that return to a Hassidic past destroyed by Hitler. Cohen shares both the emptiness the Hassid had felt after the Holocaust and the mystical presence that later filled him in Montreal. These orphans and immigrants look for substitute fathers in their grandfathers' texts, and reject real uncles in favour of the mythical. Disciples of this rich anarchy step from the vanguard of postmodernism backward to Klein's grandfatherly journal and Kafka's parable: "Leopards break into the temple and drink the sacrificial chalices dry; this occurs repeatedly, again and again: finally it can be reckoned on beforehand and becomes part of the ceremony."[32] Klein, Cohen, Kafka, and Derrida open the ceremony of the Diaspora where meanings shift, outsiders are admitted as insiders, and dramatic beasts exchange places with priests in a typically Jewish conflict with Jewry. The Torah procession may recede for these secular writers, but they retain just enough of the fervour of Hassidic joy on one side, and moral outrage or prophetic indignation on the other. In exile they write home.

Much of this equivocation in negative dialectics and deconstruction derives from the uncertainties and insecurities of exile. A classic modern statement on homelessness appears in Freud's essay on "The Uncanny" (1919) with its lengthy etymological opening equating *heimlich* and *unheimlich*, home and homelessness, canny and uncanny. After quoting extensively from dictionaries in several languages (including Hebrew), Freud concludes: "Thus *heimlich* is a word the meaning of which develops towards an ambivalence, until it finally coincides with its opposite, *unheimlich*."[33] If deconstructors mine this essay for its reversals of "uncanny," so too do modern Jewish hermeneuts, as Freud's essay masks his attitude to a Judaic past. As Charles Péguy has said of the Jews, "Being elsewhere [is] the great vice of this race, the great secret virtue, the great vocation of this race."[34] This "being elsewhere," this *différance*, constitutes the unresolved ambivalence of otherness in a ubiquitous diaspora from Europe to North America. Jewish-Canadian literature, in particular, turns back to a lost European tradition to help forge a new identity in its relatively unsettled Canadian homeland of vestigial ghettos.

In "Autobiographical" Klein proceeds "out of ghetto streets," wanders away from "home and the familiar" to seek a fabled city in "Space's vapours and Time's haze," but his passage from home is indeed a "dying off." Sensitized to exile, Klein pauses to observe the Indian Reserve at Caughnawaga, just outside of Montreal: "This is a grassy ghetto, and no home."[35] What for Klein had been a physical reality in his childhood, takes on figurative nuances in later writers. George Woodcock, for instance, relies on this metaphor to underline Canadian themes of isolation and division: "Jewish writers have also revealed with a peculiar force and sensitivity the tensions that are characteristic of Canadian life ... It might be a metaphorical exaggeration to describe Canada as a land of invisible ghettos, but certainly it is, both historically and geographically, a country of minorities that have never achieved assimilation."[36] Mordecai Richler delineates Montreal's invisible ghetto: the "ghetto of Montreal has no real walls and no true dimensions. The walls are the habits of atavism and the dimensions are an illusion. But the ghetto exists all the same."[37] Demonstrating that atavistic habits die hard, no less intrepid a *voyageur* than Irving Layton sketches his view of Hochelaga: "In Montreal the dominant ethnic groups stare at one another balefully across their self-erected ghetto walls. Three solitudes. I remember this feeling of anxiety I had as a boy whenever I crossed St Denis Street. This street marked the border between Jewish and French-Canadian territories. East of St Denis was hostile Indian country densely populated with church-going Mohawks somewhat older than myself waiting to ambush me."[38]

At the very heart of Jewish-Canadian literature, this tension between erecting and destroying ghetto walls, between constructing boundaries and assimilating territories, between *voyageur* and blind *voyeur*, preoccupies the major poets and novelists who, for the most part, originate in Montreal's third solitude. They mediate between English and French solitudes, and Klein's "schizoid solitudes." Out of St Denis, St Dominique, and St Urbain, Layton, Bellow, Richler, and Klein dream pavement into Bible-land, combining street savvy with

a transcending tradition where one-armed jugglers, tightrope walkers, pole-vaulters, dangling men, gymnasts of the spirit, and ambivalent acrobats defy gravity. From their intermediate vantage point,
these writers and their ironic personae survey a Montreal which is at
once both more and less than home, charged with more reality and
human feelings than any other place.

Exile within Montreal's narrow ghetto may be carried over to the
broader prairies, that other centre of Jewish-Canadian creativity. In
"Driving Home," Miriam Waddington traverses prairie grain
elevators and drives to the Volga on the world throughway to unearth
ancestral roots. At the end of the Wandering Jew's peregrinations, the
poet turns *schlemiel*, adopting a self-ironic persona in dispersed free
verse:

> I am on my way home:
>   home?
> Fool
>   you *are* home
>   you were home
> in the first place.[39]

But in tracing roots towards an origin, the displaced poet may discover that the first place is an illusion no longer retrievable, the nameless expanse of prairie and Diaspora. Waddington arrives at the same
conclusion or unknown destination in "My travels" where she repeats
that uncanny feeling of being at once lost and at home:

> I am homesick I
> am packing up
> I am going home
> but now I don't
> know anymore
> where home is.[40]

Home may be dispersed among the Promised Lands of America,
Jerusalem, the *shtetlach* of Eastern Europe, or the capitals of Western
Europe. If the modernist Jew perceives this century as a global
ghetto, then he maps lines of demarcation, borders, boundaries, margins of discourse, and walls to contain his homelessness and childhood memories. In "Fortunes" Waddington is "untraditional, North
American / Jewish, Russian, and rootless in all four," seeking "a
homecoming / for my homeless half-and-half soul."[41] Culturally
hyphenated in schizoid solitude, Jewish artists grapple with the

paradoxes of ghetto cosmopolitanism or urban regionalism, of multiplicity and nothingness, rich sources and lack of status. Like Montreal's writers recapturing home, Waddington, Adele Wiseman, and Jack Ludwig travel across the prairies, the Atlantic, and Europe with an uncertain passport and burdensome baggage.

One of Richler's protagonists, another homeless half-and-half soul, thinks of himself as a guilty Diaspora Jew, carrying his double burden of the past and a copy of Maimonides' *Guide for the Perplexed*:

Canadian-born, he sometimes felt as if he were condemned to lope slant-shouldered through this world that confused him. One shoulder sloping downwards, groaning under the weight of his Jewish heritage (burnings on the market square, crazed Cossacks on the rampage, gas chambers, as well as Moses, Rabbi Akiba, and Maimonides); the other thrust heavenwards, yearning for an inheritance, weightier than the construction of a transcontinental railway, a reputation for honest trading, good skiing conditions.[42]

More than just the shoulders of this Jewish-Canadian anti-hero are dislocated. As in Richler's dualistic confusions and cultural hyphenations (Canadian-born, slant-shouldered), and in response to an unstable inheritance, Jewish-Canadian literature mediates between marginal man and his discourse. Following Maimonides, authors of latter-day guides for the perplexed — Kafka, Derrida, Klein — advocate negatives, non-literal approaches to a modern diaspora, and a subversive resistance to closure. Their shoulders provide a unique slant or critical perspective on the dominant culture that articulates both an inside and outside view. In the absence of absolutes, their jeremiads and secular Hassidism offer an ethical and spiritual dimension that weighs them down and buoys them up. Breaking and joining with tradition, Jewish-Canadian memory rises out of lost homes and voices to populate a no-man's land with figures of the imagination.

CHAPTER ONE

Doublecrossing the Atlantic in A.M. Klein's The Second Scroll

In any case we Jews are not painters. We cannot depict
things statically. We see them always in transition,
in movement, as change. We are story-tellers.

Kafka

When Klein saw the cover design of his book, he wrote enthusiastically to his publisher: "The Second Scroll bursting forth — as from flame — from behind the curled parchment of the first — that was an inspiration! A new and improved form of the palimpsest! Above all, a commentary."[1] Endless commentary, in the form of five glosses in *The Second Scroll*, is in a talmudic tradition of explaining and amplifying the first scroll, and in turn Klein's exegetical peregrinations match the endless wandering of his narrator and Uncle Melech throughout the Diaspora. As Klein travels through the first half of this century, he is caught between two theories of history — cyclical and dialectic — one corresponding to the curled design of scroll, the other corresponding to an improved palimpsest where seconds progress from originals. History may repeat itself cyclically or it may advance to new stages in a Hegelian dialectic, but Klein is not fully at home in either theory as he breaks circles, negates dialectical synthesis, and seconds "a testament already seconded."[2] Always in a double bind, Klein's nameless narrator admits that he is "bound to the country of my father's choice, to Canada," just as he is bound for Israel; and his narrative ends inconclusively as he turns from Safed, one of his fabled cities.[3]

The first epigraph to Klein's text comes from Milton's *Areopagitica*: "And ask a Talmudist what ails the modesty of his marginal Keri that Moses and all the prophets cannot persuade him to pronounce the textual Chetiv." *The Second Scroll* pronounces textual *Chetiv* (the Five Books of Moses) in the immodesty of its own marginal *Keri* (added commentary). Klein's re-reading of the original consists of marginal discourse — footnotes leading to glosses of poems, aesthetic essay, play, and prayer. And the philosophy of marginal discourse is well suited to the subject of his text — the sociology of marginal man, in the person of Melech Davidson, a messianic figure forever disappearing throughout twentieth-century diaspora. Thus, Klein's second epigraph, Rabbi Levi Yitschak of Berdichev's Hassidic questions, ("where shall I find Thee? where art Thou not to be found?") refers not only to man's quest for the divine, but to all other senses of Buber's "I-Thou" relationship. The question applies to the narrator's search for his Uncle Melech, his genealogy, and his Jewish-Canadian identity, as well as Klein's quest in communicating with his reader. Derrida also uses one of Rabbi Levi Yitschak's sayings as the basis for linguistic theory: "Polysemy is the possibility of a 'new Torah' capable of arising out of the other."[4] This statement applies precisely to Klein's polysemous new version of the Bible with its omnipresent absence, its invention of a new identity out of an old tradition, and its striving after an over-determined representation in the face of a second commandment which inhibits representation.

From the very beginning of *The Second Scroll*, Klein announces a fraternal conflict between the narrator's father and Uncle Melech, a family feud that goes as far back as Cain and Abel, Jacob and Esau, Joseph and his brethren. Wishing to emulate his uncle, the young narrator asks for a photograph but is reminded of the second commandment forbidding such a practice. He is thus forced to imagine and "retouch" the photograph of Melech Davidson: "this afforded me an interesting pastime, for as the years went by and I myself changed from year to year, the image of Uncle Melech that I illegally carried in my mind also suffered its transformations" (20). If Klein's imagination transgresses visual prohibitions, so too does he "illegally" carry his burden of the past as he tries to revise the first scroll. Indeed, if the original *Genesis* offers numerous examples of the struggle for primogeniture, Klein's version more than hints at his own anxiety of influence. Compounding these visual restrictions is the silence of the opening words ("refused to permit in his presence even the mention of that person's name") and of Klein's final years. These audio-visual taboos range from his father's frozen face with its "stony stare Semitic" to the double or multiple exposure of Melech's photograph to his unrecognizable corpse. Klein wrestles with blindness and silence, unseen voices and spectres of anteriority. In his universe of absence presided over by an eclipsed God, he seeks memory and metaphor for a photograph fraught with background.

Instead of indulging in iconography, the young narrator is forced to decipher letters. The letters of the Hebrew alphabet, like the four-legged aleph, are "mystic blocks" which send "angel pennies" during the boy's lessons. These lessons, in turn, sensitize the boy to European letters with their strange script and unfamiliar numerals. While

Melech is so far removed from worldly matters that he cannot identify the countenances on coins, his brother-in-law points to the coin
image of a more material *melech*, King George V. Yet when Melech
lapses, his nephew internalizes the strange metamorphosis: "I made
myself a new image of the uncle who together with angels had stood
invisible and auspicious over my Hebrew lesson" (25–6). Where
Abraham smashed his father's idols and Moses smashed the tablets,
Abraham Moses Klein inherits iconoclasm but turns it against these
very forefathers in his desire to create new images and visibility. Since
the post-office, like fate, plays blindman's buff with Melech's letter,
and since another of his letters with a missing first page is purloined,
the obstacles to image-making are insurmountable. Uncle Melech,
the object of Klein's quest, is hidden but not lost (52). Just as
Michelangelo shows (and does not show) the face of God, just as
Maimonides' circular pentimento sentence (52, 111) "covers" the ceiling of the Sistine Chapel, so Klein's scroll acts as a palimpsest over
earlier testaments. And that palimpsest blurs images, retaining
irreconcilable differences of a heretic hermeneutics.

One method of unraveling *The Second Scroll* is to examine the
autobiographical "Gloss Aleph," for it contains some important
themes developed throughout the rest of the book:

> Out of the ghetto streets where a Jewboy
> Dreamed pavement into pleasant Bible-land,
> Out of the Yiddish slums where childhood met
> The friendly beard, the loutish Sabbath-goy,
> Or followed, proud, the Torah-escorting band,
> Out of the jargoning city I regret,
> Rise memories.

Like Milton in the opening lines of *Paradise Lost*, Klein suspends the
subject of his first stanza by preceding it with a triple parallelism,
"Out of," a phrase with three-fold connotations of space, time, and
transformation. In the spatial interpretation, a wandering Jewboy
travels out of Montreal's ghetto to an external diaspora, between
oriental and occidental realms as he encompasses the twain; temporally, memories rise out of the poet's childhood as he recalls his nonage
days, shifting from origins to messianic deferment; the metamorphic
interpretation includes an imaginative transformation of Bible-land
out of pavement, as language transcends physical deprivation. His
three-fold emergence nevertheless renders him marginal as a poet,
a Canadian, and a Jew awaiting his autobiographical agon through

misdirected letters like "four-legged alephs" which slouch towards a fabled city, neither Bethlehem nor Byzantium. Klein interweaves all three interpretations in his novel and although the temporal is the most important, it may be useful to begin with an investigation of his spatial odyssey through the Diaspora.

Where Joyce focuses on a single day in Dublin, Klein scatters his encyclopedic knowledge around the Diaspora. Lacking the unities of time and place, *The Second Scroll* uses two symbols to emphasize spatial dissemination — the ocean and the airplane. The narrator must overcome the vastness separating new world from old, his Canadian origins from Uncle Melech's European boundaries. Melech, who "had completely weathered the ocean of the Talmud" (30), refers to the Atlantic as "that futile bucket" which is unable to extinguish the fires of the Holocaust, and concludes his letter with a description of the blue and white colours of the Mediterranean where the Israeli Navy of Redemption sails. If the Atlantic is powerless to douse the genocidal fires, it also cannot dissipate the odour of Casablanca's *mellah*: "Not all the breezes of the Atlantic, less than a mile away, have yet effected a purification" (60). While a marine abyss contrasts with a land-locked ghetto, it acts as a counterpoint for the dispersal of the Diaspora. In his allusion to Jonah in the whale, Melech repeats the ocean's destructive power: "The waters compassed me about" (112), which is echoed in his nephew's poem, "And in that Drowning Instant," where the poet fades and vanishes in ghettos from Amsterdam to Cordova. Ultimately he reaches the Temple at Jerusalem, "For the third time my body rises / And finds the good, the lasting shore!" heterodoxly on the margins of oceanic exile (141).

To counteract the water's separation and demonic force, Klein employs the airplane as an apocalyptic symbol which shrinks diasporic distances. "Leviticus" begins with the narrator's plane roaring over the Atlantic. In addition to its Daedalus-Icarus associations, the flight is eschatological: "on the wings of eagles" the narrator is "borne" to his destination, oriented in perverse oriental directions, going forward and backward synchronically and diachronically. In the Diaspora's *deus ex machina*, he is transported and transformed. "My very levitation seemed a miracle in harmony with the wonder of my time; through my mind there ran the High Holiday praise of God for that He did 'suspend worlds on without-what,' even as my plane was suspended, even as over the abyss of recent history there had risen the new bright shining microcosm of Israel" (39). "Levitation" picks up the title of the chapter, while his miraculous flight is a "re-enactment" or rebirth with an obvious play on "borne": the *luftmensch's* suspension between ancient and modern testaments finds its transcendence in another scroll and another kind of epic after Homer, Milton, and Joyce.

The opening of the final chapter parallels "Leviticus": "Warmed by the sun beating through the porthole, my mind was dreamily in communion with the murmur of the motors humming through aluminum. They made me whatever music my mind willed, ululative, Messianic, annunciatory. It was as if I was part of an ascension, a going forward in which I was drawn on and on." Like the earlier "levitation," this "ascension" is highly charged with meaning as are the leviathans of the Mediterranean which, covered by "white horses," recall Melech's description of the sea with other leviathans. An old man from Safed makes the final connection between the messianic airplane and its ability to diminish distances, to cross oceans almost instantly. When the narrator announces that the airplane makes the transatlantic journey "not so great a distance," the venerable sage begins his explication:

It is the Messiah's days because we see his signs and portents everywhere. Thus it is written that when the Messiah will come there will be the wonder of *kvitzath ha-derech*, the curtailment of the route. What does this mean? It means that a route which but yesterday was long and arduous suddenly becomes short and speedy. Is this not the experience of our time? Is it not the experience of the Yemenites who, located as if on another planet, as if in another century, are brought by planes to this our century and to this our planet, our country, our home, in the space of but eight hours?" (88)

By shrinking time and oceanic distances, Klein's airplane fosters an illusion of centring, but the old man's interpretation must be taken with a grain of salt. Since he appears "bearded like antiquity ... not of this world," he is not of "our century." Thus, rather than being brought together by the airplane's speed, the Diaspora's time zones prolong routes, messianic presence, and redemption.

Indeed, how does Klein reconcile this sage's eschatological "curtailment of the route" with his own experience of a deferred quest or prolongation of the diasporic route? The very contradiction is built into the word "route" itself, which means to break — breaking new ground, pathfinding, earth-shattering. *The Second Scroll* breaks with earlier sacred texts in its attempt to stake out new territory, to discover new directions for Jewish-Canadian literature. The distances between the old man and skeptical narrator, between first and second scrolls, and between curtailment and prolongation of routes cannot be resolved; instead, Klein invokes poststructuralist *aporia* or talmudic *taiku*, the "magic cataleptic word" whose initials stand for *Tishbi yetaraitz kushioth v'abayoth* (the Tishbite would resolve all problems and difficulties). In his epiphany of the epic revealed, the narrator notices poetry everywhere, even in the secularization of the Hebrew language; for instance, from its talmudic sense, *taiku* has come to indicate a tied football score in modern usage. Since ultimate answers must be held in abeyance, the best the narrator can hope for is the act of translation, but Klein is engaged in far more than translating from Hebrew to English. He translates from first to second scroll, creating new contexts, mediating between multiple experiences of time and place. Having visited the Arch of Titus in Rome which becomes "an irony directed against itself" (like so many other ironies in Klein's purview), the nephew recalls Uncle Melech's cabbalistic phrase about fashioning "Aught from Naught" (86). Waiting in Italy for his turn to board a ship for Israel, Melech pauses over his hope and "revolves" it, "as ben Bag-Bag was wont to do to the texts of Holy Writ — about and about." Out of this decentring, he makes "an introspective game ... a sacred play," not unlike the Israeli football game. His textual revisions commence with the Bible as he imagines the command to leave his father's house in Russia or Canada for his forefather's home in Israel. To follow the route is to break the routine of ghetto regionalism, to go from Montreal's familiar streets to a fabled city. Melech then supplements his biblical scroll with talmudic commentary: "a benediction not yet composed, the Tishbite Elijah will compose it." Klein translates texts and traditions while waiting for the Tishbite's resolution of divergent routes (37).

While the narrator quests for his uncle through a diaspora separated by oceans and joined by airplanes, the temporal separation of nephew and uncle forms part of a larger historical pattern. Klein incorporates two fundamental theories of history in his book — the cyclic, which he may have derived from Vico, and the progressively linear, inherited from the dialectics of Hegel and Marx on the one hand, and talmudic *pilpul* on the other. To the rationalism and resolution of dialectics he opposes his own negative dialectics; to cyclic completion he opposes more "open" mystical circles; and both remain irreconcilable in Klein's aesthetics of fluctuation.

On a literal level, *The Second Scroll* covers events from 1917 to 1949, from the Russian pogroms to an Arabic "pogrom" in which Melech is murdered. Thus, Klein implies that history is cyclical; history oscillates between these demonic moments and the "apocalyptic dream of a renewed Zion" (27). From the outset Klein emphasizes the temporal, not only in his apocalyptic reference to Eden which reminds the reader of the historical distance between first and second scrolls, but in the simultaneous review of the narrator's childhood. This positive mood continues at the Feast of Rejoicing in the Law when his father's happiness is interrupted by the arrival of Uncle Melech's letter which brings news of the pogrom in Ratno. "Genesis" ends with a further descent into the diabolic as the Nazis invade Poland. Yet this demonic "cloud" over Europe changes to a redemptive dream of a renewed Zion at the beginning of "Exodus" as the narrator envisions the battle of Gog and Magog: "I saw through my mind's eye a great black aftermath cloud ... The cloud then began to scatter ... until revealed there shone the glory of a burnished dome." "Leviticus" begins with an apocalyptic flight, but is followed by a demonic descent into Casablanca's *mellah* in "Numbers": "we slid into the mellah ... descending into the ... centuries" (62). "Deuteronomy", however, remains optimistic from the opening flight to the transformed Sephardic elevator-boys ("whose houses but a year ago must needs be lower than the lowest Arab's") to the Safed scholar who expatiates on messianic resurrection.

But Klein's cyclic view of history goes beyond this vertical pattern of the rise and fall of life. In Miriam Waddington's words, "For Klein, as for Shelley, language itself is a vast cyclic poem."[5] Perhaps the most recurrent image in *The Second Scroll* is the circle or cycle used either in an historical sense of a wheel come full circle or in a mystical geometry as with Yeats's gyre;[6] moreover, centre and circumference symbolize the relationship of Zion to Diaspora. In "A Psalm Touching Genealogy" Klein sees himself as part of the historical circle of the risings and fallings of his forefathers:

They dwell in my veins, they eavesdrop at my ear,
They circle, as with Torahs, round my skull,
In exit and in entrance all day pull
The latches of my heart, descend, and rise —

The same metaphors appear early in the novel: "A year of the reading of the Law had been concluded, a year was beginning anew, the last verses of Deuteronomy joined the first of Genesis, the eternal circle continued. Circular, too, was the dance, a scriptural gaiety, with wine rejoicing the heart, and the Torah exalting it to heights that strong wine could not reach" (20). The annual cycle and the circular scroll of the Pentateuch are followed by the Hassidic circle which, in its most extreme form, verges on the mystical. This joyous celebration contrasts with its tragic counterpart in Europe when the Nazis force Jewish women to strip and circle the synagogue in vulgar imitation of the *hakofos*. The "corpuscular" image from Klein's "Psalm" is used as well in *The Second Scroll* when Melech expresses the cyclical unity of Jewry during the Holocaust: "the numbered dead run through my veins their plasma, that I must live their unexpired six million circuits" (30).

Klein's interpretation of Christianity is circular too, as seen in the nephew's dream of Melech as Pope, a transformation borrowed from Joyce's conversion of Bloom into Leopold the First: "he performed the annual cycle of religious rite. ... the long round of his encyclicals" (45). But Melech confirms his faith in Judaism by including the thirteen credos of Maimonides at the end of his letter to Piersanti: "In a single circular sentence, without beginning or end, he described God coming to the rescue of His chosen." The mystical circle reappears in the theorizing of the Zionist journalist beside the narrator on his flight to Israel: Jewry "lost itself in the contemplation of the One; with commentary hooped upon commentary it constricted Him until from Circle He diminished to Dot" (72). This self-ironic deflation applies both to the creative artist and his work which shrink from periphery to nothingness — lost, lacunal. Portraits of poets in the Israeli landscape belong to this mystical circle: "In adamic intimacy the poets had returned to nature ... the marabou, amorphous, mystical, circling ever in a round" (81). In the novel's final scene the narrator, "As at the centre of a whirlwind," prays for his uncle and watches "the beacons announcing new moons, festivals, and set times"; though not as circular as the beginning and end of *Finnegans Wake*, these concluding words of "Deuteronomy" act as a *ricorso* for a return to "Genesis." And at the end of "Gloss Beth" the poet prays to God, "Circled and winged in vortex of my kin": "Again renew them as they were of old, / And for all time cancel that ashen orbit / In which our days, and hopes, and kin, are rolled."

Thus, history, literature, and religion form part of a universal circle. Furthermore, the two-fold quest at the novel's core is cyclical: nephew and uncle, seeker and sought, are identical; language and poetry reside in a ubiquitous miracle — words made flesh. That the narrator and his avuncular double are the same is evident when the nephew repeats, "I was like one that dreamed. I, surely had not been of the captivity; but when the Lord turned again the captivity of Zion, I was like one that dreamed," (28) which is soon echoed in Melech's letter: "When the Lord turned again the captivity, I was like one that dreamed" (31). The distance between the two men diminishes until, in Israel, the narrator discovers that "A change in our relationship had ensued; it was he, I felt, who was now pursuing me" (78). The doppelgänger, or its Yiddish equivalent, the obsessive *dybbuk*, serves Klein well in a work about doubling or seconding. In Safed, the thirteen-year-old boy with his *Baba Kama* parallels the narrator at the same age with his *Baba Bathra*, and the venerable sage, like Melech, is an "anticipatory figure, an image of the boy an era hence" (88). Similarly, in the cyclical and deferred quest for "the poetry of the recaptured time," a key image is the miracle where centre and periphery interact.

Running counter to this cyclical view of history is a progressive philosophy which proceeds through dialectic. Malcolm Ross summarizes the stylistic tension in Klein's poetry: "Klein has come close to creating the archetypal Canadian pattern — a dense organic fusion of traditional idiom, ancient myth and cult, the contrapuntal dialectic of our French-English relationship, the sophisticated technical reach of man alive in this age and in whom all ages are alive."[7] The opening conflict between lapsed uncle and orthodox father commences the dialectics. The father maintains primitive notions about the philosophy of Marxism; he displays his antipathy to dialectics in the *reductio* "Hegel-baigal," a rhyme combining the notion that *The Second Scroll* constitutes an *Aufhebung* over earlier scrolls with the notion of a circular *ricorso*. Both notions are, however, equally ironic. So too does the father remain unimpressed by the Russian *pilpul*. In direct opposition Melech, transformed into Comrade Krul, exploits his linguistic, polemical, and talmudic talents in a dialectical essay: "it constituted a remarkable instance of what happens when the Talmudic discipline is applied either to a belletristic or revolutionary praxis ... his argumentation was like nothing so much as like the subtilized airy transcendent *pilpul* of Talmud-commentary commentators" (26). Indeed, the polemical content of *The Second Scroll* includes Melech's letter which occupies most of "Exodus," the narrator's political argument with Settano and Melech's religious disagreement with Monsignor Piersanti in "Leviticus," Melech's letter of protest against the treatment of Jews in Casablanca which appears dramatically in the gloss to "Numbers," and the narrator's encounter in "Deuteronomy" with the Zionist journalist who expounds a theory of history. Thus, much of the book is taken up by letters, essays, and philosophical debates which account for didacticism within the novel which itself becomes a text for teaching dialects and second languages.

No sooner does the nephew complete his uncle's essay in "Genesis" than he receives, in the next chapter, a letter in which Melech notes "the abandonment of the Marxist jargon. Instead Uncle Melech had reverted to the epistolary style of his Talmudic days." This letter denounces "those two-faced masters of thesis and antithesis": "In the midst of our anguish we were regaled with a dialectic which proved that fascism was but a matter of taste" (31). The long letter concludes with a dialectic game proceeding from Bible to Mishna to talmudic commentary, but the rational, linear progression is undercut by the "revolving" circular "cumuli of Cabbala" with its *creatio ex nihilo* — a swirling desert anticipating the imaginary "whirlwind" at Melech's death. Waiting his turn to board a ship, Melech remembers ben Bag-Bag who used to turn about endlessly the texts of Holy Writ, for the meaning could never be exhausted (37). So, unlike the two-faced masters of thesis and synthesis, Klein offers a multi-faced waiting game, a patient negative dialectic where restless images cannot be fixed. "This lends to negative dialectics the quality of quicksilver: just when you think you have grasped the point, by turning into its opposite it slips through your fingers and escapes ... Only by keeping the argument in perpetual motion could thought escape compromising with its revolutionary goal."[8] One reverses Comrade Krul to discover what will always lurk behind his disguise of negative dialectics and hermeneutics. For a modern Jewish writer this juggling of legalistic talmudic sources, anti-rational Hassidic opponents, and the secular rationalism of the *Haskala* (the Enlightenment) results in a simultaneous rebellion against continuity and tradition. Cyclical and dialectical interpretations of history provide appropriate vehicles for exploring this rich discipline where ultimate answers are ironically postponed.

Klein collocates the narrator's argument with Settano (the satanic tempter) and Melech's disagreement with Piersanti to show the kinship and unity between nephew and uncle. The shifting grounds of their argument reflect their ever-changing conditions of exile. Although Klein treats his Satan with linguistic humour, the Italian begins his attack in a manner which parodies Piersanti's proselytizing: "he had scoffed at me, styled me a typical emissary of the new religion, a sound, orthodox Coca-colian" (45). In low imitation of the Sistine evaluation, the narrator retorts aesthetically: "I had spitefully accepted the compliment and — *pour l'épater* — had expatiated upon the beauty of the Coca-Cola bottle, curved and dusky like some Gauguin painting of a South Sea maiden, upon the purity of its contents, its ubiquity in space, its symbolic evocations — a little torchless Statue of Liberty." Like Jews in the Diaspora, these bottles are omnipresent. Every time Settano polarizes East and West, communism and American capitalism, his adversary deflects his thrust by praising Canada's northern qualities and annexing the United States to Canada, for Klein's cultural sense of occident and orient transcends political considerations. While Settano with his dialectical smile dogmatically asserts his materialistic interpretation of history, the narrator presents himself as an example of spirituality and later imagines himself to be John the Baptist. Klein's double subverts duplicity and decapitates two-faced authority.

In comparison with his uncle's epistle to the Romans, the narrator inquires, "Whither, O Romans?"; in comparison with Settano's polylingual autodidacticism, Melech's letter is dominated by a polyphonous evocation of Aramaic; and in comparison with conflicting directions of conversation, Melech "was southing; other parts of his letter might be ambiguous, but that was orient clear." Stylistically, there is little difference between the homily, or sermon, and the narrator's appraisal of it. The basic premise of the letter is the divinity of humanity in contrast with the Christian humanity of divinity; and the syllogisms lead to the conclusion that "Since man is created in the image of God, the killing of man is deicide" (51). At the centre of the novel, Melech's critical interpretation of the Sistine Chapel is a rejection of Christian doctrine; Klein thus offers a defense of Jewish faith through personal hermeneutics of revision.

Melech's description of the Sistine Chapel combines cyclical, labyrinthine, and dialectical modes. The passage begins and ends with the outer marble corridors; Melech circles the chapel gazing at the "whirlwind of forms" which are "circle-racked"; and in place of Michelangelo's "magic circles" he substitutes Maimonides' thirteen credos which appear in the form of a single circular sentence. Like Joyce's "Oxen of the Sun" episode in *Ulysses*, the letter imitates embryology: "the long umbilical cord of corridors behind me, pressed forward with infant eagerness to enter this new world" (103). Like "Gloss Aleph," "Gloss Gimel" examines how ontogeny recapitulates phylogeny, the marble corridors recalling "childhood's ogred corridors," and the "ghostly gauntlet" echoing the journalist's interpretation of Jewish history — "a gauntlet to be run" (72). Once again, Klein's concern with origins reflects both his childhood and his original place within Jewish-Canadian literary history.

The ceiling is a heaven which "breaks even the necks of the proud" (103) (a literal reference to the stiff-necked pride of Jews). Melech's study of the ceiling juxtaposes classical and biblical allusion but, unlike Milton who blends these elements harmoniously, Klein has a different purpose in mind. The classical list within the Christian setting includes the alexandrine floor, Euclidean geometry, the chapel's empyrean, januarial, Atlas-shouldered, lyre-chested, adonic figures, a pantheon of gods. These Greek and Roman references deflate the Christian content as Melech substitutes a secular aesthetic which somewhat reduces the religious subject. In addition to classicism, Klein employs a linguistic dialectic of wit to undercut Christianity: "adonic-adonaic," "adamic-seraphic," "damonandpythias-davidandjonathan," "Michael Angelo-Archangel Michael." Klein's classical allusions clash with Christian context, and his marginal notes reveal a Hebraic-Hellenic dialectic in which the sons of Jerusalem are victorious. The method then shifts from pre-Christian history to Melech's personal history which is the suffering of all Jews during World War II as Klein's reinterpretation replaces the Christian interpretation of the Pentateuch. Seen in this light, *The Second Scroll* is an *apologia* which, in its support of the Old Testament, rejects the other second scroll, the New Testament. Negative hermeneutics forestalls Hegelian synthesis.

The narrator reflects this polemic not only in his debate with Settano, but also in his understanding in Rome of "the miracle of the transformed stone." The final words of Melech's letter of affirmation ring in his ears as he realizes the historical truth: "The Arch of Titus, from being a taunt, then, had become an irony, an irony directed against itself; the candelabrum, set against the new light that had been kindled across the Great Sea, had turned into satire; the trumpets, symbolic now of jubilee, really taunted Titus!" Through the narrator's "appreciation" of the bas-relief and through Melech's analysis of the ceiling, Klein celebrates the victory of Israel over its foes — a projection of self-irony, hermeneutic dexterity, historical revisionism, and syntactical subversions, the only weapons available to the uprooted Other (*acher*), a belated alter ego splitting Gods and words (41).

"Gloss Dalid" also presents an *apologia* in dramatic form in a manner not unlike the most famous medieval defence of Judaism — Rabbi Yehuda Ha-Levi's *Kazari*. Indeed, the narrator refers to Ha-Levi, and Klein wrote a poem entitled "Yehuda HaLevi, His Pilgrimage." Desmond Pacey suggests that *The Second Scroll* is the fulfillment of Klein's partial failure in this earlier poem, but the connection may be more substantial than Pacey implies.[9] In the *Kazari*, HaLevi depicts a mighty king who searches for the true religion; representatives from Islam, Christianity, and Judaism try to persuade him of the truths of their respective religions, and in the end the Kazar is convinced of the merits of Judaism. In "Gloss Dalid," the *Cadi* replaces the Kazar as three judicial cases are brought before him; by the end of the play, the Jew adapts the moral from each case to argue for freedom, understanding, and brotherhood. The Jew sees himself as the "plaintiff" while Hassan, Marouf, and Ibn Aziz are "but proxies." The parable of the lamp manufacturer and the light at the end of the play iterate the image which Klein uses in "Yehuda HaLevi":

Did he not also in that wondrous script
Of Al-Kazari chronicle that king,
The heathen begging of the godly-lipped
Some wisdom for his pious hearkening, —

A candle for the dark, — a signet ring
To make the impress of the soul, — that prince
Who covenanted with the mightiest King,
Abjured false testaments and alcorans,
Accepting only Torah and its puissance.

With its own king, Melech Davidson, *The Second Scroll* abjures false testaments and builds upon the Torah in its author's personal covenant.

In another defence of Judaism the nameless journalist, like the nameless narrator, presents another view of Jewish history. His theory borrows the Hegelian "Judaic Idea" and the essence-existence terminology of Existentialism; in place of the Christian Incarnation he substitutes the miracle of the "Discarnation," a kind of deconstruction of Christianity. Like Joyce, Klein resorts to medical and physical metaphors to examine spiritual, historical, and metaphysical theories. In his analysis of the Sistine ceiling Melech discovers the key word for Michelangelo — the "Flesh" — and then proceeds to give his own version of the Discarnation from the concentration camps: "the flesh dwindled, the bones showed" (106). Linguistically, and ironically for this poet, the Word-made-Flesh is the "four-legged aleph." The Diaspora infection is reduced to the lowest common denominator as Klein "overdoes" the preparations for Israel: "Scarified ... against smallpox, punctured against typhus, pierced for tetanus, injected for typhoid, and needled with cholera ... they pointillated upon my arms their prescribed prophylactic prayers" (29). Prophylactic phylacteries, wearing one's heart on one's sleeve — this dualistic tension between physical and metaphysical manifests itself in Klein's excessive *écriture*. Through Melech's veins run the plasma of six million souls, and he is "inoculated against the world" with the Star of David, just like his nephew, his alter ego. When the latter discovers the "miracle" in Israel, "It was as if I were spectator to the healing of torn flesh, or *heard* a broken bone come together, set, and grow again. Wonderful is the engrafting of skin, but more wonderful the million busy hushed cells, in secret planning, stitching, stretching, until — the wound is vanished, the blood courses normal, the cicatrice falls off" (85). The individual Jew is part of a body politic that has survived the vicissitudes and cycles of history, unwilling to accept the Christian elements in itself.

The difference between Judaism and Christianity revolves around concepts of the Messiah, Incarnation, and the Word-made-Flesh; the difference between Islam and Judaism concerns the difference between magic and miracle. In "Leviticus," Klein defends Judaism against Christianity using the Italian Renaissance as an aesthetic and historical medium; in "Numbers," he reverts to Dante and the Middle Ages to support Judaism against Moslem persecution. Just as Melech discovers his own Jewish reality behind Michelangelo's art, so his nephew perceives the truth behind Casablanca's false front. Casablanca, "arrayed in all the colours of Islam, stands mirroring itself in the mirror of the Atlantic. As upon some Circean strand magical with voices" (56). In contrast, Melech "naturalized the miracle" and "had become a kind of mirror, an *aspaklaria*, of the events of our time." The mirror of art and the mirror of history reflect analogous events: Casablanca mirrors "false music" and "hollow art" while Israel reflects truth. A series of oxymorons depicts Arabian deceptions: "unlucky-lucky Negro," "possible-marvellous," and "old-new affinities." History becomes regressive in the Dantesque descent into the labyrinthine *mellah* which reveals the reality beneath an appearance of beauty in the city. The Virgilian guide remarks that space deceives the stomach; the visitor from the West cannot believe it real. "Some magician out of the *Arabian Nights*, I thought, had cast upon me a spell and conjured up with sinister open-sesame this melodramatic illusion. Or perhaps it was a desert mirage that was playing tricks with my vision. Or I was dreaming" (64). Like the "miracle of the transformed stone," the magic in "Numbers" is transformed into the miracle in "Deuteronomy."

Similar to the photograph of Melech Davidson, history is a double exposure or palimpsest with the present second scroll superimposed on the past in a recurrent cycle. Amalgamating cyclic and dialectic theories of history, Klein offers simultaneously an *apologia* and a linguistic *tour de force*. Even as the wandering Jew passes through the labyrinths of the Holocaust, the Sistine painting, and the *mellah* to emerge from space into time's eternal cycle, so he wanders through language and argument. Melech's double or multiple exposure results from a narrative camera which attempts to capture its subject just at that time when a second almost meets an absent first.

Once in Israel, the narrator ironically continues his diasporic quest, wandering from place to place where all the names recall his childhood studies in Montreal. He longs for the impossible gift of ubiquity, for only thus would he be able to accomplish his twofold mission of discovering Israel's poetic statement and Uncle Melech's whereabouts: like the Hebrew language, "to look for Uncle Melech was to suspect him everywhere and to find him nowhere" (75). He encounters Sephardic Jews in Tel Aviv who have been transformed from black-clad inhabitants of the Moslem *mellah* to white-clad elevator-boys of the modern Israel. He becomes a kind of census-taker, searching official records and lists of refugees: "Uncle Melech was nowhere listed, yet each name somehow seemed his alias" (76). Klein supplies a list of thirty-six names, the *lamed vav*, those thirty-six pious, unknown Jews for whom, according to legend, God continues the world. Most of the names have a meaning related to absence: the first name, for instance, Lazarus Achron, means last and appears ironically at the beginning; Moishe Anav means modesty; Samuel Galut, the Diaspora; I. Iota precedes Kalman Klain, incognito, lost, lacunal, diminished to nothing; Abraham Nistar, hidden; Yidel Nebich, diminutive, unfortunate nothingness. The nephew concludes that Uncle Melech is "present yet evanescent," and that "it was he, I felt, who was now pursuing me," as in most literary quests where the roles of pursuer and pursued interchange (78).

The narrator's quest for the essence of contemporary Hebrew poetry is beset by similar difficulty. He rejects one group of poets who advocate, in reaction to their own European exile, "the negation of the Diaspora." Not only does the nephew reject this kind of poetry as alien to the essential way of thought of Jews, but "Uncle Melech, I was certain, would read this literature but once" (80), an indication that any worthwhile work requires a second reading, for only through repetition can complexity be created and interpreted. Happily, the narrator rediscovers the pastoral in Hebrew poetry, so long dormant in urban ghettos: "In adamic intimacy the poets had returned to nature; the sulphur-crested cockatoo, the golden pheasant — they called them by their names — and the marabou, amorphous, mystical, circling ever in a round" (81). Naming, cyclical repetition, and origins — these three qualities meet with Klein's approval and form part of his fundamental poetics. In Tiberias, the nephew meets a fairly underivative poet whose writing resembles Uncle Melech's: "a poem is not a destination, it is a point of departure. The destination is determined by the reader. The poet's function is but to point direction" (82). With this invitation to reader-oriented criticism, Klein seems to repeat Milton's discontent with the marginal *Keri* in the face of the textual *Chetiv*; simultaneously it reminds the reader that the destinations of nephew, uncle, and *The Second Scroll* are constantly delayed, and that each chapter is but a point of departure, a vehicle for Klein's meaning.

The narrator finally realizes that modern Hebrew poetry belongs to the people and is housed in everyday language — a democratic, yet somewhat anti-climactic epiphany. "It was there all the time — the fashioning folk, anonymous and unobserved, creating word by word, phrase by phrase, the total work that when completed would stand as epic revealed!" (84). Words that had been confined to the boy's religious texts in Montreal are now miraculously transformed in secular Israeli usage: "Nameless authorship flourished in the streets." Klein's anonymous poet rewrites a poetics of absence in the almost meeting between language and translator, uncle and nephew, seeker and sought, beginning and end of a circular scroll.

Now that the narrator has found the answer to his linguistic quest, he concentrates solely on the pursuit of Melech Davidson whose messianic presence is ever blurred and deferred. Klein's quest ends in Safed as he enters the synagogue of Rabbi Isaac Luria, the great cabbalist known as Ari (the Lion). In comparing this humble house to any place of worship in the poorer quarters of the world's ghettos, he re-establishes a link between Israel and the Diaspora that carries through to the final words and by a *ricorso* to the opening of the novel. Just as the end of the first scroll returns the reader to the beginning, so *The Second Scroll* ends cyclically: the closer Klein comes to Safed or a New Jerusalem, the more we wonder whether he ever left Montreal. No sooner does the old sage in the synagogue mention *gilgul m'choloth* (the cabbalistic rolling of bodies in resurrection) than we learn of Melech's martyrdom. The old man who looks like Elijah describes the *gilgul*: "cadavers and corpses of Jewry deceased in the Diaspora would roll and strive and roll through subterranean passages ... directed all to rise at last and stand erect on the heights of Carmel, on the hillocks of the Negev, on the mountains of Galilee" (89). Melech's "strange" funeral or "high mythic rite" exemplifies Klein's *apophrades*:

In clouds of dust they came, from all parts of the country and from all classes of the population, corteges of cars and pilgrimages on foot, climbing the hills of Galilee ... As the banners and slogans were raised aloft, announcing the names of settlements in the Negev, in the Emek, in the Galil, each with its own exclamatory reaction to these obsequies which transcended their immediate purpose, it was as if the tribes of Israel had come to life again and were travelling as in olden times, each with its devices and gems. (91–2)

And Klein goes on to list each tribe's emblematic jewel, paradoxically heralding one of his own hidden "devices."

Just as Milton in *Paradise Lost* uses the "shield" and "spear" to transume his epic precursors, so Klein's *apophrades*, or *techiyat hamaitim*, projects his precursors into belatedness in order to transcend his own immediate purpose.[10] Since both "second" and "scroll" are already tropes, *The Second Scroll* is entirely metaleptic in its troping upon a trope, in its seconding of a scroll already seconded. In alluding to the Bible, Maimonides, Michelangelo, Joyce, and a host of other codes and traditions, Klein's old-new alphabet transumes its precursors: his scroll or *megillah* with its subterranean passages parallels the *gilgul*. Since "scroll" establishes and confuses the metonymy between container and contents, books and glosses, Klein's metalepsis emphasizes the cyclical experience of revisionary ratios. "The name that had once rung for me with angel pennies was resounding now to the conning of a new alphabet" (93). And that name is concealed in the Sabbath melody, *L'cho doidi* (a Hebrew play on "my dear, my uncle, my David"), which acts as a transition between the nephew's departure from the synagogue and the announcement of his uncle's death. These verses also act as a transition between profane weekday and holy Sabbath, past boyhood and present quester: "but now the words regained their original significance" (90). In the shadows of Sabbath and words lost and regained, Klein overcomes his Miltonic belatedness and agon. In Safed, as the crowds disperse, the quester turns for the last time from the centre of a whirlwind where "once were kindled, as now again, the beacons announcing new moons, festivals, and set times" (93). Klein swerves from Melech's last look at the Sistine Chapel and from the lasting shore of "that Drowning Instant."

Through the swerves and turning points of dialectics and mystical cycles, the nth Adam, Abraham, Moses, or marginal ephebe serves as an origin, a new covenant, for Jewish-Canadian literature. Klein's palimpsest results in blurred and double vision, returning to a religious past even as it progresses toward a secular future — a pattern followed by later Jewish-Canadian writers. *The Second Scroll* charts a perilous course between the Scylla of repetition and Charybdis of invention; it is an archi-text through which gleams that untravelled world and fading margin of Jewish-Canadian literature.

CHAPTER TWO

Canadian Poetry after Auschwitz: Layton, Cohen, Mandel

This past beginning, [the Holocaust,] this primitive
experience beyond which it is impossible to go,
constitutes, in effect, for Jewish consciousness, a
method of somber initiation; it is the apprenticeship
of wisdom and fear ...

Robert Mirashi

Before writing *The Second Scroll*, A.M. Klein published *The Hitleriad*,
a mock-epic poem contravening Theodor Adorno's famous injunction, "No poetry after Auschwitz."[1] But *The Hitleriad* lacked the necessary historical distance for coping with the enormity of the
Holocaust: satiric, Augustan rhyming couplets proved inadequate to
this unparalleled tragedy, and by the time Klein had grasped the
historical perspective, he succumbed to silence, as if in obeisance to
Adorno's prophetic caveat. Klein's successors — most notably Irving
Layton, Leonard Cohen, and Eli Mandel — with the advantage of
historical distance have achieved some of the means of expression for
arriving at a phenomenology of the Holocaust. A. Alvarez suggests
one way out of Adorno's *huis clos*: "The difficulty is to find language
for this world without values ... Perhaps the most convincing way is
that by which dreams express anguish: by displacement, disguise,
and indirection."[2] If Alvarez's tentative "formula" seems to provide
one way out, then Eli Mandel, in a description of his own poem, has
found a similar solution: "It would be a series of displacements ... It
would be a camp poem by not being a camp poem."[3] Mandel's theory
of "derealization," disorientation, and fragmentation echoes not only
Alvarez's suggestion, but also Klein's epigraph, "Where shall I find
Thee?" This cabbalistic quest becomes more acute during a period
of God's eclipse when absence dominates the universe so that the
question of God's whereabouts may be displaced by the poet's linguistic question: where shall I find the words to express this absence?
Fragmented verse and negatives begin to explore a poetics of absence
where memory must somehow fill the historical void created by
genocide and deicide. Through Alvarez's oneiric techniques that displace the Europe of the forties to a later Canada, Jewish-Canadian
poets find a language for this nightmarish, valueless world.

Emmanuel Levinas, a French philosopher who survived the Holocaust, writes extensively about the absence of God and the need for dialogue or discourse to mediate this absence.[4] Where Orthodox Judaism relies on the Torah, secular poets offer their writing as a mediation to overcome absence in this "I-Thou" relationship. To counter this universal void, in his verse Irving Layton projects a self-image who participates in a dialectic of potential and completion much like Klein's "pilpulistic antitheses."[5] As Seymour Mayne perceptively notes, "The 'I' or persona is almost invariably involved in the poem itself. It is at the center of the action, and this encounter of the persona and experience, of the personal and the world, suggests that some suspension of disbelief is involved."[6] In theology, the poet suspends disbelief in an eclipsed God; in poetry, he creates metaphor where tenor and vehicle almost meet. "Analogy as dialogue with God" is Derrida's formulation of this "I-Thou" relationship.[7]

Where Klein resorts to medieval parallels and historical allusions to contemporary atrocities, Layton relies on more modern techniques for grasping the horrors of the Second World War. In place of Klein's traditional couplets, the younger poet's free verse in such poems as "Ex-Nazi" attempts to come to terms with the psychological complexities in the aftermath of the war. Drawing on a poetics of absence, Layton dramatizes the hide-and-seek relationship between himself and his neighbour, poet and ex-Nazi, victim and victimizer, in order to comprehend the latter's guilt. In the first stanza, the poet plays blindman's buff with "scarred bushes" — the child's game suggests the blind fate awaiting those hunted, innocent Jews in European woods, and prepares for the "sacrificial smoke" at the end of the poem. In addition to the disguise of the child's game, Layton makes extensive use of simile to equate through indirection the poet's experience with anti-semitism and his relationship to the ex-Nazi for the same reason that he develops contrasts between darkness and light, blindness and revelation:

> I come sharp at this unguessed-at pole
> Spooky as an overturned ambulance;
> Like a sick anti-semite
> The morning struggles to reveal itself.[8]

The blind poet's strong visual sense creates a macabre, surrealistic atmosphere as he suddenly discovers a pole (possibly a Pole) that conceals hidden meanings and deaths. Who would have guessed that an ordinary neighbour could once have been a Nazi? Evoking Eliot's image of the evening which begins "The Love Song of J. Alfred Prufrock," the second simile prepares for the stanzaic progression from morning, to night, and finally to noon when revelation of guilt and absence occurs. Layton's verbs heighten the antitheses of potential and completion in this encounter between the poet's persona and his neighbour's artificial mask which conceal morning, history, and truth. Just as the poet "comes" at the pole, so his neighbour "comes" toward him; the identical verbs with varying prepositions further the poem's dialectic.

The second stanza begins prosaically with the neighbour's approach, his namelessness suggesting the universality of his guilt and banality of evil. Can an ex-Nazi disavow his past affiliation? Once a Nazi, always a Nazi, for his veins stagnate with pus and his demented brain transforms nature into "a March landscape / That's ravaged like the face of Dostoievski." In contrast to the poet's transformations in similes and metaphors, the neighbour's "turns" are untrue. Like the autumnal bushes, this wintry vision is "scarred" by the grotesque face of an earlier anti-semite. Yet another simile adds to the dislocating, surrealistic effect: "At night the whitened streets / Lean into his dreams like a child's coffin." Internal rhymes and similes create a Munch-like canvas as the frozen scene melts into summer heat with a crescendo from innocence to guilt:

> But now at noon he meets himself
> In the summer craze of the sun,
> Boy eager, as springy as grass,
> Innocenter than his bounding mastiff
> Whose tail flicks from conscience
> The yammering guilt.

Whereas in the first stanza poet meets pole and in the second poet meets neighbour, now the neighbour confronts himself in a dialectic leading to their final relationship — a convergence of absence. The reflexive pronoun links Nazi to the anti-semitic morning's concealment of identity as man and nature intertwine in an atmosphere of masked, sinister guilt. While Layton heightens this "innocentric" universe by comparing the Nazi with his dog, the rhythm and movement contrast dramatically with the closing, and suspend the relationship between hunter and hunted:

> The hot sun desiccates his guilt.
> Between us the pale dust hangs

Like particles
Of sacrificial smoke.

Suspension of disbelief, history, and landscape informs Layton's poetics and unresolved masquerades. The concluding smokescreen conceals and exposes historical guilt, memory, irreconcilable otherness, and a dialectic of incomplete potential, much as Melech Davidson's Europe is at the mercy of Canada's game of blindman's buff. "Ex-Nazi" examines an almost meeting between neighbours separated by the ashes of the Holocaust in an absent gulf which time fails to diminish.

Similar sentiments between the poet ("I") and an ex-Nazi ("*Ich*") constitute the subject of "Das Wahre Ich," a banal statement on the nature of the German woman of twenty years ago: "*Wahre*" (truth) plays on existential and historical illusions. Outside, "Ex-Nazi" creates a claustral atmosphere through nature and dramatic confrontation; meanwhile the interior setting of this poem closes in on the poet and his hostess. The opening confession is prosaic, matter of fact, and the distance between the present, hospitable proximity and a violent past, which would have cast hostess and guest in much different roles of murderer and victim, creates the tension in the poem:

> She tells me she was a Nazi; her father also.
> Her brother lies buried under the defeat
>   and rubble of Stalingrad.
> She tells me this, her mortal enemy, a Jew.[9]

In contrast to the buried past, the present is imaged and mediated by floating mobiles that she makes for this salon setting reminiscent of Eliot's "Prufrock":

> We are twenty years removed from the war.
> She urges on me candied biscuits and tea,
> and her face is touched by a brief happiness
> when I praise her for them and for the mobiles
>   she has herself fashioned
> in the comfortless burdensome evenings.

This domestic innocence continues in the third stanza while the mobiles hover symbolically over the historical gap and absence between Nazi and Jewish persona:

Her face is sad and thin as those mobiles
moving round and round in the wind
my voice makes when I thank her
and she bows her frail proud head into her hands.

The oxymoronic "frail proud" underlines the disparity between her failure and her once powerful illusion. These disguising and dislocating mobiles and the final stanza resemble the pale dust and particles of sacrificial smoke at the end of "Ex-Nazi":

The terrible stillness holds us both
and stops our breath
while I wonder, a thrill stabbing into my mind:
"At this moment, does she see my crumpled form
                        against the wall,
blood on my still compassionate eyes and mouth?"

Thus, through dramatic irony and "near" encounters with one-time Nazis, Layton as would-be victim freezes time and faces the post-Holocaust world; through the impossibilities of these "I-*Ich*" confrontations, he strives for a transcending "I-Thou" relationship.

The memory of the slaughtered six million pervades "Rhine Boat Trip" where beauty is marred through the perspective of recent history. The aesthetics of leisure and scenery in the first half of each stanza is undercut by the lingering tragedy of past frenzy in the second half culminating in the opposition of the noise of the cattle-cars to the serenity of the boat on the river. In these juxtapositions of guilt-ridden past and a disguising present, Layton controls his passionate lyricism between outright silence and an outraged scream. The absence of punctuation imitates the smooth, synaesthetic gliding of the boat and allows the past to flow into the present as spectres of absence witness what the poet sees:

The castles on the Rhine
are all haunted
by the ghosts of Jewish mothers
looking for their ghostly children

And the clusters of grapes
in the sloping vineyards
are myriads of blinded eyes
staring at the blind sun

The tireless Lorelei
can never comb from their hair
the crimson beards
of murdered rabbis

However sweetly they sing
one hears only
the low wailing of cattle-cars
moving invisibly across the land.[10]

An impersonal persona, "one," intrudes at the end of the poem to contrast with history's myriads who forbid failure of memory and metaphor. Man's violence can become so extreme that even the landscape is permanently tainted; invisibility and silence, two forms of absence, cling to Germany's void in time and place. Beneath Layton's sharply etched images lies the blurring palimpsest of history, an abysmal impress simultaneously distancing and involving poet and reader.

This spatial-temporal projection into the European past recurs in the five paragraph-like stanzas of "The Shadow." Here the poet is transformed into a ubiquitous shadow — mankind's absent, displaced conscience — both in familiar Canadian surroundings and in a Viennese *hofbrau*, where he observes the merriment of Austrians whose bowels are reactivated through *brauten* and *schweinerfleisch*:

I sit at my table, *nein* excuse me,
lie flat against the wall and manipulate
my filled glass like an aging acrobat
taking care not to spill a single drop
on their mothballed Nazi uniforms.[11]

Ironic contrasts between spilling a mere drop of beer on Nazi uniforms and the blood shed by six million Jews, between the ghost-like poet as survivor and the dense substance of the beer-swilling, decadent masses, create a grotesque Baudelairean atmosphere. The poet transcends human boundaries when he composes metaphors of mediation: "I release my shadow like a switchblade / or the cavernous grin of a ghost / as it spreads across the polished bannister." Relative absence of punctuation results in flowing free verse which accentuates the dialectic of potential and completion in this poetry of process; the reader participates in this flow of past and present drama as Layton's cutting edge stabs the mind. The poet cannot help but be a censorious moralist in the midst of all the camaraderie, for he must come to haunt even as he has been haunted by his massacred kin in this counterpoint between shadows of past and present. The shadow — a mask within a mask — shouts to be taken off the wall (as in the conclusion of "Das Wahre Ich") to disturb amnesiac complacency, invisibility, and false innocence:

> teach me indifference to great events
> your boisterous pinkfaced affability as you slam
> down your cards on the table as if they were fists
> on an old Jew's skull.

Once again Layton the prophet declaims against forgetfulness in order to avenge the ghosts of innocent children, while Layton the poet employs metaphoric disguise to imprint images of absence, like tattooed arms, indelibly in his reader's mind.

When Layton the preacher ascends the pulpit, exhorting his followers to a kind of muscular Judaism replete with tight-rope dancers, one-armed jugglers, and pole-vaulters, he occasionally eclipses his metaphoric impulse. In his own negative dialectics, mobiles, and particles of sacrificial smoke, he suspends reconciliation, forgetfulness, and disbelief. Layton's Lorelei recall Heine's prophecy that German armies will tear up the roots of the past and revive the forces of paganism. To revive his own roots, the Canadian poet places himself in a line with his forbears, but the post-Holocaust poet can no longer rely on the Romantic lyricism of Heine.

If Klein belongs to the first generation and Layton to the second, then Leonard Cohen represents the third generation of Holocaust poets; while *The Hitleriad* is Klein's attempt to come to terms with the Holocaust, *Flowers for Hitler* contains many poems in which Cohen confronts the ultimate evil of the Nazi regime. Like Layton, Cohen experiments with free verse fragments, identifying victim and victimizer. Just as Klein empathizes with his tortured brothers who enter his bloodstream, so Cohen feels that he is an inmate of a concentration camp twenty years after the war. But while Klein refers specifically to Nazi crimes, Cohen uses these as pretexts for a more generalized probing of the evils of modern society. In constructing his own corporal and cerebral Auschwitz, Cohen is both German and Jew. Citing the epigraph to the volume from Primo Levi's *Survivor in Auschwitz*, critics neglect the poet's note on the title:

A while ago
this book would
have been called
SUNSHINE FOR NAPOLEON,
and earlier still it
would have been
called
WALLS FOR GHENGHIS KHAN.[12]

Although most theologians insist that the Holocaust was unique, an extreme instance of malice and atrocity, Cohen implies that evil is relative, part of an historical continuum. Even if Cohen's note is ironic, nevertheless the casual "while ago" and the links with Napoleon and a remote Ghenghis Khan deny the singular, unprecedented nature of Hitler's methods.

Yet "Lines from my Grandfather's Journal" seems to contradict this relativism as Cohen searches for a phenomenology to approach the deaths of six million: "It is painful to recall a past intensity, to estimate your distance from the Belsen heap, to make your peace with numbers." Cohen deliberately indulges in "pain" whenever he recalls the Holocaust:

I saw my brothers dance in Poland. Before the final
destruction I heard them sing. I could not put away my
scholarship or my experiments with blasphemy.
    (In Prague their Golem slept.)
    Desolation means no ravens, no black symbols. The
carcass of the rotting dog cannot speak for you. The
ovens have no tongue ...
    Desolation means no comparisons ...[13]

He lists painful images of destruction and absence, continues his secular revisions in place of the Golem's revenge, and concludes that because of its absolute horror the Holocaust brooks no metaphors — a conclusion shared by Uri Zvi Greenberg in his poetry of the Holocaust: "There are no other analogies (all words are shades of shadow) — / Therein lies the horrifying phrase: No other analogies!"[14] If desolation means no comparisons, no black metaphors, we seem to fall back into Adorno's trap ("No poetry after Auschwitz") and all we may expect are fragments of blindness, silence, and mutilation — the ghosts and shadows that Layton and Cohen resurrect.

Cohen emphasizes these shadows when he differentiates between private art and public politics, between German culture and Nazi

barbarism, in "Goebbels Abandons His Novel and Joins the Party."
The disjunction between the two activities in the title is recapitulated
in the key verb in the poem, "broke."

> His last love poem
> broke in the harbour
> where swearing blondes
> loaded scrap
> into rusted submarines.[15]

Like a wave, the poem "breaks" in the harbour, but the verb also
signifies a breaking away from truth — the man "broke" or bankrupt
of values. The "blondes" of the Aryan race prepare for the "favourite
hair" which appears later in the poem, while the "rust" and "scrap,"
favourite foci for Cohen, are ironic inversions of the Nazi's ordurous
language of derision for the Jews. The mechanical destroys any ves-
tiges of humanity:

> the pieces of iron
> broke whatever thous
> his pain had left
> like a whistle breaks
> a gang of sweating men.

"Thous" rather than vows are broken in a world devoid of humane
dialogue; the pronouns are instructive, for after repeating the third
person throughout the poem, the poet shifts to the first and second
when he addresses his pupils. The authoritative whistle can "break
down" the slaves or it can restore them through a temporary "breaking off" from labour.

In contrast to this "breaking" is the joining of the party: "Ready to
join the world," to become the public figure of power. As if to mock
the idea that there is a moral to this account, Cohen concludes with
a rhetorical question:

> Ah my darling pupils
> do you think there exists a hand
> so bestial in beauty so ruthless
> that can switch off
> his religious electric Exlax light?

Ambiguity arises from the oxymoronic "bestial beauty" of black
romanticism and from the shifting pronominal referents: the hand
may belong to Goebbels, the poet, or Everyman. Yet to envision

Hitler and Goebbels as Everyman seems an inadequate, reductive response. George Woodcock aptly summarizes Cohen's unstable phenomenon if not his failure of nerve: "when he faces the phenomenon of the Hitler terror, he withdraws from partisan involvement, and either adopts the style of Gothic macabre which is one literary way of dealing with fundamentally indescribable human aberrations, or he extends through satire the argument, not that *all Germans* are responsible, but *all men* are responsible for what happened in the concentration camps."[16]

Both strains are visible in "It Uses Us!" as the poet and his lover practice their erotic art on a cadaverous mound. Voyeurism and gothicism coalesce in the opening stanza where the simple rhyme heightens the surrealistic effect:

> Come upon this heap
> exposed to camera leer:
> would you snatch a skull
> for midnight wine, my dear?[17]

Cohen projects himself as Nazi and Jew, victimizer and victim in *l'univers concentrationnaire*, for his sexual and morbid explorations allow him to approximate the pornographic mentality of his persecutors. Not only does the camera "use" the lovers in demonic photography, but the dead bodies reverse utilitarian order. The living cannot use the remains of the dead; death uses the living, the living abuse death, and the survivors merge with the slaughtered in a grotesquely tragic almost meeting:

> Can you wear a cape
> claim these burned for you
> or is this death unusable
> alien and new?

Deploring the past and erasing memory, the leaders celebrate the victory of freedom, but for the poet who identifies with the powerful and the oppressed, freedom can only be an illusion:

> In my own mirror
> their faces beam at me:
> my face is theirs, my eyes
> burnt and free.

Cohen chooses martyrdom in his poetics of absence and indirection.

Atop this phantasmagoric charnel heap, distinctions dissolve between eros and *thanatos*: "from this height we thrill / as boundaries disappear." Nihilism and chaos are infernal extensions of freedom, in the poet's vision, because combat combines in twentieth-century post-gothicism: "*All things can be done* / whisper museum ovens of / a war that Freedom won."

That memory of the war cannot be erased may be seen in "The Invisible Trouble" where the poet empathizes with a survivor whose indelible tattoo will always distinguish him from the rest of society. If the branded number on his wrist is the visible trouble, the invisible is not so much his attempt at anatomical concealment, as the world of terror hidden beneath physical reality. As in Layton's poetry, invisibility signifies absence, disguise, and indirection — the essentials of Holocaust literature. Hiding the concentration camp tattoos, the survivor wants to forget the past and participate in the bachannalian illusion of the surrounding bar:

> His arm is unburned
> his flesh whole:
> the numbers he learned
> from a movie reel.
> He covers his wrist
> under the table.
> The drunkards have missed
> his invisible trouble.[18]

Cohen deliberately distorts illusion and reality: whole flesh replaces fragments, cinema replaces history, and drink replaces truth for those who avoided the tragedy. But the survivor cannot lift his cup to join in the chorus for fear of revealing the reality of the mark; instead, alone, a specimen of absence, he must confront silence and the void. Thus Cohen takes literally the maxim that to understand another person one must get under his skin. He uses the body as a means of entering the world of the other; only by getting under the other's skin can Cohen empathize and grasp his own guilt as another kind of survivor, one who almost meets himself at the brink of an abyss.

This process of entering another's body takes on a different form in "Hitler the Brain-Mole," a witches' brew of human anatomy in which Nazis torture the poet and become part of his body:

> Hitler the brain-mole looks out of my eyes
> Goering boils ingots of gold in my bowels

My Adam's Apple bulges with the whole head of Goebbels
No use to tell a man he's a Jew
I'm making a lampshade out of your kiss
Confess! confess!
   is what you demand
although you believe you're giving me everything.[19]

The metamorphoses and torture machines are Kafkaesque; the shifting pronouns implicate everyone in hideous, surrealistic cruelty. The shift in the latter half connects sexual intercourse with the physical interchanges of the first half; Cohen thereby implies the pornography of existence. Similarly, the synecdoches of the first half undercut the final "everything" to suggest the absurd nothingness of being.

"Hitler," however has a much calmer tone; atrocity is recollected in tranquillity as Cohen tries to upset apathy without resorting to hysteria. The emotional control brings a clearer, though no less frightening, portrait of the *führer*.

Now let him go to sleep with history,
the real skeleton stinking of gasoline,
the mutt and jeff henchmen beside him:
let them sleep among our precious poppies.

Cadres of ss waken in our minds
where they began before we ransomed them
to that actual empty realm we people
with the shadows that disturb our inward peace.

For a while we resist the silver-black cars
rolling in slow parade through the brain.
We stuff the microphones with old chaotic flowers
from a bed which rapidly exhausts itself.

Never mind. They turn up as poppies
beside the tombs and libraries of the real world.
The leader's vast design, the tilt of his chin
seem excessively familiar to minds at peace.[20]

While history has destroyed some Nazis, their spectres haunt the survivors whether through surrealistic nightmare or documentary —two opposing modes of indirection and literalness that Cohen exploits in his Holocaust poetry. From a casual imperative opening in hypnotic, monosyllabic, iambic pentameter to the repeated "peace" at the end of the second and fourth stanzas, the four symmetric quatrains create a soporific illusion. This illusion underlies madness, as silence stifles a scream like flowers stuffing a microphone. These flowers for Hitler are funereal and perennial, and they smell like the skeleton which stinks of gasoline; the "bed" is both a flowerbed, the graves of victims and victimizers, and the survivors' bed of nightmares. The "real skeleton" and the "real world" interchange with nightmare and shadow for the disguise of absence reveals that an "empty realm" may be "actual" in this mock elegy. The ambiguity of "minds at peace," as opposed to peace of mind, completes the prosaic "Never mind" just as the grandiloquent "vast design" fizzles into a familiar, banal profile in which the nose above that tilting chin sniffs in uncanny recurrence the opium of history.

Like his fellow poets from Montreal, Eli Mandel, an isolated, semitic voice of the prairies, gropes for the appropriate forms to express his response to the Holocaust; unlike Layton and Cohen, however, who have written many shorter poems on this topic, Mandel concentrates his efforts in one long poem. "On the 25th Anniversary of the Liberation of Auschwitz: Memorial Services, Toronto, January 25, 1970 YMHA Bloor & Spadina" is an occasional poem in which Mandel casts about for his own reactions to the Holocaust. The complete revision of the original poem a few years later for publication in *Stony Plain* indicates the problematic nature of the poet's confrontation with his subject, which is not only Auschwitz, but the process of writing about the Holocaust. Thus, the opening line "the name is hard" refers not only to the "German sound made out of / the gut guttural throat / y scream yell ing," but also to the emotional and aesthetic difficulties the poet has in even pronouncing the name "Auschwitz."[21] The onomatopoeic stammering of the split syllables in the third and fourth lines suggests both the primitive barbarism of the Nazis with their cacophonous "growl," and the faltering hesitancy of the victims being led to slaughter. The repeated "out of," which Mandel plays upon in the title of another book, *Out of Place*, carries the twofold meaning of space and transformation. Thus, while the word itself is formed phonemically from the throat, the emotional response comes from the "gut" — a reminder of what will be "made out of / the gut" of the victims in the ruthless dissection.

The poem also explores the temporal relationship of the survivors to both the victims and victimizers twenty-five years after the event, and to the writing of the poem some time after the memorial services. Mandel's phenomenological fragmentation breaks down the historical separation of Europe in 1945 from Toronto in 1970. On the platform at the Y, Sigmund Sherwood (Sobolewski) — the survivor's name transformed — speaks in the present tense to dissolve the twenty-five-year gap between destruction and survival: "the only way out of Auschwitz / is through the chimneys." The poet comments on the spoken sentence: "that's second hand that's told / again," which is a warning against the use of cliché that can turn tragedy into banality. But Mandel is also telling again, repeating a repetition of the original, and is aware of the moral imperative of re-telling the tragic story, or "bearing witness" as he writes at the beginning of another poem, "For Elie Weisel."[22] Apparently Sobolewski was fortunate to get "out of" Auschwitz and now by way of contrast he is "twisting himself into that sentence" as a means of getting back to the original experience. The poem comes as a response to a response, for the process begins at the Y but the form appears afterwards: "the poem / shaping itself late in the after / noon later than it would be." Dispersing the moment into past and future, Mandel suffers from the double burden of poetic belatedness and guilt-ridden survival.

For the memorial service, the poem continues, slides are shown; Pendericki's "Wrath of God," framed by the name "looking away from / pretending not there / no name no not name no," is played. Mandel applies his interest in naming and un-naming as a means of confronting that which is painful to behold. His dislocated sounds and forms distance the poet and his audience from the excruciating content. The name "Auschwitz" appears on the screen in gothic lettering while in the poem the word "gothic" is capitalized to emphasize the gothic nature of the event and its remembrance, as well as the iconoclastic roots of the early Gothic invaders. A poetics of absence, silent spaces between words, fragments, disguise, indirection, dislocation, and almost meetings between event and expression inform Mandel's lines.

As Mandel vacillates between exile and origins, the YMHA hall becomes "a parody a reminiscence a nasty memory" of similar settings of violence from the poet's childhood in Saskatchewan which was filled with the guns of cowboy killers. Like the nomadic procession of Polish Legionnaires, the process of "the poem gradual / ly insistent beginning to shape itself / with the others," uniting the poet to his fellow sufferers and the individual poem to the collective work. Thus, through its process the poem, though written later, becomes simultaneous with the anniversary. In turn, both poem and anniversary become contemporaneous with the history of the genocide as the wanderers' march at Bloor and Spadina recalls the march at Auschwitz:

thinking apocalypse shame degradation
thinking bones and bodies melting
thickening thinning melting bones and bodies
thinking not mine / must speak clearly
the poet's words / Yevtyshenko at Baba-Yar.

"Thinking" dissolves into "thickening" and "thinning" as the poet's mental process reflects the apocalyptic marches of 1970 and 1945. Furthermore, the poet identifies both with the victims and with his fellow Russian poet who has also written about the massacre of Jews. The heat of the crematoria overwhelms the pathetic fallacy of a Canadian January; even identities melt under the extremity of genocide where humanity and individuality are denied.

Identities are further confused in the hallucinatory verse: the prisoner in the YMHA hall is a prisoner of the past and the present, and with "arms wax stiff body stiff unnatural / coloured face" he resembles the Nazi generals with "their stiff wax bodies their unnatural faces / and their blank eyes and their hands their stiff hands." That the slide presentation dissolves identities is reflected in the breaking down of lines and the scattering of words:

this is mother
this is father
this is
        the one who is
waving her arms like that
is the one who
                like
I mean running with her breasts bound
ing
    running
            with her hands here and there
with her here and
                        there
hands
        that   that is

The failed similes and attempts at doubling link the poet's personal background with the larger family of Jews, while synecdoche underscores the catastrophic fragmentation and mutilation. The poet gropes for the language and form just as the woman flails her arms, and their suffering is united in the poem itself:

the poem becoming the body
becoming the faint hunger
ing body
      prowling
         through
words the words words the words
opening   mouths ovens

Just as the poem becomes the body of the concentration camp, so the poet as silent, suffering spokesman becomes the poem. "Becoming" refers mainly to the creative process, but the second meaning, that of matching appropriateness, carries a grim irony of poetic form which suits the historical subject. Another inversion of identity appears in the "god-like" generals who are figuratively intertwined with their Jewish victims through black leather phylacteries. The poem becomes the film, the film is transformed into the poem, the audience is on screen, and the reader participates in the memorial service through the poem's self-consciousness:

the poem flickers, fades
  the four Yarzeit candles guttering one
     each four million lights dim
my words   drift

The poem, like the film and the memorial flame, "flickers," "fades," and "gutters" — the last verb echoing the "gut guttural" at the beginning of the poem. The synaesthetic quality of the sights and sounds furthers the melting identities, as does the reintroduction of the boyhood memory of Saskatchewan. The words drift as the poem reaches its end, drifting like the smoke from Auschwitz to Estevan. The badly reproduced picture and failing electrical power reflect the poetic process of the voyeuristic "jewboy yelling" at the western slaughter — a commentary on the brutality of European civilization as viewed by the not-so-innocent child:

the gothic word hangs
over us on a shroud-white screen

we drift away
      to ourselves
        to the late Sunday Times
        the wet snow
        the city

        a body melting

The final line contrasts with the "hard" name at the outset, and the concluding images hover between indelibility and evanescence.

Written almost a generation after Klein's *The Hitleriad*, Mandel's revised "Auschwitz" demonstrates some of the postmodernist innovations in poetic technique that ease the expression of the ultimately ineffable. Beginning in the fifties with Irving Layton, the "School of Klein" gave voice to the silent legacy of the father of Jewish-Canadian literature.[23] Layton's fairly direct poems attack all those implicated in past or present guilt by presenting clearly dramatic situations that unearth the ghosts of the six million dead. A decade later, Leonard Cohen couples more experimental verse forms with a black romanticism to explore the universal ramifications of evil in a postmodern world. Experimenting with form to an even greater degree than Cohen's "Hitler" poems, Eli Mandel's single long poem goes to extremes of consciousness and linguistic torture. Out of the ashes of the Second World War, these poets have created monuments to the memories of their innocent brethren and their destroyed European culture. Through displacement, disguise, and indirection, Jewish-Canadian poetry reduces the historical gulf separating the European battlefield from more fortunate Canadian ghettos where a silent scream keeps memory awake. Mandel's Toronto march, Cohen's "silver-black cars / rolling in slow parade through the brain," and Layton's hide-and-seek exemplify the ways Jewish-Canadian poetry trespasses on history, seeking silence in vocal paralysis and a home in time's demonic haze. If the centre cannot hold, modern Jewish poets shore these fragments against their ruins.

Mandel's theory of "derealization" and disorientation in the composition of his poem summarizes the evolution of Canadian poetry after Auschwitz:

It would be a series of displacements: structurally, grammatically, imagistically, psychologically. *It would be a camp poem by not being a camp poem.* Stuttering. All theatricality. All frantic posturing. All pointed to a resolution that would not be a resolution, a total ambiguity in which two different moments (Toronto, 1970 and Estevan, 1930) dissolved into one another seamlessly, becoming at that instant another time, the unimaginable place of the killing ground itself.[24]

What Lawrence Langer says of Holocaust literature in general applies to Mandel's statement and poem: "The reader is temporarily an insider and permanently an outsider, and the very tension resulting from this paradox precludes the possibility of the kind of 'pleasure' Adorno mentions, while the uncertain nature of the experience recorded, combined with the reader's feeling of puzzled involvement in it, prohibits Adorno's fear that the reader may discern in the inconceivable fate of the victims 'some sense after all'."[25] In Canadian Holocaust literature this puzzled involvement, decentring reader and writer, begins in *The Second Scroll*, develops in the poetry of Layton, Cohen, and Mandel, and culminates in the fiction of Henry Kreisel. Klein's Yiddish spirit shines through the syntax of these ghost writers in the haunted wilderness of history; their fading faces emerge in negatives behind the film of unresolved representation.

In the Hebrew temporal agon, not the Hellenic spatial icon, Jewish-Canadian poets strive with Klein and other biblical precursors. Melech Davidson is quintessentially Jewish in leaving no belongings; though Klein may never look upon his face, he may scan his sole legacy, the penultimate poem, "And in that Drowning Instant." The poet's "preterite eternity / the image of myself intent / on several freedoms" fades to earlier faces, metaleptic moments:

> the face
> is suddenly beneath the arch
> whose Latin script the waves erase
> and flashes now the backward march
> of many.[26]

This erasure of signifiers by the palimpsest of history creates a blank and a blindness to be restored by Klein's biblical precursors and his Canadian followers who revise and revive him. Layton's morning struggles to reveal itself but the pale dust of history conceals presence. The Rhine is empty (*rein*), blind, invisible, defaced and effaced. For Cohen, "no black symbols" "exposed to camera leer," "eyes burnt," "invisible trouble." For Mandel, black and secret blanks, fading poems and faces on a shroud-white screen. The leaves cry when their verse turns to the immediate past and to a more remote biblical horizon. With Klein, they barely see "as on a screen," "dark against blank white / The bearded ikon-bearing royalties," eclipsed in "Diaspora-dark."

The examples of Edmond Jabès or Paul Celan demonstrate how writers cope (or fail to cope) with the Holocaust and postmodernism: they write neither *about* the Holocaust in traditionally representational forms nor do they write themselves in intransitive, non-referential solipsism. Instead, they write-the-Holocaust: the object writes itself, the narrative voice is the voice of history.[27] Layton, Cohen, and Mandel move in this direction, but Klein's inability to reconcile moral and aesthetic questions, to find sanctuary in mediated or unmediated dialogue, may have led to his final silence, a silence echoed in Celan's suicide.

In *The Exile of the Word* André Neher traces this theme of silence from the Bible to Auschwitz, refers to Adorno's *Negative Dialectics*, and concludes that "relationships after Auschwitz are possible only in a vacant area, in a sort of philosophic no-man's land."[28] In the void of a Jewish-Canadian no-man's land after the Holocaust, words are in exile and people "mismeet." Elie Wiesel writes in the same vein: "I'd like you to know only this: separation contains as much of a mystery as a meeting. In both cases a door opens: in meeting it opens on the future, in separation on the past. It's the same door."[29] Silence from the first to *The Second Scroll* and beyond is the threshold for these almost meetings.

CHAPTER THREE

From Vienna to Edmonton: Henry Kreisel's Almost Meetings

"To be a Jew" is something that cannot be defined for the cultured, assimilated Jew, except paradoxically and circuitously: by the *mere fact* of always being susceptible to gratuitous murder "because of being Jewish."

Robert Mirashi

Like Freud, Hermann Broch, Elias Canetti, Stefan Zweig, Martin Buber, and many other Jewish-Austrian writers, Henry Kreisel fled the Anschluss in 1938, leaving behind a highly developed European Jewish culture on the verge of destruction. After settling in Canada, Kreisel had to learn a new idiom for his fictional world, and he turned to Klein's writing as one model. *The Second Scroll* provided him with a transatlantic quest motif that combines Jewish roots in Canada and Europe — a diasporic response to Kreisel's own wandering. His short stories and novels explore a poetics of absence, the doppelgänger motif for doubly marginal man, and a return to the Holocaust through indirection. In "Homecoming" (whose title recalls Harold Pinter's play, Kafka's sketch, and the final section of Hermann Broch's *The Death of Virgil*), Kreisel describes a prodigal son's return to his Polish village after World War II only to discover that his family has been destroyed: "The way seemed endless, the goal impossible to reach."[1] These words apply equally to Klein's quest for Uncle Melech and the infinite questioning of homeless survivors in Europe and Canada, the settings for both of Kreisel's novels.

If the opening sentence of Kreisel's first novel, *The Rich Man*, sounds ominously like the beginning of Kafka's "The Metamorphosis," the reader is soon reassured that its protagonist Jacob Grossman, unlike Gregor Samsa, will not be transformed into a gigantic insect. Yet Jacob does undergo certain transformations upon awakening *in medias res* when he finds that his alarm clock has not gone off. He has decided to break his thirty-three year working routine in Toronto and return to Vienna to visit his family; in so doing, the poor labourer will be transformed into an illusory rich man, the old man will regress to childishness, and the New World revert to the "old country." His sleeping-in is but a prelude to his belated awakening to a grim historical reality that opens his eyes just prior to the final darkness of the night, the void into which he flings his painting at the novel's close.

Once out of bed, he hears music over the radio, the first song, "Swing Low, Sweet Chariot," sung by a Black quartet with deep, sad voices: "Coming for to carry me home."[2] This background music sets the mood for Jacob's return to Vienna, his questionable Austrian homeland, and is immediately followed by a modern jazz arrangement of the Blue Danube Waltz, as if to emphasize the contrast between old and new worlds. A news report follows these songs, announcing Goering's intention of rearming Germany, British Commonwealth preparations for the twenty-fifth anniversary of King George V's accession to the throne, and the opposition of the United States' Chamber of Commerce to President Roosevelt's reform legislation. These political events help establish Kriesel's international theme as well as Jacob's various loyalties; disruptions in Jacob's own family reflect impending catastrophe in Europe. The gulf between illusion and reality widens as the novel progresses, demonstrating an absence in the life of Jacob who is an exile on both continents. As a result of tragic historical events, and the lie that his life has become, his meeting with his family never amounts to more than an almost meeting in which characters are paralyzed.

From the very first paragraph the reader encounters the immigrant's problem of linguistic homelessness: "It was difficult to find the right words." Ironically, the only right word for Jacob is the monosyllabic Yiddish "*noo*," the perfect vehicle for child, immigrant, and "new" man who is at home only in the barest phonemes of his "modder language."

The word *Noo* was the richest and most expressive word in his vocabulary. He could play with this little word like a virtuoso. He could thunder it in a loud bass, and he could whisper it softly, drawing it out gently. He could pronounce it sharply, almost threateningly, like a stab, and he could speak it lightly and playfully, modulating his sing-song, his voice wavering and trembling until it died away like the closing notes of a sad aria. In the mouth of Jacob Grossman this little sound was capable of expressing the profoundest emotions and the most delicate shades of meaning. (16)

The rich man's richest word contrasts with the voices heard on the radio, the demonic voices encountered in Europe, and the voicelessness of his painting. Indeed, Jacob's final utterance as he abandons his family to their tragic fate at the novel's end is "*noo*," repeated in exasperation, despair, and resignation to his own inability to aid those with whom he has been so involved. For the self-proclaimed *shlimazl*, a Jewish anti-hero caught lucklessly between two traditions, an ironic *noo* may be a futile gesture — a primitive, childlike howl fraught with ambiguities — but it remains one of the few ways to transcend oppression.

An ironic artist of the monosyllable, Jacob becomes an *artiste manqué*. He is in exile from his mother tongue, and thus experiences a verbal absence whenever he tries to express himself in English. When he asks his boss, Mr Duncan, for permission to take a few weeks' leave, a comical dialectic ensues between his hands and his voice; he needs manual gestures to assist him where words fail. But this comical drama has a more serious dimension in the conflict between labour and management, a struggle central to the historical and economic issues raised in *The Rich Man*'s occasionally Marxist orientation. The dialogue between employer and employee is matched by a dialectic between hands and voice: Jacob "did not use his hands. They lay stretched out on the desk now, rough hands, hands tired after a lifetime of labour. And now they looked like strangers because he was expressing something in which they had no part" (18). Like a child, the immigrant labourer who is at a loss for words requires the assistance of mother tongue and expressive fingers; later those same hands, synecdochic parts that play no part, suffer from paralysis when they confront his family's adversity. Like his voice in the wilderness of history, Jacob's hands come up empty in the same void.

Jacob runs into the same problem aboard the ship which takes him across the Atlantic when he encounters the French artist Tassigny. In this almost meeting between painter and presser neither marginal figure understands the other's English, so they communicate more with sweeping, expressive gestures than with words. The gulf separating artist and immigrant widens, like the ocean which separates North America from Europe, when Tassigny tries to explain his vision of the sea, the background music — the Blue Danube Waltz — adds to the unreality of the luxurious passage. The Frenchman's impressionistic description of the waves carries prophetic overtones of the tide of history preceding the war. "Sometimes the waves come quick, so quick you cannot see, one behind the other as if they cannot wait, as if they have lived enough, and now want only to destroy themselves. And it seems as if each wave wants to be the first to die" (32).

Unaccustomed to metaphors, Jacob senses the limitations of his own language once again when Tassigny describes one of his paintings, *L'Entrepreneur*. The cubist canvas displays a cylindrical, megaphone-like contraption for the head, and behind the right leg a thin, distorted female face — the anima behind the animus. "It means a man, who … who … who … how shall I say, *Monsieur,* who … who has something to show off and he shouts and screams so people will hear and come and pay to see. They come, they pay, sometimes only money, sometimes more, the whole body and soul" (36). *L'Entrepreneur* reveals a Marxist critique of capitalism, comments on Jacob's illusion of the rich man, prepares for the circus barker in Vienna, and symbolizes the fascist demagogue who captivates his audience through his powerful voice. In waves, the crowd follows this false, empty face like a herd of sheep.

Transforming the aesthetic into the materialistic, Jacob buys the painting for thirty dollars, thereby furthering his illusion of himself as a rich patron of the arts. He responds to this symbolic world in a surreal, cubist dream. He is all alone at night in his factory faced with a huge pile of white suits to be pressed before morning. A cloud of steam envelopes him. "Suddenly a faceless giant with enormous legs came stalking through an open window, roaring, 'There's no percentage working for somebody else, you gotta go in business for yourself.' The voice grew louder and more insistent and more threatening" (39). As the monster approaches, Jacob tries to flee but is paralyzed; then he is grabbed by two powerful arms. In this ghoulish nightmare, destiny overpowers the individual who has lost his free will to the forces of history; the nightmare becomes reality so long as Jacob maintains his illusions about wealth in an impoverished world. Jacob's dream fits into Alvarez's formulation of Holocaust literature by disguising the fate of paralyzed marginal man.

No sooner does Jacob arrive in Europe than he is confronted by ominous signs of anti-semitism. As his train passes through Germany's borders, he encounters one sinister manifestation of *L'Entrepreneur* in the person of a stormguard with his black swastika in a white disk and the insignia of his cap — two crossed bones and a leering death's head. The reality of Austrian politics — beggars in the streets, a failing economy, and anti-semitic outbursts — soon dispel any romantic illusions Jacob may have held about Vienna. Surrounded by his aged, fawning mother, Jacob becomes even more of a child with his family, especially when he accompanies his two young nephews to their secret cave. When a gang of ruffians hurl anti-semitic remarks at them, one of Jacob's nephews retaliates with the threat that his uncle has come all the way from Canada, near Al Capone's Chicago. His family's picture of wealthy Canada with Niagara Falls and Chicago gangsters parallels Jacob's fantasies of the blue Danube — a false meeting between two *terrae incognitae*. The cave episode represents a retreat into primitivism where the innocence of childhood may be corrupted; escape from pervasive racial hatred proves impossible even in this natural ghetto where shadows on the wall forebode catastrophe. In contrast to the openness of the Atlantic crossing, claustral spaces in the cave or factory suggest the central element of the rich man's enclosed ego — the inability to enter into an "I-Thou" dialogue.

After escaping from this cave of the Cyclops, they head for the Circean enchantment of the circus at the Prater; they move from isolation to crowds. The decadence portrayed in the film *Cabaret* or the propaganda in Leni Riefenstahl's work is analogous to Kreisel's implicit comments about the manipulation of irrational crowds with Wagnerian sensationalism: "From all sides came the tin-clang of weary Wurlitzers, accompanying the endless circles of merry-go-rounds. In the beer-gardens and in the open-air cafés loudspeakers blared out the latest jazz hits, newly imported from America. It was a mad, whirling, strident cacophony" (120). Old and new worlds almost meet through the medium of jazz imported, like Jacob, from America; a musical counterpart of the cubist *L'Entrepreneur*, this scene is an echo of the novel's opening juxtapositions — the jazz version of the Blue Danube Waltz alongside the announcement of Germany's rearmament. Cacophony within this microcosm extends not only to Viennese society but to all of pre-war, out-of-tune Europe; cacophony in the outer world parallels Jacob's own linguistic paralysis, his stammering inability to communicate. Like the clown's faces, the circus itself becomes a mask behind which society escapes from the burdens of reality. For the diabolic undertones associated with the illusory circus world, one need only think of Coketown in *Hard Times*, Archibald MacLeish's sustained metaphor in "The End of the World," Robertson Davies' Faustian troupe in *Fifth Business*, and Gunter Grass's *The Tin Drum* where circus costumes hide a demonic nightmare.

At the circus, the bugler and the barker, yet another in the list of *les entrepreneurs*, draw the unsuspecting masses as if by dictatorial suasion. "The crowd gathered round the platform ... like a lowing herd of cattle waiting to be led to pasture" (120). With its intimations of cattle-car mortality, this pathetic pastoral simile repeats Tassigny's image of people who witness *l'entrepreneur*: "One goes and all follow, like a herd of sheep" (36–7). The victims of this mesmerizing propaganda may become the tormentors who seek other victims, the innocent scapegoats; political parallels are all too evident when all the world becomes a circus in which fantasies whose consequences cannot be foreseen are performed. The deluding marginal circus, effete yet childish, ends with a grotesque act, *die Dame ohne Unterleib*, the lower half of the distorted legs of *L'Entrepreneur* — a symbol of deception and paralysis in an imperfect society.

The circus also serves as a refuge for Robert Koch, a former journalist forced into hiding for exposing political corruption. Koch first appears in the bookshop of Albert Reich, Jacob's brother-in-law; his eyes reveal a clarity of vision in marked contrast to the blindness of Jacob and the crowds. "A thin, filmy layer seemed to veil them, spanned across the pupils like a protecting screen, as if to prevent people from detecting everything that went on in them" (128). As a clown in the circus and as a foil for Jacob, he both protects and detects, for he is cursed with too much conscience and must occasionally fantasize about being a wealthy foreigner visiting Vienna. If Koch's game comments ironically on Jacob's role, it also points to Koch's disguise as clown, for, as he describes, the bugler pushes and pulls him in the side-show. Koch's prophecy prepares for Albert's death and his own arrest: "out of all the suffering, a new state of mind, a new world-spirit will eventually be born, even though I will probably not survive the holocaust" (133). After Albert's death, Jacob meets Koch at the circus to report the tragedy. "The two men looked at each other in silence. They were now an island within themselves, isolated and far away, and the noise which raged all about them came to them, muffled and indistinct, like the sound of little waves lapping and breaking themselves against a desolated shore when the sea is calm" (158). Silence and noise, isolation and crowds, the ocean separating European tragedy from American innocence — all of these themes and images surface as Jacob prepares to depart for Canada's distant shores and abandon his family to Hitler.

In Jacob's almost meeting with his family, the rich man is unable to lend any help to those who will perish. Returning to the safety of Toronto, Jacob realizes that his family was born neither at the right time nor in the right place; like them, he remains incongruous in an indifferent universe. Jacob takes Koch's advice about the fascist stream: "The best thing therefore, for those who can, is to get out of the water and wait on the bank" (163). A procrastinator, Jacob waits on the other side of the Atlantic, that futile bucket which has soiled his white suit of innocence; a lost child, Jacob will experience absence in Canada as in Europe. Poverty, unemployment, visual and aural symbols, family disputes, the motif of the crowd, difficulties in the exchange of language from character to character, the decadent world of illusions closing its eyes on unbearable realities, and lengthy political debates — by these means Kreisel hints that the fate of the Jews is similar to that of Austria: "And to us here who had to look on helplessly it seemed that nobody in the whole world cared. This is such a little country. Only six million people. We don't matter" (63).

Always in exile, doubly alienated Jacob Grossman looks on helplessly at his origins from the margins of a distant shore as Jews and Austrians suffer.

Where *The Rich Man* deals with events leading up to World War II, *The Betrayal*, Kreisel's second novel, approaches the aftermath of the Holocaust. In place of the naive immigrant of the first novel, Kreisel now substitutes a more sophisticated protagonist/narrator in a shift from third- to first-person narration. Mark Lerner, a professor of history at the University of Alberta, becomes involved in a triangular relationship associated with the Holocaust. As in *The Rich Man*, Kreisel relies on a quest motif, only this time he reverses the direction westward to the Canadian prairies. When Lerner becomes involved with one of his students, Katherine Held, he meets Theodore Stappler who wants to take revenge on Katherine's father for having betrayed him to the Gestapo thirteen years earlier. The psychological complexities of this pursuit, the suffering and guilt in the experience of the Holocaust, appear in the form of a labyrinth, one of the images Klein uses for his motif of quest and doppelgänger. "But always, no matter how I started, no matter how I twisted, I always ended up in the same narrow alley, and I had to go up this alley and at the end of it there wasn't Held, there was just Stappler ... I myself, facing an emptiness."[3] The meetings between characters in *The Betrayal* are never more than almost meetings, desolation in unheroic deserts, exercises in emptiness, absences in labyrinths where origins and margins become confused as pursuer and pursued interchange. The doppelgänger loses itself both in claustral settings such as narrow alleys as well as in the wider expanses of the prairies, thus reflecting how the debilitating effects of the Holocaust manifest themselves in dispersal and deferment through history's maze.

Kreisel's image of the labyrinth allows for a play of ambiguities and contradictions: "It led me out of the *cul de sac* ... It led me deeper into it" (126). When confronted with his act of betrayal, Joseph Held responds, "It is true and it is not true" (177). Even the simple hotel clerk, Sam, a keeper of the keys where the transient Stappler resides, complains to Lerner about linguistic ambiguities shared by the double: "You and he brothers or something? Why'n't you talk like ordinary guys? You do and you don't! You know, when he first got here he told me he was everybody and nobody" (143). As a Jew and as an immigrant, Sam is also everybody and nobody, Everyman as "a number, an x, / a Mr. Smith in a hotel register, — / incognito, lost, lacunal." Sam, who recognizes hotel guests by their footsteps, also recognizes, like Lerner and Katherine Held, that he has been fortunate enough to have escaped the fate of other European Jews. Kreisel employs labyrinthine symbolism and contradictions to encompass the complexities of responses to the Holocaust making the impossible possible. To render the Holocaust in fiction, Kreisel uses those techniques of displacement and indirection (outlined by Alvarez) both to distance himself from his subject and to involve the Canadian reader who seems so far removed from the European tragedy. To gain this double perspective of distance and involvement for himself and his reader, he displaces space and time, and disguises the experiences of his characters.

Spatial perspective enables Kreisel to distance his story geographically from the European tragedy by contrasting the guilt of the older civilization with the innocence of the New World. Not only the Atlantic separates these two worlds, but, in addition, thousands of Canadian miles — the metaphoric sea of the prairies.[4] In choosing Edmonton as the setting for this novel, the author emphasizes the vast differences between an ahistorical western Canada and a burdened Europe. Lerner comments on the sheltered life of Canadians who are removed from wars and revolutions: "It is hard, for instance, to walk the streets of this growing, unselfconscious western city, where I have been living for two years, teaching the turbulent history of Europe to young western Canadians, and to realize that elsewhere the past is not merely history but something that touches sensitive nerves, evokes powerful responses" (2). As a Canadian, Lerner the *arriviste* senses that the west is marginal to historical reality; as a Jew, with sensitive nerves and a growing self-consciousness, he converts Edmonton's streets into a labyrinthine ghetto. He immediately qualifies his generalization to demonstrate the universal implications of evil whose tentacles span even the greatest distances, regardless of borders:

For here, too, in this western city, so peaceful, stodgy even, in spite of all its activity, its growth, its feeling that the world has only just begun and history is a tomb, a collection of dry bones, here too the old ghosts stir, walk beside many a man or woman on the crowded, peaceful pavements or stand beside them as they look down into the river valley and see the great Saskatchewan River flowing dark-grey in the summer or lying stiff and white and frozen in the long winter. (2)

The recurrent image of the "old ghosts" in the novel's haunted wilderness reminds the reader not only of the nightmarish quality of the experience, but also of the impossibility of escape from mankind's universal guilt in origins anterior to the new west.

Reflecting the paradox of aesthetic distance and existential engage-ment, the ever-present Saskatchewan River becomes the spatial back-drop of everywhere and nowhere, as well as the temporal symbol of arrested history — the flux of events frozen for scrutiny. "Lying stiff," this hibernal river mirrors the paralysis of the major characters caught in a "dead-end" quest. The Saskatchewan resembles, or almost meets, the Danube, as Theodore Stappler — the second nar-rator and Lerner's double — links the forces of liberation and entrap-ment between the two rivers with his father's drowning in the treacherous eddies, the undercurrents of demonic history. Lerner's attachment to the river demonstrates the extent to which it partici-pates in the lives of the two narrators: "I look down on the magnifi-cent river winding its way through the city, and watch the changes of the seasons as they reflect themselves in the mirror of the river, until I think that I could not live without the river" (205). *Aspaklaria* and labyrinth without origin or end, the Saskatchewan accepts and con-ceals the empty pill bottle which is evidence of Held's suicide. This act complements Stappler's father's suicide, thereby completing the Held-Stappler-Lerner axis of guilt, betrayal, and involvement; Edmonton's great divide winds absently through a labyrinth of paradoxes.

The Chinese restaurant beside Stappler's hotel also divides the city and suggests an almost meeting between oriental and occidental, the everywhere and nowhere of universal nothingness: "right on the dividing line between what seemed to be two different parts of the city, a green and red neon dragon above what appeared to be a Chinese restaurant" (59). Ever sensitive to dividing lines and to ways of overcoming them, Kreisel colours his stop-and-go lights as emblems of paralysis and movement. In a reversal of the St George legend, Stappler sleeps protected by the dragon which, like the demonic, apocalyptic, and magnetic forces of the river, attracts Lerner and Stappler; participating in the quest, this dragon breathes the fire of the Holocaust and beckons the Lerner-Stappler doppel-gänger. Kreisel develops the religious implications of the protecting dragon during Lerner's and Stappler's "last supper" as they discuss crucifixion, martyrdom, and an Austrian Corpus Christi parade: "And then Kretschmar, the lover of the saints and of the martyrs, forgot all about love and everything else the saints and martyrs might have taught him, and became the soldier of his lord, just as many years afterwards he became the loyal servant of his earthly Messiah, Adolf Hitler" (157). The evils of the past with their global conse-quences invade the purity of Edmonton: through a bitter but muted irony, Kreisel is not simply accusing the Roman Catholic Church for its complicity with Nazism; rather, he is implying the universal guilt of mankind as victimizer.

Like the river and the dragon, Emily Carr's painting of a British Columbian forest scene lures both characters toward a labyrinth of paralysis. The painting resembles the river in its paradoxical combination of stasis and flux; furthermore, both represent spatial perspective — the vanishing point of convergence for the winding water and tangled trees — which, in turn, reflects internal, psychological depths. For Stappler, as he analyzes its subtleties and ambiguities, the canvas expresses "tangled emotions," the entanglement of Held, Lerner, and Stappler: "Everything seems quiet ... But that is only the surface. Below, everything is in motion. The landscape is static, but the colours are dynamic. So everything is still, and yet everything moves" (33–4). Surface and depth, stasis and motion — these contradictory poles encompass the complexities of Carr's picture and Kreisel's narrative, yielding a negative dialectic and negative capability for grasping the Holocaust. As spatial symbols of displacement and indirection, the painting, the Chinese dragon, and the river serve a twofold purpose: first, like the two narrators, they mediate between Kreisel and the Holocaust; second, they include the Canadian audience by associating the West with the evil of the Third Reich.

Aside from these specific instances of spatial dislocation, a general sense of Canadian vastness and dispersion emerges in Stappler's arctic quest at the end of the novel. A haunted haven, the liberating, infinite Canadian wilderness stands in marked contrast to his claustral hotel room and to his earlier European experience of persecution where space contracted as it pursued its victim. The perspectives of time and place converge, approaching the infinite: "you are really close to the absolute elemental quality of nature. It takes some time before you become aware of any variation in the landscape at all. After a while you see that the surface of the ice is constantly changing. So all is movement and yet all is still ... Time and silence acting together have produced a no-time" (217). Thus, the paradoxical landscape parallels Emily Carr's sylvan stasis and kinesis, as well as the movement of the Saskatchewan River with the repeated "no-time" and no-place of existential nothingness of *l'univers concentrationnaire*. Trained in absences and *différance*, the Jewish survivor braves both the Canadian problem of survival in silence, exile, and cunning, and the dilemma of representation in disfigured canvases.

For Lerner, Stappler, and Held the way seems endless, the goal impossible to reach, since they are entangled and paralyzed by paradox. What fascinates Lerner about the French Revolution in par-

ticular and history in general are "all the ironies, all the paradoxes
... sometimes the divine and the satanic are so finely balanced that
no ultimate judgement is possible, and the figure remains forever
paradoxical" (4). Accordingly, Stappler satisfies a certain desire in his
Canadian brother whenever he uses "irony as his shield" (96) and
through an ironic twist gives "an ambiguity to his words" (108). Irony,
ambiguity, and paradox protect Stappler from his own inability to
save his mother at the train station. Paralyzed by fear at the Austrian
border, paralyzed by Held in Edmonton, Stappler spreads this
paralysis to infect the other characters: "If Theodore Stappler and
Joseph Held had paralyzed each other, they had paralyzed me, too"
(196). This contagious paralysis makes the plight of the Wandering
Jew an impossible one. All that Lerner can do when Katherine introduces the spectre of Auschwitz into his office is blurt out a platitude,
"The refugee is the everyman of our time" (16). But Stappler, the
uprooted wanderer, has learned history differently: "we used to be
told about what was called the *Voelkerwanderung*, the migration of
whole peoples. But what happened then, in that distant past, was
nothing compared to what has been happening in Europe in the last
twenty years" (39). Paralyzed wanderers in the Diaspora *almost* meet,
but their convergence can never be complete; *The Betrayal*'s central
experience resides in the gap.

Another almost meeting appears in the doppelgänger motif which
links Lerner and Stappler, and implicates the Canadian in the
Holocaust by shrinking the phenomenological distance between
Edmonton and its shadows in Vienna and Auschwitz. Lerner and
Stappler are identified through their acting abilities, and the dramatic metaphors which run through the novel underline at once the
relationships between reality and illusion, and involvement and
detachment. Both the content and style of Lerner's lectures reflect
his double identity: his academic interest in the French Revolution
contrasts with his existential implication in more recent history. Stylistically, however, Lerner sees himself as an actor whose lecture hall
persona disappears in his extracurricular life. While lecturing about
the "high dramatic moments" of the Revolution, he values his experience with drama societies as an undergraduate at the University of
Toronto which have taught him "that there is such a thing as an audience, and that this audience needs to be captured and held" (1). Just
as Lerner's acting instinct arouses in his students a sense of participation in the past, so Stappler, like Kreisel, is a very effective teller of
stories: "At one point I asked him if he had ever been an actor ...
there was no doubt that he had a fully developed sense of the dramatic, and he could project the personality of others, mimic their speech

and imitate their mannerisms" (53–4). Forced to adapt to varying conditions throughout the Diaspora, these masters of mimesis act well on stage, but freeze in the face of tragic reality.

Lerner's involvement in this drama represents the attachment of all those who consider themselves innocent — whether Canadians or the majority of mankind who remain neutral, blind, indifferent, or act in bad faith by not combating evil. That the dramatic parallels afford one perspective for historical phenomenology may be illustrated in an example which acts as an ironic, though tragic, play within the play. When Stappler's middle-aged father, Dr Stappler, "became involved with a young actress," the son watches her in the roles of Desdemona, Ophelia, and Gretchen. "I used to sit there in the theatre and feel myself torn in two. Because I identified myself with my mother ... I felt that my father had betrayed her ... And I used to sit and watch that young actress going through the agony of betrayal and despair on the stage" (159). The constant repetition of "involvement" and "betrayal" serves as a linguistic trap from which character and reader never escape, while Stappler's split indicates the shifting identities between actor and audience — two halves of an aesthetic doppelgänger. The affair has ramifications beyond Dr Stappler's subsequent suicide: his widow "mourned also a lost world, until she herself was lost in the chaos and in the total corruption of that time." Thus, the individual story forms part of the larger history that immediately precedes the war; the postwar continuity appears immediately when Lerner announces that Stappler is leaving Ophelia replying "Horatio will be kind to her" (160). The full range of the dramatic allusion is thereby extended.

The first stage of Lerner's participation occurs in his office with Katherine's introduction of the Holocaust; the second stage takes place with Stappler in his apartment: "Here it was, the whole horror of the recent European past, in this apartment, where on the whole I live a peaceful, contented, relatively happy life. Here now were the old ghosts, and I was, whether I liked it or not, involved" (43–4). With the introduction of the spectre of Auschwitz, the here and now reverse to nowhere — the dissolution of the gateway to the North. This intrusion of the Holocaust firmly cements the doppelgänger as does the repetition of "whole" and "involve": "Somehow, though I had resisted it, a bond had been unquestionably established between us ... That was ironic, since my intention had been quite the opposite. For I had no wish to become involved with him ... The truth is that I resented having become involved" (46). Deterministic forces of destiny paralyze free will; mystical forces of the doppelgänger, however, also cripple.

The divisions within Lerner match those within Stappler whose Jewish mother, Protestant father, and Catholic teachers make him "a little bit of everything. Everybody and nobody. Everything and nothing" (60–1). Like the spatial and temporal extremes of everywhere and nowhere, eternity and the moment, this existential paradox underlines the dualisms within *The Betrayal* and the universality of extremity outside the novel. In addition, both brothers share a dream that can be interpreted as an unconscious reaction to the horror of the Holocaust. Stappler dreams of a man (obviously himself) wandering through a desert in search of water and seeking refuge in a cave where he soon observes his mother approaching. He tries to follow her through his surrealistic landscape:

> Then suddenly he found himself by the shore of a stagnant lake. Along the shore stood petrified trees, and from the lake itself gaseous fumes arose and poisoned the air. And he saw his mother in the middle of the lake, and he cried out to her.
>
> Only the wind answered, and the fumes from the lake enveloped him, blinding and choking him, and, like a drowning man coming up for air, with arms flailing, he awoke from his dream. (63)

His claustrophobic nightmare refers to the fate of Mrs Stappler in the Nazi gas chambers and reappears later in Lerner's sleep:

> By a stagnant lake I lay entangled in roots. I struggled to free myself. On my left and on my right there were two men whose faces never came into clear focus, although I kept looking at them, staring and staring ... They stretched their arms out towards me, as if beseeching me to help them, to get them out of the bog, to free them from creeping roots that were threatening to strangle them. But how could I help them? I was myself entangled. (194)

Kreisel's dreams of anguish depict paralysis in racial roots; this entanglement, like the one represented in Emily Carr's painting, relates to phenomenological involvement: "The more I tried to detach myself, the more involved, the more entangled, I became" (196). Ultimately, Kreisel is caught in his phenomenological labyrinth among racial roots in his attempt to comprehend the Holocaust through fiction.

The Betrayal begins and ends with the word "strange," for it is a story of estrangement, defamiliarization, paradox, and paralysis without resolution. "Everything seemed jumbled; event melted into event. I no longer knew where dream ended and reality began ... I could no longer differentiate the past from the immediate present.

Everything was now, and yet everything seemed to have happened somewhere in the distant past" (195–6). The survivor suffers for not having suffered enough; he recounts a tale of silence, absence, and absurdity; and he learns not to differentiate — to allow for the freedom of *différance* because answers falsify the fiction. Homeless words and outcast meanings almost, but not quite, meet as the ghosts of Auschwitz respect no borders, especially those of consciousness. Shades of the ghetto stir from Freud's fabled Vienna to the exposed shelter of Edmonton, gateway to the North's untravelled world, where marginal man and his discourse fade. Both of Kreisel's novels end without closure: in *The Rich Man*, Jacob Grossman leaves his European roots to return to Canadian marginality, disburdened of his painted albatross but weighted down with memory "into the darkness of the night"; in *The Betrayal*, Stappler's Arctic nomadism lingers after his death in the memory of Lerner, his celibate double who has learned about stillness in the city and wandering in the Diaspora. *The Betrayal* also ends with Stappler's first and last Yukon letter promising to tell Lerner "all" after a long period of silence. But Stappler, like Kreisel, cannot tell "all," for much remains concealed in the witness's silent language between nostalgia for a lost home and the nightmare of Hitler's war against the Jews.

CHAPTER FOUR

Between Ottawa and St Ives: Norman Levine's Tight-Rope Walkers

The true way goes over a rope which is not stretched
at any great height but just above the ground.
It seems more designed to make people stumble
than to be walked upon.

Kafka

In his short story, "A Canadian Upbringing," Norman Levine invents a writer, Alexander Marsden, a composite of A.M. Klein (similar initials) and Mordecai Richler (similar scansion). Marsden's short book, *A Canadian Upbringing*, describes Montreal's warm, lively ghetto atmosphere — its strong family and religious ties as well as its prejudices and limitations. By the end of the book, he decides to leave Canada for England where he hopes to find for himself a wider view of life: Marsden's pattern provides the blueprint for Levine's Jewish-Canadian upbringing — up from the ghetto, out of the streets, down and out across the Atlantic through a diaspora of perplexing dimensions and directions. Marsden advises the young narrator to go home, and the latter returns to silence and homelessness. Through muted long-distance dialogues across the Atlantic, Levine tries to give voice and vision to a realistic slice of life, reserving a hidden dimension in his flat representation of reality.

Born in Ottawa, Norman Levine left the colony's capital at the age of twenty-six to begin his self-imposed exile in St Ives, the mother country's artistic outpost. With such a dislocation, where is the centre, where the margin, where the ironic edge? Judging from some of his titles alone — *The Tight-Rope Walker, I Walk by the Harbour, The Angled Road, From a Seaside Town*, and *One Way Ticket* — one can see Levine's preoccupation with seascapes, journeys, and divided directions which recur in most of his work. Though known mainly for his fiction, he began his career also with poetry; indeed, some of his early poems introduce themes and images which are developed in the short stories and novels.

The first poem of *The Tight-Rope Walker* (1950) explores the dichotomy between life in Canada and in England, the coast of Cornwall being an appropriate setting as it points westward towards the poet's Canadian origins. St Ives and the Cornish coast protrude from England, suspended in transatlantic tensions just as the tight-rope walker's foot hangs in an airy void. Levine sketches his portrait of the poet as seascape or escape:

> He came as a child taking a journey,
> High above the water, in the midst of darkness.
> He separated the cliff and began to walk.
>
> There was no rejoicing at his leaving.
> There was no sorrow.
> He was neither proud nor famous.
> The wave that swept him to this cliff
> Passed many a sea-wall.
>
> He did not know why he was led to the cliff.
> Being a child
> He knew that if he swayed and plunged into the water
> He would have no final reward.
>
> Alone and above that land paling and sick of strength
> He was not lost. Only a little lonely
> He walked as a graveyard while around him
> Cities were no more than small lights
> Severed at the head by fog.
>
> Would he find responsibilities in yesterday's dream,
> Or would his religion be part of that landscape,
> Of boys throwing pebbles, hitting rain-drops?[1]

The tight-rope aptly figures Levine's dual predicament, his division between land and sea, Canada and England, Jewish minority and the larger Anglo-Saxon world, past and present. By using the third-person pronoun in this autobiographical sketch, the poet distances himself in his lines as he separates himself from Canada. Form and content reinforce one another to create the persona of the tight-rope walker, a hyphenated Icarus-like child at the cliff's edge. The child-poet on his unknown quest defies gravity and society: his directions are unknown, he is alone and unknown, and the poem's final stanza remains suspended in the mystery of his questionable future. As passive as a graveyard, driven by an indifferent wave, and separated from nature and society, the tight-rope walker in his rite of passage enters a precarious manhood in an unaccustomed setting — the mist or midst of darkness. Having abandoned his ghetto wall for a sea-wall near a darkling plain, Levine is swept with confused alarms of struggle and flight as ignorant armies clash. To the rhetorical question about the place of religion posed at the end of "The Tight-Rope Walker," Levine provides an answer in his next poem "St Ives Cornwall": "The boats were old jews praying in the Sabbath wind." This metaphor suggests that on land or at sea, in England or Canada, his Jewish roots accompany him and tighten the rope so that even when he sways he will not plunge into the sea.

The third-person distancing of the first poem becomes more complicated in the penultimate "Letter from England," which resorts to the second person with the addition of other personal pronouns; the "I" disappears after the first stanza so that the focus is on the "you" of the poem. Levine seems to be writing a letter to another part of himself, the Canadian part perhaps. The poet becomes disoriented in Trafalgar Square's Canada House:

An empty room filled with provincial papers
Telling me home-spun news
Pulled the magnet in all directions,
And this day became the same as that day
Wobbling along amputated stilts.

In the midst of London's imperial centre, an empty room is filled with provincial papers that scatter the Wandering Jew throughout the Diaspora and Commonwealth; the Canadian intrusion, a centrifugal force, dismembers the poet, and cripples the tight-rope walker; the vertigo of "home-spun" news for the homeless letter writer serves as a fading device for the flashback that takes over the rest of the poem. With the dissolution of time, one day melts into another, "then" into "now," and dates are determined by nature alone; thus the poem is dated "Saturday the trees". Similarly the magnet spins a number of pronouns in the poem, resulting in a "wobbling" I, you, she, and we.

The St Lawrence River occupies most of the second stanza, but instead of the Leviathan which swallows a Canadian immigrant, it now expels an emigrant toward the sea. The sense of division or amputation introduced in the opening stanza reappears in the wake seen from the freighter's deck: "Watching the big knife cut that water until / Bleeding white the sea became the colour of two gulls." This parting of the waters mirrors the parting of the poet who is cut off in schizoid solitude. The last rhetorical question in the stanza also combines his Canadian and Jewish heritages: "Would you return to parchment summers and merchant eyes?" An answer to these hidden allusions to Shylock's merchant and dry biblical scrolls follows in the third stanza which describes the poet's return to New Brunswick: "When by Piccadilly Circus she stood and wept. / But her exodus discovered no Babylon." Levine answers his question ironically and ambiguously, for he supplies no clear antecedent for the third-person exiled female who has left England for Canada; "she" finds no home in Canada just as he remains rootless in England — both are lost in their transatlantic quests.

No sooner does the poet return to Canada than he is back in Cornwall, England, this time in the first-person plural, the shifting pronouns suggesting a multiplicity of personae. Despite the presence of Cornish fields for the uprooted wanderer, "the roots you needed were not there."

> But Canada still called
> Across that sea-weed,
>   A horn fogged in the night.
> You added new things, but in translation
> They dissolved into provinces:
> Into Montreals, Torontos and Ottawas.

Words get lost in translation while the poet gets lost in atlantic transition between capitals and provinces (whether Canadian or British). London life makes him forget the contentment

> Of grey merchandise spawning in parchment summers.
> An exile you were then,
> As you are now,
> Wanting roots and living on an island.

The ambivalence of his nostalgic view of a Canadian past is incorporated in maritime "spawning" as opposed to arid heat, the land-sea pull throughout the poem. On his British island Levine remains an exile, lacking and desiring Jewish-Canadian roots, a hollow, reversed "Norman" conquest; without a destination, his letter and its message stay at sea.

These divisive tensions between land and sea, Canada and England, past and present, Jewish particularism and universal assimilation all reappear in Levine's short stories and, as the title *One Way Ticket* suggests, return journeys are unfulfilled, deferred necessities for his various directions. Most of his fiction may be characterized by a bare style that reinforces the sense of absence in his characters' lives. Yet out of this sparseness, Levine fashions his blend of ghetto regionalism — a self-enclosed Cornish world (or global village) with its eccentric inhabitants which is disturbed and decentred when one of its denizens leaves or when an outsider intrudes. On the one hand, this world is a clearly-demarcated region (whether in Cornwall or Ottawa's Lower Town) with stable memories, photographs, local dialects, enclosed rooms, gardens, streets; on the other, simple intrusions upset regional routine: an unexpected letter calling away the insider, or a stranger briefly visiting the area and threatening the established balance.

The central focus for Levine's Canadian regionalism is Lower Town in Ottawa, not so much a nation's capital as a lesser version of Montreal's St Urbain ghetto. Marginal with respect to the Canadian mainstream, this carefully delineated ghetto from Guigues Street to Murray Street was the centre of the lives of European immigrants in Ottawa, and central in the memory of the narrator who looks back nostalgically at a world that no longer exists. The eccentrics with their dialects have disappeared: pregnant Ethel "looked a bit scatty with her blond fuzzy hair that she had difficulty in combing" and complained about her labour pains, saying *"Me hoits. Me hoits."*;[2] or, Zaydeh Saslove, who spent days carefully piling blocks of wood in the backyard, only to knock them down and rebuild them neatly. Within this familiar microcosm these grotesques are accepted, recognizable features of the ghettoscape, their eccentricities and Yiddishisms taken for granted. When the narrator's father, a fruit peddler, returned home after a day's work in the larger, external world, he "was the same self I had known before, in his chair, in the corner, by the hanging Morning Glory, drinking Kik. And looking at the families sitting outside on the other verandahs doing much the same" (110). Where time in the pastoral world is governed by nature's cycles, in the ghetto the familiar routine of the rocking chair rivals "the mere stuttering clock": "A whole street sat on the wooden verandahs, in rocking-chairs, on the verandah steps, in the shade of the hanging Morning Glory" (5). Midway between cradle and throne, the rocking chair elevates the peddler to regal status, but in a democratic kingdom where everyone repeats the same pattern. As in Alice Munro's stories, the verandah becomes a stage between the private interior of the house and the public domain of the street, a common ground for displays of community.

To make this internal world stand out in relief, ghetto regionalism invokes the larger world outside. Levine uses the wooden wagon — a kind of moving verandah — as his vehicle in and out of the ghetto: "It was painted a bright red. And it had, on its sides, wooden steps and iron rungs to help him get up to the driver's seat and to the wooden boxes where he kept the fruit and vegetables" (5). Although Levine does not animate these objects to a Dickensian extent, he does humanize this horse-drawn world, doomed to be replaced by modern metallic transportation. Riding in a taxi along Murray Street a generation later, the narrator notices the houses, boarded up, "Solemn boxes with wooden verandahs" (11); like the fruit on the wagon, these coffin-like structures are peddled away to modernity. In his fiction, Levine is able to kill off his parents, along with the street of peddlers' horses, wagons, and the eyes of middle-aged women staring from behind lace curtains. Shedding his heritage and horses, the Jewish-Canadian writer comes of age when he returns to these roots and meets the gaze of neighbours' ghosts from behind the scrim of his own seasoned consciousness.

Once these wagons convey their peddlers to the outer world they export their comic values as well. The narrator's father jokes in vulgar Yiddish to an uncomprehending customer, the language of the ghetto levelling the more fashionable world on the other side of the Rideau Canal. The child notices the bizarre behaviour of his neighbour Mr Pleet who, instead of calling out "rags for sale" from his wagon, recites in a slight sing-song the evening service of the synagogue. "Mr Pleet was miles and miles away" (110), dislocated from his region. Another peddler, Mr Slack, resorts to Yiddish in the wealthy Rockcliffe area: "Thieves. Thieves. Nothing but a bunch of thieves live here." Robbed of their inheritance, these immigrants use linguistic wit, their only legacy, when they confront a decentering macrocosm. "I guess they knew that once away from Lower Town they might as well have been in a foreign country. And they also knew that they could never become a part of it" (111). Forever crossing borders, these marginal wanderers peddle their wit, comic resentment, and eccentricities to the external society. To lighten the burden of their own poverty, they may take solace in stories of Chelm, the archetypal ghetto which houses halfwit *schlemiels* who make the residents of Lower Town seem all the wiser. Their offspring will become part of this foreign territory, leaving the Lower Towns of America to be resettled by Greeks, Italians, or Portuguese. For centuries, European Jews were displaced from the ghettos of one nation to those of another; in North America, Jewish migration to golden and greener suburbs left empty pockets that were ironically filled by ethnic groups who may have forced the Jews out of the European world. Inheriting rich blood and two contradictory testaments, Jewish history has a way of meddling, peddling, and repeating itself with a vengeance.

As a child, the narrator day-dreamed about having other parents, pretended to live somewhere else, and wondered when he could escape; as an adult, he cannot stay away from Lower Town. "It's become like a magnet. Whenever I can, I return" (112). For the child, reality is elsewhere; for the adult, however, Lower Town is over-charged with reality. This paradoxical magnet of ghetto regionalism continues to disorient the inhabitants of Lower Town, St Urbain, and Winnipeg's Northern Island. But these photographs fade by the end of the story into an absence that can be restored only through mem-ory. Wrecking machines tear down buildings. "And the houses, on either side, in shadow, appeared even more boarded up, as if you would have to go through several layers before you found something living" (11). An archaeologist of the ghetto, Levine must dig through several layers of experience rather than remain on a surface of emp-tiness and absence. Everything is neat and in place in his mother's apartment, but looking for an old photograph, he sees to his relief "that the neatness, everything in its place, was only on the surface. That in the drawers, in the dresser, things were still jumbled up" (115). Surface neatness hides messy depths; the reader often longs for Levine to enter that jumbled world hidden in the drawers or inner recesses of characters' minds. Frozen photographs capture Lower Town's regional states of mind while creative memory thaws them and guards against mechanized destruction, modern amnesia, and universal homogenization.

In "The Playground" Levine switches from Canadian regionalism to English regionalism, from Jewish Lower Town to Gentile St Ives. Nar-ration shifts from first person to third person depending on the nar-rator's point of view. Bill Stringer, the Canadian narrator, lives in St Ives where his attempts at writing a book about an Irish immigrant trying to survive his first Montreal winter are unsuccessful. An Irishman in Quebec, a Canadian in Cornwall for the summer — these two fictional halves (or have-nots) splinter the narrator: "at the time I wasn't interested in this place. I was living in a book I was working on, set in winter, in Montreal."[3] Boundaries between life and art dissolve in this story about Stringer's difficulties with writing. His name heads most of the story's sections or sub-sections since he is responsible for "stringing" together (like a tight-rope) characters and events. So, at the end of section 1 he lists a dramatis personae that is ripe for onomastics:

These were the people Bill Stringer met at the round of parties in the summer of 1959. Abe and Nancy Gin — Baby Bunting — Rosalie Grass — Jimmy Stark (whom everyone called Starkie) — Julius and Bernice November — Albert Rivers — Carl Darch — Helen Greenway — Nat Bubis — Oscar Preston. As the professional writer he took pride in being he had them down for characters that he would someday use. (24)

Indeed, what links the empty lives of these characters, their empty names, and the emptiness of the landscape are lines of narrative description based on contiguity of event, character, and picturesque landscape. Like the local artists, Levine paints his seascapes with brushstrokes that either omit verbs or use the copula at most: "the long line at the bottom of the dazzling sand" (12). In his metonymic mode, Levine juxtaposes characters and scenes, and eschews metaphor or symbol, concentrating instead on filling absence by combining lines. The "tide-line," "water line," "dark line," the "line of dead seaweed," and the "line-ups" of tourists fill the seaside town. A "single-line train" from the mainline station conveys the tourists from centres like London to the village where they inundate and decentre its residents. One of the cottages is called "Cat's Cradle," a playground for intermeshed lives. In turn, one of the gulls that appears at the outset of "The Playground" gets "caught in between the electric wires, hung head down, the neck arching with the wind like the neck of a kettle" (65). While this bird gets stuck in the cat's cradle, Stringer manages to emerge from the regional wedge.

If the "play" involves the roles of characters, then the "ground" for these figures is both painterly line by line description, and the more sombre burial ground. As early as section 1, Levine juxtaposes playground and burial ground, yoking them together metonymically rather than metaphorically, relying on line more than on imaginative leaps:

Just above me, on the slope of earth above the beach, was a cemetery. Around me, scattered in clusters on the strip of hot sand, families were stretched out. Surf boards were standing upright, stuck in the sand, by their heads ... They looked like the tombstones on the slopes.

I told myself, I must remember that, and use it some place. But I should have given it more thought. For the kind of images that one finds in a particular place are not as accidental as they appear. Surf boards around people lying on the sand getting brown — tombstones in a cemetery. (17–8)

The "like" in the first paragraph functions metonymically, not metaphorically as in the usual simile, because the definite articles link the two parts of the landscape; in the second paragraph, a dash or line of thought connects the two disparate images that Stringer will use just as he will use the list of characters at the end of the section. While Levine may ultimately strive for the "essential," his writing depends on the accidental and contingent of metonymy.

St Ives is fraught with ambivalence for the artist: while it provides a descriptive, regional setting with some eccentric characters, this playground may deny the writer a true room of his own in which to create. The obstacles at the outset of the story — noisy gulls, summer heat, noisy tourists, and passing cars which block the light and sea — prevent Stringer from writing yet ironically provide Levine with raw material for his narrative. The transience of the setting emerges through the temporary tourists, the French crabbers, gulls which hover between land and sea, and the pervasive tidal rhythm; the rootless, fortnightly tourist stands in relief against the narrator's slightly more permanent residence, though he too departs in an empty train at the end. This contrast between permanence and evanescence appears in the initial dialogue between the elderly tourists who praise the beauty of St Ives and the local girl who is bored by the place to which she is tied. Like the comparison between surfboards and tombstones, this juxtaposition of playground and burial ground demonstrates the passing of seaside hedonism: a two-week routine of bronzing accompanied by ennui, absence, emptiness.

If Bill Stringer inhabits two worlds, Abe Gin (né Ginsberg) also remains very much attached to his birthplace — the ghetto of Winnipeg — even though he has resided in England for ten years. When swimming, Abe realizes that there is nothing between him and North America, for the C-shaped beach is like "a small bent finger flung out from the mainland into the Alantic" (18). Abe's nostalgic longing for his Canadian past is matched by his attitude towards his Jewish roots: as he becomes less Jewish, his non-Jewish wife deliberately cultivates Jewishness by cooking latkes and affecting Yiddish attitudes. Abe, like Levine's other exiles, looks across regional absence for Jewish-Canadian roots even when trapped in an actionless Chekhovian setting. One-way tickets do not suffice for these vagrants or Wandering Jews: the return ticket of memory, or ghetto regionalism, completes their lives.

Transatlantic tight-ropes between England and Canada, cosmopolitanism and provincialism, Jew and Gentile, and regionalism and universalism reappear in *From a Seaside Town* (1970).[4] Joseph Grand — tight-rope walker, narrator, travel writer, liar, adulterer, marginal man, and dweller of coastal Carnbray and of absences —

describes his narrative as a series of "confessions." In his confessional or garret, a diminished Grand shrives himself:

I went up to this room, looked at the collection of picture postcards stuck on the large mirror. (When I look in the mirror, to see myself, the postcards give a 3-D effect.) They were from people scattered over North America, Africa, Europe ... I've stuck them on with sellotape with spaces of glass in between. I even have a postcard of Carnbray in with the others ... As a postcard, I thought, I could like this place. (71–2)

While Levine's writers usually offer a mimetic view of a linear landscape from the windows of their garrets, Grand complicates this mode of perception through his looking-glass which reflects more than just his narcissistic self. Also on the wall facing him is a sign which states "You've got to get out of here"; for this latter-day Lady of Shalott, the way out of imprisoning ego and region is through postcards which (like the diasporic letters in *The Second Scroll*) cover continents and mirrors. But these postcards create a *trompe-l'oeil*: they give the illusion of a third dimension for flat, static two-dimensional characters; they offer the fantasy of escape for someone trapped "in between" various modes of existence; and they dislocate the regionalist, dispersing him throughout the globe.

In his day-to-day existence, Joseph has a confused love-hate relationship with Carnbray as with other places. As a postcard, though, he finds Carnbray bearable. Postcards combine both photograph and letter — *ut pictura poesis*. On one side, the picture captures in miniature the subject matter of the travel writer, the metonymic descriptions in Levine's photographic realism and naturalism; on the other side, the verbal experience appears in miniature, unlike a letter which may be more revealing because of its privacy. Indeed, Grand's affair with the actress Anna Likely is carried on through a series of illicit letters the eventual discovery of which jeopardizes his marriage. For those isolated, inert regionalist writers in Levine's fiction, life revolves around postal routines:

I found the whole day centred around the postman coming. I'd get up early and wait anxiously until I saw him in the street opposite. Then stand by the window, to the side, so he wouldn't see me. I watched him as he worked the street opposite, before he came here. And hid until I heard the release of the letter slot. I got to know all the postmen's habits. Who was fast. Who dawdled. Who talked. (31)

Joseph's daily confessions begin when the postman delivers words from the outer world which decentre the region just as the arrival of guests from outside disrupts local patterns. Joseph, the *voyeur*, spies on and shadow boxes with the letter carrier — an intermediary between writer and the rest of mankind. At the margins of his window or mirror, the self-confessing tight-rope walker projects his vision of absence, addressing empty letters, unable to live in and by postcards alone.

Joseph doesn't just tell time by the comings and goings of these men of letters; instead, he keeps a double standard of time (in exactly the same manner as Jake Hersh in *St. Urbain's Horseman*): "I have these two wrist watches on my desk. One is set at the time in Ottawa and Montreal, the other the time here" (170). Split between two time zones, two ways of life, the past and the present, Joseph nevertheless tries to be precise when asked the time. His wife Emily, however, complains: "As if time matters here" (177). Time matters, time doesn't matter — caught on this temporal tight-rope, Joseph struggles to keep a balance on time while Levine tries to balance temporal and generic distinctions between short story and novel. If Joseph is dispersed in space between the mirror's reflection and the postcard's projection, then he is also disoriented in time: "It's the business of having to live with two calendars" (39). Like the two watches, these calendars point to Joseph's bifurcations. As fastidious as he is, he can never quite gain control over time, just as he never manages to jettison his regional insulation. In narration, he demonstrates chaos by beginning *in medias res* and often interjecting into his narrative, "But that is going ahead" (44, 106, 110). Time-stitching in the narrative, flashbacks, an inset short story ("A Trip to London" in chapter 7), frequent parentheses and footnotes attest to structural disorder. In the face of naturalism's deterministic forces the Grands' free will is severely limited.

Levine's novel opens with a warning to Joseph to leave his wife: "Clear out. She'll only drag you down." And indeed much of the novel is about this paralytic dragging down, the inability to clear out of inert regionalism: one person drags down another, a character drags himself down, poverty drags the Grands down physically, sexually, and mentally, and footnotes scattered throughout the chapters drag the reader's eye down to the bottom of the page. Dragged down and out in Carnbray, "half way" between Canadian ghetto and British colony, these marginal characters, always in a state of chaos, live their lives at the edge. Thus, the depressing routine of the Grands' isolated lives in Carnbray is constantly being broken either by the sudden appearance of guests or by their own departures to Penzance, London, or Canada. Similarly, the narrator reveals from the novel's outset Emily's careless habits of leaving everything in disarray, "half way over the edge so that they fell ... I was always going around after her moving things away from the edge" (7). Emily leaves objects where they don't belong; in turn, she and her husband don't belong wherever they find themselves. Joseph's absent friend Albert (another marginal Jewish writer who serves as Joseph's double in his quests for Polish roots) keeps a garret in Soho "in complete disorder ('don't tell anyone about this')" (12) — the parenthesis pointing not only to Albert's shame but to Joseph's habit of exposing private details in his discourse. Albert's Kensington flat displays more of the chaos of a wandering Jew: "And the overcrowding, the haphazardness ... only heightened the feeling that something was lacking. As if the accumulation of all the years was waiting for something to come along to make sense out of it" (13). Emptiness in the midst of plenty, and deferment in meaning characterize this Jewish writer so obsessed with tracking down ex-Nazis. The room of another London friend, Charles, a homosexual painter and therefore an outcast like the Jewish writer, is a "mixture of disorder ('but I know where things are') and neatness," (23) — the parenthesis once again qualifying and protesting too much against a void. By the end of the novel, Joseph accepts Emily's "jam jars at the edge." She, however, attaches much significance to a particular red French crabber which she goes down to the bay daily to watch: "I know it doesn't belong here. It looks so gay. And I know that one day I'll go down. And it will be gone" (220). The boat forms a recognizable part of the seascape, yet offers the possibility of escape from regional suffocation. Or does its disappearance symbolize death?

In the face of all this disorder, and paralyzed by his inability to escape from a milieu to which he doesn't belong, Joseph can only write or give a semblance of order to this formlessness. He frequently describes the problematics of travel writing and short stories: "As a travel writer I have always depended on externals. Let me alone in a place, especially one that has no past associations, and I can go to town. I need the excitement of the unfamiliar, of being on the move, in order to function" (36–7). The travel writer, a kind of Wandering Jew, remains on the surface while the novelist depends on the illusion of a third dimension — hence, those mirror postcards for the craft of fiction. A metonymic writer of contiguous lines without metaphoric or historical associations, Joseph may be able to "go to town" in a place without past associations, but he cannot get out of his seaside town, nor can he escape his past associations with Canada. Trusting his eye, the voyeuristic narrator in a cut-off, empty town feels compelled to confess about his self-conscious art:

Although I'm doing confessions, I feel I'm still thinking as a travel writer. Am I not using "being hard-up" (it's my main excitement) the way I used travelling before? I tell myself, I have to go deeper. But am I going deeper? Or am I just behaving like a travel writer and, instead of a landscape, skimming over Emily's life and mine. Are things "deeper" just because you go into yourself? Perhaps a writer wasn't what I was cut out for after all. I feel I was meant to be on the move. (69)

Forever on the horns of a diasporic dilemma, Joseph tight-rope walks between genres, traditions, and contradictions. He is a two-dimensional travel writer or three-dimensional novelist, static regionalist or universal wanderer, Jewish or Gentile, Canadian or British, the mirror along the roadway or the mirror with the postcards in his room, mimesis or self-reflection. This rhetorical questioner protests too much in his own fiction, successful at painterly brushstrokes but a failure in the psychology of character development in the manner of Chekhov rather than Tolstoy or Dostoyevsky: "I have always found it difficult to describe people. Put me in front of a landscape ... and I feel immediately at home" (105). Escapist and landscapist, Joseph feels at home in language, but only in a specific kind of language, one suited to the paradoxes of diasporic regionalism, not the *unheimlich* of icons.

Joseph, then, is suited to Carnbray's regionalism which Levine accentuates by devoting a full chapter to the town's eccentrics: The Voice of Calcutta, who tells ludicrous jokes and hates the privileged; the Russian Lady, who feeds butter to her "Poosie" cats and alcohol to herself; Miss Edwards, the tall thin spinster who emerges half-dressed on cold winter days; and the short woman further down the road with her absurd conversations. Aside from this list of eccentrics, regionalism may also be characterized by the disruptive effects of characters' exits from and entrances into the self-sustaining region; and this decentring of the peripheral centre cannot be accomplished without irony. Emissaries from the Canadian town of Meridian, in the person of Mona and Oscar, arrive unannounced in Carnbray at Christmas time; Joseph's sister and brother-in-law upset regional routine. Not having seen them in ten years, he describes their appearance with an irony that treats them as total strangers, unconnected with his way of life. "It was a wizened, hunched-up little woman, determined, thrusting her face forward. It was not a pretty face" (73). And the narrator continues to describe his sister with these simplistic "it was" constructions which reduce Mona from Meridian and all her bourgeois Jewish-Canadian values. The Meridianites bear gifts of Hanuka *gelt* instead of Christmas presents, and when Mona speaks to her brother in Yiddish, Emily breaks down because she feels like an outsider in her own house. In the same manner there follows a visit from a Canadian academic whom Levine satirizes for his shallow values and interference with Carnbray: "there's nothing here. It just goes through your fingers" (103). In the next chapter the Likelys from London shake up the inertia of the seaside town and fill its emptiness when Joseph conducts his affair with Anna Likely. Ambassadors of embarrassment from the periphery fail to appreciate Carnbray, while the more creative central Londoners value the seaside artists' colony.

The converse of these entrances into the region occurs when Joseph abandons Carnbray for the larger world outside. He makes trips to London because he has to get away from Carnbray's isolation, but when he returns he brings back delicatessen food — rye bread, salami, cream cheese, herring, chick-peas — which just as easily could have been imported from Montreal's ghetto. But London's ghetto proves to be as much a trap as Carnbray's regional isolation; in London, Joseph immediately goes to Bloom's which reminds him of Waxman's in Montreal. "I thought I put the Jewish business behind me by marrying the English girl. Just as I thought I could forget about Canada by going over to live in England" (44). But ghettoism and provincialism cling to him stubbornly; memory overturns the present as much as exodus from regionalistic habit. When he returns to Canada he feels a confusing emotional combination of isolation and happiness. On the luxurious train between Montreal and Ottawa he expects "a different kind of human being to go with it*" (135), the asterisk cleaving the text through a footnote of mental association: "* I thought of the other trains ... And music was piped in: *This Way for the Gas, Ladies and Gentlemen*" (135). This sudden allusion to Tadeusz Borowski's book about the Holocaust disorients the reader who has been led from innocent regional trains to demonic ones.[5]

Once in Ottawa, nostalgia overtakes Joseph as he passes stores and streets: "They have meant more to me than anywhere else I have lived" (136), the same emotions expressed by Saul Bellow in his recollections of Montreal childhood.[6] The list of Jewish relics overpowers Joseph, displacing Carnbray regionalism with ghetto identification: "the nickel-plated samovar, the silver candlesticks used every Friday night, the brass drinking cup once used for Elijah's cup at Pesach. When I see this — and the rubber plant, the drawers packed tight with Ashkenazi prayer books, my father's tallis — I know that I once belonged to something" (140). In this family museum Joseph belongs to the past, not to the present whether in England or Canada; remembrance of things past leads him beyond Ottawa towards his

Polish origins. What begins as a trip outside of a region, ends up as a voyage into personal history where time is constantly chronicled through a tracing of origins — two watches and two calendars for the tight-rope walk between modern margins and ancient origins. The metonymic spatial chain of description for the Cornish regionalist yields to a metaphoric train of memory, that third diasporic dimension. The samovar brought over from Europe evokes another memory that requires a footnote, time-stitching between Russian music in the present at Carnbray to a song from Joseph's childhood in Ottawa. His Polish roots cause narratological, textual, and psychological decentring — "I thought of concentration camps, gas ovens" (41). As a travel writer, the narrator is often asked for a short biographical note from his editors. "Of course I change the details depending on who is getting the biography. But what a lot is left out" (38). Homeless Joseph does not know where he was born, and, concealing as much as he reveals, this unreliable narrator must be read for his omissions — absences between the lines that complement his sparse style. As he wanders through the Ottawa of his childhood he questions why he had run away to a cut-off seaside town, but he cannot find the answer to this geographical castration. Instead he offers another footnote, dissecting his text and postponing any ultimate answers: "I remember the early travel articles about Canada that I wrote in England. I wrote about the violence, the mediocrity of the people, the provincialism, the dullness ... And all the time I wanted to be there" (150). Joseph has simply transplanted one provincialism for another, Canadian colonial mentality for Carnbray regionalism.[7]

Joseph is schizoid because of his travels in and out of regionalism: outside he is carefree, inside he is all caution, always typing new lists and noting everything down. The regionalist writer protects his marriage through seclusion and irony: "the only way of keeping something one values intact one needs to be isolated, cut off" (161). Yet Joseph has to run away from Carnbray just as he had to run away from Ottawa. "Even if it is only for those few days in London, or those few weeks in Canada ... Part of me wants the conventional and some other part wants to be outside society. Yet I cannot take one without longing for the other. And so the only way seems to be to live these separate lives" (162). Jew, writer, regionalist, outcast, itinerant repeater, Joseph walks the tight-rope of ambivalence: "Or was another reason why I don't live in Canada because I didn't want to become a *Canadian* Jew. I couldn't make the change from what my parents were to what I see walking in Montreal and Ottawa. When it was necessary, at the start, to change one's name, to live with two calendars, and tell little lies about oneself — I told whoppers" (162). The changing tenses indicate the different perspectives between past and present, Canada and England, while the lies, like irony, become defenses against root-lessness and instability. Writing cancels all of these boundaries. The platonic lies of literature break down the falsehoods of life as we are constantly reminded by Emily who repeatedly warns that her husband will translate everything into a story about writing and difference. Joseph sees "nothing wrong in writing about it because I saw writing as something different than living. I mean I tell the truth in writing. But in life I live it in different ways, with different people, full of evasions" (216).

The truth in Joseph's writing or in Levine's is deceptive: it "lies" in the lines between postcard and mirror, self-conscious reflection, travel literature and short stories, Ottawa's ghetto and Cornwall's artists' colony, absences and regions decentred. Levine's amphibious tight-rope walkers wander through the Diaspora to climb marginal roofs and window-sills, and to defy with irony the drag of gravity; his linear sense of observation and obsessive regional lists make for a literalness "in the cleanness of the prose" (146). His third dimension lives *in absentia*. A thin line divides the pared-down prose and characters from "home recognized: there: to be returned to —." Out of Ottawa's streets Levine turns to Albion's literary heritage before returning to his Yiddish slums, curtailing the long journey into a short story.

CHAPTER FIVE

Homeward Unbound: Jack Ludwig's American Exile

In an introduction to his first novel, Jack Ludwig invents a beginning in his frozen city teeming with a northern immigrant mix: "I sing confusion, I, Jack Ludwig, myself confused, or, to put it another way, a come-home Winnipegger. Half my adult life I lived in Canada, the other in the U.S.A., is it any wonder that when I say *I'm going home* I don't know where I'm heading?"[1] This mock-heroic testimonial to Homer and Whitman announces Ludwig's North American split, a rupture further complicated by his Jewish background where a highly developed ironic sensibility guides him through multiple confusions. Janus-like, facing Canada and the States, Ludwig's homeless half-and-half soul deliberately makes it unclear where he is heading.

Consider, for example, his award-winning short story "Requiem for Bibul," which first appeared in 1960. Set in Winnipeg during World War II, the story establishes an American polarity when Bibul goes to New York to study at a Yeshiva, a Commonwealth axis when the narrator dreams of Oxford and when Winnipeg is invaded by aircrew trainees from New Zealand, South Africa, and India, and a Yiddish background when mothers of the northern ghetto haggle with Bibul, their fruit peddler. The title itself indicates a kind of oxymoronic mix of high and low brow — a Roman Catholic religious service for a Yiddish peddler, high mass for lowly Jew midway between Bible and Babel, the religious and secular poles of the protagonist's life. Indeed, if we accept a portrait of the semite as a split man — one who "sits in a cloaca up to his neck, but his brow touches the heavens"[2] — then most of Ludwig's fiction, like Bellow's and Richler's, seeks a middle ground between high-brow erudition and low-brow coarseness, between a transcendent Bible-land and street-savvy pavement. "Requiem for Bibul" fulfils precisely the criteria of this portrait because Bibul's devotion to pavement peddling will yield enough money to enable him to become a rabbi: "Bibul immersed himself in the practical, pedestrian, material life because of a Great Cause — the Yeshiva in New York, eventual immersion in a spiritual life."[3] Immersion imparts transcendence: "Hip deep in ... effluvium Bibul ... in reality's ooze of tomato" (213). Bibul fluctuates between his peddler's notebook and God's prayerbook. What complicates this dualistic caricature of fruit-and-vegetable reality is the perspective of the narrator who belongs to a group of high-school students intent on avoiding the ghetto's cloaca and achieving recognition in the larger world. These competitive academic sharks of St John's High believe that they have surpassed their teachers in know-how, and dream of graduating from Oxford: "We were out to save the world, Bibul a buck" (213). For all the narrator's insistence about his group of theoreticians being lost in abstraction in contrast to Bibul's practicality, the opposition does not hold by the end of the story when we see Bibul the *schlemiel* drown because he never learned to swim. Hip deep in the reality of Winnipeg's "island" slum, his own *terra firma* of pavement and street savvy, Bibul survives and thrives, but in the heat of New York at the Y's pool, he sinks absent-mindedly. The ghetto's Lycidas immerses himself in effluvium up to his neck, but in cleaner waters, his brow which touches the heavens loses sight of reality and destroys him on earth; amidst island sharks, he is a fish out of water.

"Requiem for Bibul" opens conventionally — "Once upon a time" — but soon becomes an anti-convention which immediately calls to mind Joyce's *Portrait*, and therefore deconstructs its own temporal layering. Before the reader gets to "*that* kind of time" about a boy and his horse, he must wade through a lengthy historical list which precedes the subject of the opening sentence and paragraph: "if we counted time not by calendars but by assimilated history and scientific change I'd be tempted to say four or five thousand years ago: before total war and all-out war, before death-camps." Those complicated Jewish calendars create a "time-sorrowed perspective" from Biblical origins until the Holocaust, for Bibul's drowning in New York coincides with Hitler's Final Solution in Europe. But Ludwig's "Requiem" salvages the memory of Bibul. Although the narrator cannot find Bibul's like in Winnipeg today, he concludes: "In love and the joy of remembering I sing you this Bibul and all that's past and passing but not to come." This mock epic style runs through the story and is well suited to the disjunction between Hebrew high-brow and Yiddish low-brow, for St John's peddler is the forerunner of St Urbain's horseman. The Bibulophile transforms the ordinary into the extraordinary, immortalizing 1939 from a twenty-year distance and heightening the time scale through medieval comparisons.

Winnipeg as a village exhibits elements of ghetto regionalism in its "island" slum north of the CP railway yards. To leave it is to become lost, as Bibul tragically discovers, and as the narrator warns prior to his departure: "doesn't the idea of a city the size of New York scare you? You'll be strange" (221) — as if he weren't strange enough on his own island. With his twisted dialect, fearless Bibul brushes aside the narrator's concern: "Wadz t'be asgared? ... Beoble iz beoble. I zeen all ginds aready." With such wordly wisdom and pronunciation of "people," he becomes identifiable with Everyman in this "Requiem for Beoble." At the same time that he leaves for the Jewish capital of America, his own region becomes disturbed by the war. "Winnipeg was transformed, full of aircrew trainees from places I knew about before only through postage stamps, men with yellow skins, red, brown, black, Maori tribesmen from New Zealand, bushmen from Australia, strange-sounding South-Africans, carved-faced Indians thronging the streets and beer parlors" (221). The Jewish regionalist on his way up from the ghetto toward universalist assimilation recognizes estrangement and defamiliarization, and ironically exchanges his tribalism with the primitive bushmen from down under. As the empire descends on the colony, Bibul expands outward to the Diaspora — equally strange, out of place, different.

If the war temporarily invades the region, modernism destroys it permanently: "Somebody waved a T-square wand over the old 'island,' bringing in the ninety-degree angle unknown in Bibul's far-off day. Progress pretends Bibul's 'island' never really existed; the lanes are paved, the rotten wood of wall and fence has been sloshed over with paint" (223). The ghetto's architect laments this kind of demonic transformation from eccentricity to electricity, centralization, prosperity, motorized trucks, River Heights, Silver Heights, Garden City, places of togetherness, spotlessness, the polite answers comfort has given to the sad old questions of civilization. Right angles are wrong for a dislocating nostalgia: Ludwig, like Levine and Cohen, would prefer dissemination, unanswerable questions, Yiddish slums that remain in writing that is about time's haze.

Aside from these disconcerting exits and entrances into ghetto regionalism, Ludwig focuses on the eccentricities of his protagonist, a Yiddish picaro with "his ticlike blink, his coal-black hair in bangs over his forehead, his emery-cloth shaver's shadow, his ink-stained mouth, his immutable clothes that wouldn't conform to style or seasons: always black denim Relief-style pants whitened by wear and washing, always a brown pebbled cardigan coiled at the wrists and elbows with unraveled wool, always a leather cap with bent visor, split seams, matching the color and texture of Bibul's hair" (212). Even in life, Ludwig seems to set up his heavily-hyphenated, disheveled subject — quasi-cadaverous Bibul — for a requiem, but come to life Bibul does with his everlasting "yeh-yeh" — a Yiddish double affirmative that perversely makes a negative. "Bibul had a grand gesture to sweep away our irrelevance, a sudden movement of the hand like a farmwife's throwing feed to chickens, his nose sniffing disgust, his sour mouth giving out a squelching sound, *aaaa*. Sometimes he sounded like a goat, other times a baby lamb — just *aaaa*, but enough to murder our pushy pretensions" (213). Ludwig has warned his reader from the outset that this is no pastoral tale, but at times it resembles a barnyard fable in which Bibul levels and democratizes with a gesture or a Yiddish monosyllable, a vehicle for comic revenge, a demolition of the established by a nomadic wit. When his fellow students question him about semantics, "'Aaaa,' *aa*ed Bibul, and his chicken-feeding motion sent us back to ivory towers" (213), for the tower of Bibul confounds the third-floor kings of St John's High School. The low brow unmasks the high.

Instead of doing battle against the intellectual kings of St John's, Bibul rides out with his horse Malkeh (Yiddish for "Queen") to challenge his female customers, those abusive, haggling, thieving *schnorrers*. Drawing ironically on epic and picaresque traditions from classical to medieval to the Renaissance of Cervantes, Ludwig juxtaposes sublime and bathetic in his detailed description of Malkeh who is long past her galloping prime. "And what a riding-out that was! His painted wagon listed like a sinking ship" (215), preparing for Bibul's eventual drowning. "As grim as Don Quixote's Rosinante would look next to elegant Pegasus, that's how Malkeh would have looked next to Rosinante; she was U-shaped in side view, as if permanently crippled by the world's fattest knight lugging the world's heaviest armor" (215). In his mock-epic simile Ludwig compares mythologies, suggesting that Bibul's hyperbolic ghetto chivalry belongs in the tradition of Sancho Panza and Falstaff, while the detailed list of Malkeh's features belongs to ghetto regionalism and epic battles, commercial rather than courtly. Although Malkeh is purblind rather than purebred, Bibul covers her eyes with fancy blinkers, hinting at his own ultimate blindness when the swimming attendant warns him not to enter the pool. "Who can be blind to Bibul's response?" (222). Heaven hinders vision as strongly as the cloaca impedes movement and transcendence. Malkeh symbolizes the entire immigrant predicament, for on the "island" she suffers no invidious comparisons, "but on a main thoroughfare like St John's High's Salter Street, Malkeh was exposed to the cruelty of horse hierarchy, and her submarginal subproletariat hide was bared" (216). Ludwig's irony, his mock-heroic stylistics, comes to Malkeh's aid, undermining a Canadian code of honour with its class-ridden boundaries, by inverting and displacing hierarchies, by elevating the "submarginal" to olympian heights of literary recognition. Ludwig's naturalistic humour restores the likes of Bibul and Malkeh to the centre of Canadian focus, exposing traditional authority. "Into the lists Malkeh dragged the keening wagon, onto the 'island' in ruins like a medieval town (Canadian history is short, but our buildings add spice by getting older faster)" (217). The old mare enters ghetto and courtly lists, low and high; if New World culture is recent, then ghetto history with its spices adds an extra dimension, a rich discipline of irony and *différance*.

"Requiem for Bibul" was first published in *The Atlantic Monthly*, bringing Winnipeg's ghetto to the attention of a wider American audience, and this dichotomy between Canadian roots and American mainstream continues in the rest of Ludwig's fiction. His first novel, *Confusions* (1963), may not be set in Winnipeg, but in his introduction to the paperback edition he confesses: "I wrote *Confusions* in the reading rooms of the New York Public Library, in various apartments scattered around New York City and New York State; it contained stuff I had jotted in notebooks years earlier, while in Massachusetts, California, Minnesota, Puerto Rico; but the novel proper was written during a long hot summer — in of all places — my home town, Winnipeg" (iv). Scattered throughout an American diaspora, this marginal wanderer or pan-American Jew returns home to piece together these fragments or confusions in the empty Ryan Building, a few blocks away from where John Hirsch, an artistic "ally" against Winnipeg philistines, is trying to establish his Dominion Theatre. This need for an ally or fraternal landsman, a Sancho Panza for every Don Quixote, a double for every half or schizoid man, runs through much of Ludwig's fiction. "I am clearly a revisionist full of tricks, apologetic, and double-take. If Canada were half what I pretend it is, I wouldn't have to pretend anything at all" (vi). In league with other Jewish-Canadian tricksters, he has to revise a tradition, give and take double to compensate for halves as he crosses borders and distances himself from origins through tricks of irony. Unlike customs officials, the Manitoba mosquito pays little attention to the fact that part of this Canadian chauvinist's blood is Yankee, a continental half-breed with dual citizenship. With these insects comes the cleaning lady, a synthesis of Bibul and Malkeh, whose naturalistic presence occasions an outporing of allusiveness — Melville, Kafka, Beckett, Cocteau, Eliot, Frye, Edmund Wilson, and Erich Auerbach — which is part of tradition and authority. She "derails" him with her challenge to the superego, a substitute for any muse: "Everybody got to have a supervisor, mister" (vii). This mop-wielding Urania unsettles, unnerves, puts him into a spin with her local tales that play counterpoint against the cosmology of *Confusions*: "In Winnipeg how does one *know* the Massachusetts or California in his head *is* the one demanded by his type on paper?" (viii).

Both introduction and novel bespeak decentring, dispersal, dissemination; in the ironic metalepsis of Ludwig's motto Second Things First, revised, second scrolls come first. Expanded into an entire novel, this introduction would form a sequel or prelude to *Confusions* and, as Ludwig confesses to his "dear reader," *Confusions* is but "half a novel," the other half being the reader or the cleaning lady. "Just as two halves make a city" — past and present, inside and outside ghetto walls. This invitation to reader-oriented criticism continues beyond halves into multiples, the many-faceted, iconoclastic sub-versions of irony: "Are there *only* thirteen ways of looking at a blackbird? Maybe that's what I should have told the cleaning lady; that what I have in mind is an endlessly complex blackbird whose contradictory shapes and faces make endless possibilities for fiction?" (ix). A thirteen-dimensional diaspora holds the necessary angel and charwoman, deferred homecomings and traces of origins, confusions and contradictions, blackbirds rising from the ghetto's gutter-scattered oats, migrating across margins.

The twelve chapters and epilogue of *Confusions* amount to thirteen ways of looking at Ludwig's fictional world, a mock-epic satire of American academic life with representatives from a northern wilderness — a Jewish protagonist and a Canadian in exile. Where Levine's Joseph Grand writes confessions, Ludwig's Joseph Gillis sings confusion, split between his paleface Ivy League appearance as Joseph Gillis and Hassidic origins as the lowly Joey Galsky. "There were precedents — Abram's name change to Abraham, Jacob's to Israel, and my people have been changing their names religiously ever since" (3). These mock changes mark the changing circumstances and identities of a nomadic people on the road to assimilation, and coincide with the book's moral purpose — to change the reader's and narrator's lives: peripetia of the peripatetic. If Harvard changes the protagonist's life, he in turn transforms its walled yard into "A ghetto! A *shtetl* like Pa's small Russian hometown, Krivoi Rog, that's what my Jewish bones recognized in Harvard Yard, a ghetto where everyone knew everyone else, talked like everyone else, dressed like everyone else" (4). From Krivoi Rog to Harvard Yard in one generation, Jewish wit and irony tear down Ivy League and ivory tower hierarchies; link-

ing elbows like dancing Hassidim, Gillis, and his best friend and ally
Gabe Pulford (né Polonsky), chorus together, "So *noo*," the same Yiddish monosyllable Jacob Grossman uses in *The Rich Man* to convey
multiple nuances of meaning. Humour arises from the constant juxtaposition of the high-brow Gillis with the low-brow Galsky: instead
of unity, harmony, and radiance, he finds doubleness, confusions,
and comic blindness in the face of *différance*. On his superego board
sit his father, God, the Hassidim, Buber, Heschel, Harvard College,
Brooks Brothers, Joyce, Tolstoy, the New Critics, and Alfred Kinsey;
his id committee is equally powerful, consisting of a string of females
and a disrespect for authority; his ego is thus constantly pulled
towards two extremes.

In his thirteenth year, Gillis, then Galsky, underwent a double rite
of passage: his *bar mitzvah* at the synagogue and his sexual initiation
with his aunt's Welsh maid. His aunt, who catches him in the act,
immediately informs his mother, a dressmaker who needs help to
tzetrenn (unravel) a customer's dress, exclaiming, "That boy of yours
hot tzetrennt my *shikseh*" (9). Undressing commercial and academic
pretensions, *Confusions* is, in part, about unravelling and undoing
narratives, much in the manner of *Tristram Shandy*, for Gillis' narration exposes his character through dramatic monologues of Yiddish
rhythm addressed to the reader and heightened by rhetorical questions that are a kind of ironic mock catechism: "this confusion I sing
is as much yours as mine. In the Ur-beginning was Confusion —
remember? And only when it was recognized as confusion, and
named Confusion, could something with a little form come out of it.
Dear reader, I include *you* in" (29). Tracing origins in any direction
leads to confusion, *creatio ex nihilo*, a Sternean labyrinth of comic
chaos: "If this tale I tell seems episodic, blame my life, dear reader,
and not my technique. Tell me where to get a coherent destiny and
I'll queue up for it early tomorrow morning ... my art, mirroring my
life, emerges episodic. I myself am an imperfect prism. What you
read is imperceptible refraction of data the culture passes through
me daily. Only my confusion is consistent" (173). Neither mimetic
realism in the manner of George Eliot nor psychological stream of
consciousness à la Virginia Woolf, but diasporic narration scatters
and refracts individual episodes, incoherent fragments.

Ludwig's allusiveness and parody demonstrate the talents of Jewish
mimicry — of appropriating a host culture and mediating between
two great traditions — and almost reconcile high metaphysics and low
slang. "In this heebie-jeebie world I ride an elevator, one minute
shaking hands with the man in the moon, the next matching miseries
with that underground man of Dostoevsky" (173). Or, instead of this

vertical diaspora — Hebraic-Judaic, heebie-jeebie — the narrator may find himself trapped in the Hellenic labyrinth of language: "I see us all in that old faker Dedalus, who built himself a labyrinth so he could play at being trapped. Irony of ironies, trapped in a maze of his own making" (271). Just as the narrator exposes his function, so the protagonist displays his tradition: "I would come barefoot down from this dark hill bearing the new tablets from Sinai" (161). This Jewish prophet of second things first and newer testaments dreams, like Joyce and Klein, of a Jewish Pope, and of Moses inviting his rich Aunt Tichel of Brookline to the Promised Land. He imagines himself on Mount Sinai, but the stone in his hand is a boulder, not a tablet, and he is Sisyphus rather than Moses. Slaying Moses and slain by him, Galsky both negates and constitutes the Mosaic tradition; Gillis, however, identifies with Daedalus in his labyrinth or Sisyphus struggling, and accordingly negates and constitutes the Greek heritage. In this *Aufhebung* or ironic uplifting, Gillis-Galsky inhabits a desert, an ironic interval, a hyphenated "in-between" state.

Not only is Joey's thirteenth year "Yiddish, iddish," but the rest of his life turns into an exercise in unravelling the thread of his double hook. For Jewish-American deferment he adopts the motto Second Things First, and deflates high-brow Puritanism with low-brow Hassidism. Ludwig raises his narrator's confusions and incongruities to a mock mythical level by including a Faustian devil in a dialectic clash with a Hassidic Rabbi, both bargaining for his *tzetrennt*, schizoid soul. They accompany Joseph from Harvard to his exile in California where he continues to sing pluralism, versatility, and flexibility; as an academic deconstructor, Gillis announces, "I don't understand authority; hierarchy's plain silly" (49) — the lessons of Jewish humour. *Confusion*'s dedication to Susie and Brina, "Who break / Bread / To make / Circuses," also announces Ludwig's carnivalesque approach. He breaks bread and conventions in inviting his reader to partake of his collation, a repast that breaks with the past in its repartee.

Having dined on bear stew at Chez Dreyfus, Joseph meets the Devil who offers him "completion" and a slogan, "In God's Circus nobody gets concessions" (27), which turns into the title of chapter 11 and unsettles any chauvinistic notions of choice, chosenness, natural selection, and Kierkegaard's *Either/Or*. If the Devil advocates "unseeing the light," then the reader should follow his advice in understanding his role of mediation in the internalized mock dialectic between the protagonist's two selves. But to "unsee" the light, the reader must return to origins and examine Ludwig's satiric techniques. Harvard's world-renowned Egyptologist, Shuster Burvis, provides the necessary instruction, for he recommends dianetics as

the ultimate means of vision. In the essence of "higher-critical skepticism," Burvis performs Swedish exercises upside-down. Ludwig's
inversion reminds us of dianetics in Burvis's simian posture and
"strange goatlike keen" — a reversion to Darwinian origins. Moreover, the Yiddish translation of "Burvis" is "bare feet" so that unshod
"Shuster" is exposed. "Yet Burvis was for dianetics as if he had just
dug it out of Egyptian ruins" (31). Ontogeny recapitulates phylogeny
in Ludwig's frivolous archaelogy and Ivy carnival where dianetics is
immediately followed by comic dialectics in the person of Dr Gormand
Chargecard, the world's leading Hegelian whose dialectical materialism acts as a foil for the confusions of Doctor Gillis and Mister Galsky.
Dianetics unburdens the past, negative dialectics opens the future.

A misfit in the closed academic society of Royce Center, California,
Gillis quotes Kafka's parable about leopards which break into the
temple and drink the sacrificial chalices dry: "Royce, O Kafka, was
without leopards, though its sacrificial chalices seemed, in fact, quite
dry" (99). But Gillis does find an ally, another iconoclastic leopard,
in the person of Andrew Flamand, a Canadian exile in California.
Gillis first encounters Flamand during a departmental meeting ("Ivy
League in the Committee Room" — Ludwig's Joycean revision) where
he doodles in the face of authority, destroying professional pretense.
He next meets him in a bar after a faculty party: "Exile was banish-
ment from delicatessens" (114), whereas for Flamand, exile is banish-
ment from Canadian beer. A mesomorph Cree celebrating marginality,
Flamand is married to Annette Schwartz, a Brooklyn Yiddishist special-
izing in Sholem Aleichem — it appears that the American melting-pot
favours mixed mythologies. Torn between Thoreau's Walden and
Reich's orgones (just as Gillis is split between the Devil and the Hassid),
Flamand finds catharsis through ejaculations of untranslatable Yiddish
monosyllables, "Vei, vei." While Gillis represents palefaceless confusion, Flamand is red man "confission." Ironic fusions and fissions
constitute the dual or multiple streams of citizenship in Ludwig's
Jewish-American alliance where Spinoza's monism or Leibniz's
monads revert to perennial nomads: "I-Thou" reconciliation or negative dialectics. Philip Roth has coined the term "redface" to account
for this partial reconciliation of being fundamentally ill at ease in,
and at odds with, both worlds.[4]

In his second novel, *Above Ground* (1968), Ludwig abandons satire and
subdues his Jewish humour in favour of a lyricism that celebrates life
rather than confusions, rejecting Dostoyevsky's underground man for
an aboveground man in the moon. The picaresque episodes of *Confu-*

sions give way to more serious considerations of the *Bildungsroman* in this novel as the protagonist develops from childhood to a maturity filled with love and death. Each of the novel's three sections bears a heading along with its title — North, West, East — indicating the protagonist's growing sense of direction in the face of nomadic exile from Winnipeg to California to New York. The first section, "memos of a messenger," is set in Winnipeg though the city is never actually named, just as the protagonist's name does not appear until the final section, suggesting the formation of his identity later in life. "I was born in a cold city to a beautiful warm mother and a handsome father whose life began again every time he met a beautiful woman."[5] From his father, the narrator-protagonist inherits a love of beautiful women as well as a phoenix-like rebirth from the ashes of adversity, but where his father eventually breaks down, Josh survives. As his name indicates, Josh is both a fighter at Jericho's walls and a traverser of rivers: from the Red and Assiniboine to the Hudson in the east, he crosses time's currents on his way to the promised land of New York: "If any one wall bore a new message of Sinai I would not have been able to stop to take it in. Like the Dutch hero sailing into port to do battle with the crouching enemy, only to be swept out to sea" (232). The North American Wandering Jew defers his almost meeting with a messiah bearing new messages and newer testaments. Where *Confusions* celebrates anti-heroism, *Above Ground* praises the heroic efforts of Josh to overcome handicaps by encoding and decoding messages.

As the novel opens we find a young boy in a hospital undergoing surgery to remove his tonsils. When he wakes up after the operation he bleeds from the throat; his heroic response is to sing about love and women in vocal lyricism. When he spies a mouse under his hospital bed, he begins to hemorrhage but celebrates the epiphany of this mouse: "He was a messenger to me, gray and tiny-tailed. Gray and red. I love the colors together" (4). He identifies with the lowly creature, for both are messengers of meaning above ground in this cyclical narrative of "space spun": "Should we end celebrating the mouse we began with? ... He, poor long-dead mouse, has, alas, only me. Salute him with me" (364). If his first operation causes him to sing for love, his second operation results from, and continues to cause, his jumping for love: "I leaped over any available obstacle. No fence seemed too high" (5), yet he does trip and fractures his hip. But nothing fractures Josh's spirit, for he spends the rest of his handicapped life surmounting obstacles, leaping over routes and rooted fences, soaring upward and outward across North America.

To assist Josh in his flight above ground, a series of "European uncles" — substitutes for his weakening father — provide the necessary support.

> But when Uncle Bim stretched his long arms the way ancient birds beat their wings to soar their tired heavy bodies high over intervening mountains, he made you want to devour life.
>
> Bite chunks of blue out of the sky, I mean; flare up on fire to where the sun sits spinning. He made you want to wrap your arms around spring greenness, imprison in your ear the cry of waking birds, love and be loved by a loving lovely girl.
>
> This *imitatio* I live is a shifting fickle thing; but when I turned messenger I leaped to stride in Uncle Bim's footsteps. (6)

Immigratory birds of a feather unite in Josh's tightly-knit, extended family. Where Romantic odes to skylarks or nightingales create flights of fancy which annihilate the self — Ludwig's transcendent lyricism is more firmly rooted to the ground of mice and men like Bim. For all his flying powers above ground, Bim rises from the ghetto's "gutter-scattered oats"; a "bald eagle" who seldom bathes, forgets to wash before eating, and clears his throat in a terrible way, Bim nevertheless inspires Jewish flight between pavement and pleasant Bible-land. An eccentric prophet, he speaks in the future with similes, reassuring his hospitalized nephew: "You will glow, like sun in rubies" and "Days will pass. You will sparkle, shining, like blood." Up to his neck in cloaca, his brows touching the heavens, this Old Testament figure devours life and the *cuit* of Diaspora's delicatessen: "rye bread of a dark and snapping-crisp crust; grated black radish and Bermuda onions covered with oil and coarse salt; his taste in salami was hot, hard, dry, garlic-loaded; he prepared pickles in dill-and-red chili pepper; laid his own wine, red sweet and powerful" (7). Bim's stabilizing is a force to be reckoned with in a shifting fickle diaspora; his presence fills absence, "his singing voice mocked silence." In this brief but detailed sketch, his "beaked eagle's nose demanded a third dimension of the world," for he refuses to be just another flat minor character; instead, like a messianic Uncle Melech, "he spoke with a rush of whirlwinds and a touch of deliverer zephyrs," inspiring his nephew apostle to spread his wings and his messenger's word — flying and singing above ground-garlic zephyrs.

Uncle Bim's adversarial cousin Dobrushyn also feeds Josh's imagination, furthering his escape from casts, traction, weights, and hospital imprisonment. "I put the two of them on stage at night, when everyone slept, and no nurse came, Dobrushyn on a white steed and Uncle Bim, my Don Quixote, sitting Sancho's donkey. They tilted from the front and the back of windmills, never meeting, never hurting" (26). Imagination's free play creates a fugitive vision of an almost meeting between two quarreling relatives, *luftmenschen* slightly above ground, defying authority and providing balance for a crippled Josh. While these two quixotic characters ride horse and donkey, another uncle, Wilkoh Joe, rises out of the west on his bicycle, encouraging Josh's healing. "Wilkoh Joe and Uncle Bim, I rode off into sleep thinking of them, Uncle Joe, Wilkoh Bim, on a tandem bike, capable as Russian gymnasts, circling the moon" (27). Riding and rising in this Chagallian portrait of uncles coupled, Josh's allies and circus performers defy gravity through their lunar decentring; metaphor and imagination raise them from Winnipeg's pavement to ancestral Bible-land and origins far above ground. Yet Wilkoh Joe's life ends tragically when he hangs himself by standing on his bicycle seat and letting it roll. He commits suicide because of a Bibulesque misunderstanding with his doctor: although Dr John Dover tells his patient that he doesn't have tuberculosis, the Ukrainian immigrant in all his innocence fails to understand the English voice of authority. At school Josh has to face the bully who trips everyone during recess, but Josh manages to knock him down, and the fallen enemy is forced to shout "Uncle!" — an important part of Josh's education. A hero by accident, Josh rises from the situation above ground, always assisted by an avuncular presence. When Josh leaves Winnipeg's ghetto Uncle Bim stands on the platform, a "fierce falconer" (126) releasing his nephew higher and wider toward the west where Uncle Baer takes over in California.

If all of these uncles lend strength to Josh's body and imagination, then his seraglio serves him well in the fields of love from ghetto boyhood to diasporic manhood. Eliot's phrase, "so all women are one woman," serves as epigraph for *Above Ground*: nurses, teachers, Maggie, Zora, Alvira Drummond, Nina, Gila, and Mavra accompany Josh through his apprenticeship. He falls in love with his night nurse Miss MacLendon who removes heavy weights from his bad leg and reveals to him the larger world beyond the hospital. Engaged to Maggie, he has an affair with Zora and goes to see Don Giovanni, his hero and specialist, now an old man who knows women only in a general sense. Nina in the California library acts as a catalyst for his love: "I knew I would try to leap that fence again, the one I did not get over" (163). With Nina he breaks out, smashes the windows of his confining childhood: "That mouse, and Uncle Bim, made me *take* messages, and hug them to me. Nina made me sing them out. I ran" (174). For her, Josh turns from mimetic messenger to projective "po-et," like Coleridge whom he studies. While all of these women are life enhancing, one spastic girl threatens Josh with kinship, for her "doorway led to the underground crippled" (51). Her legs in chrome braces, she leans over a scrolled wrought-iron gate and calls his name pathetically, but ominously. "Sinister Ariadne pretending the labyrinth is a trap and she my guide out when the thread that led from me to her was a chain to drag me out of life" (51). When she trips and beckons to him, he refuses to help her: "My life changed when I decided to run" (52). During this turning point of affirmation Josh avoids her snare, but the memory of her haunts him much later, "See, Mister ... run with all your might and you will still swing on my scroll gate" (120). The lame runner vaults over gates, fences, walls, and all other boundaries, and encodes messages on scrolls; he runs away from Ariadne to run with the likes of Nina.

Joining with all these women and uncles helps heal Josh's fractured hip, not completely but enough to allow him to move upward and outward beyond hospital limits and labyrinthine corridors — "a city within a city within a city" (11). Initially only his Chagallian imagination provides escape: " I soared out the narrow windows on a multicolored Persian capet, my only passenger a dark-haired nurse. We rode together to Paris and Rome, climbed to the top of the Eiffel Tower" (8). Josh's *Bildung* involves a broadening of horizons from hospital bed to verandah windows where he rediscovers the framed world of neighbours, presence and absence: "it was Either/Or. Light or no light, sound or no sound, a human being or none at all. One window. No more. That much space. Nothing wider" (20–1). His lyrical, epistemological expansion leads him to delight in nature: "when I rose, and went out, I met my ignorance face to face. For four years I saw no river. Not till I saw the river did I know what it was like to see no river" (41). He connects the park by the river with his love for girls: "Evelyn, who like the river, I did not know without knowing I did not know" (63). Winnipeg's Red and Assiniboine rivers, like Mandel's Souris and Kreisel's North Saskatchewan, expand outward mythically from prairie regionalism to a universal river — "Shakespeare's Avon or Eliot's Thames or Joyce's Liffey" (6). Josh's early confinement and window visions create a framed mode of perception: "This square my hands frame for your eyes is a rear-view mirror" (46). To frame messages and images is to tell a story and to lend support to weaker members of his family.

Not only nature, but the city belongs to his discovery as he lists Winnipeg's mosaic from Jewish second hand clothiers to brown-shirted Nazis, Don Giovannis, Faustuses, Medeas, Cyranos, Tartuffes, Clytemnestras, punks, dolls, queans — the same mythical-realistic mix as in Bellow's Chicago or Cohen's Montreal. Josh continues expanding as he progresses from high school to university during the Depression and World War II before leaving for the States; as a narrator combining past and present tenses, he continues his childhood habit of framing scenes: "Look with me out of this high window at a town not mine, on a river neither mine nor Hermes's. There's a beat-up old slum tarpaperpatched, tilting with broken TV aerials and slanty chimeys ... My tower stands between that slum and this lovely river bridged for walking" (89–90). From his Winnipeg watchtower, an isolated Jew invites his visionary company of readers to his homeless city, an amalgam of ground, pavement, cloaca, and lyrical river. Like Levine and Isherwood, Ludwig narrates as a photographer of naturalism: "An openshuttered camera records a thousand separate moments on a single plane of film: the developed picture gives the illusion it has captured the motion of an instant: so this eye, and this imagination, and these hands which try to frame images out of what is rushing by" (91). Time's river is captured by this narrative lens whose frames, borders, and margins shape a marginal dangling man forever crossing borders towards a wider world of experience. As Jewish-Canadian protagonist, Josh expands; as a narrator, he sets limits to this experience by giving it form and frame. As an adult he returns to Winnipeg:

I sat on the porch, lay on the couch to simulate the old seeing. The world outside was a door, a gate, a blank slide flashed on a screen while the show was preparing ... The finite world fixed by the darkened houses across the street did not describe a universe which meant a thing to me. Two-dimensional memory, three-dimensional escape. Relativity's analogue in reverse, illustrating a flatworm's great liberation. (312)

Even with all the assistance of uncles and lovers, Josh has to struggle with representational dimensions of infinity, for like a Kafkaesque character, he discovers that expansion may be illusory in the face of unending deferment. "I had been allowed to reach the forbidden castle, and consider the quest at an end, to find I did not understand the rules of the world. Dark space between the castle and my feet unrolled like the black skein I saw in my dreams" (181).

The major rhythmic pattern in the novel is an oscillation between the joining of allies and the fracturing of bodies — connecting episodes and isolating fragments. Similarly, Josh when in hospital must choose between an operation or the constraining cast to heal his fractured hip — the choice is to cut or to cover. The former method is of course the more traumatic: "I had played Isaac to my surgeon, and his knife slipped" (18). The severed Jew invokes the

Hebraic œdipal precedent at a major turning point in his life, his departure from Winnipeg's ghetto:

"I now think — the worst time was not when you put that knife to Isaac's throat."
"You have left the house of your father."
"Was it sad for you?"
"Sad, and bleak, and lonely."
"With God's voice in your ear."
"I missed my father."
"Who worshipped idols."
"I missed my father's idols." (127)

By linking his personal departure with the biblical parallel, Josh adds meaning to the painful severing of family ties, that double bind, cutting umbilical cords for independence in fear and trembling. But instead of amputation and spilled blood, Josh is spared, covered in a cast. "I was spun in wet plaster, wound white like a silkworm spinning, a long sleeve ... Stiffening. Stiff ... A paralyzing cocoon" (20). From this chrysalis emerges a sensibility devoted to conquering paralysis through running and the energy of a soaring spirit. The decision to cover rather than cut has marked consequences on Josh's psyche, leading from spun plaster to "space spun" in the novel's concluding section.

Josh writes on and about his plaster cocoon, he plays tic-tac-toe on its graph and graft, so that ultimately it becomes a symbol for narrative deconstruction.

I'll stop the spool's spinning and turn back to me on that porch where, once walking, I slept on hot nights. And thought of Icarus released from a labyrinth and flying over the sun, unsinged. High-school, Depression, war, love, everything too fast. Huge ball of fate unwinding in its speedy roll down a hill, I in chase, my task hopeless — catch the ball, rewind it, come back to time's unwinding hill. (71)

From Winnipeg's regionalism, Josh's imagination projects through time and space to a mythological dimension that universalizes his own destiny. His "casting" imagination seeks to join or fuse at least two traditions — Hebraic and Hellenic, Jewish and North American, particular and universal, personal and mythical. When his mother is hospitalized his father feels "cracked" as if his collarbone has broken; when Josh encourages him that it will mend just as his own fracture mended, his father questions his imperfection:

On those concrete plaza steps that nursery tale's truth fell, and we again were shattered. And all the king's horses fell to it, to pull the vacuum-locked hemispheres apart ... Lazarus joined them, who should have known; Prince Charming did his best. Hercules, Bellerophon, Percival, and even him, Moses, and Joseph, and Jason. And when they were all gone, and had not one prevailed, he, the king, himself came and took what had fallen and held it broken in his palm, spoke gloriously to it, unchanged, in his hand. (73–4)

Falling, breaking, and shattering so that Josh can fly, join, and mend. If his "father is a river broken out of its banks," Josh will restore that river through the fullness of writing: "His city, my city is set where two rivers meet. Its two main streets hug the rivers, one better than the other. Often they wander off, but in time remember, and not much is lost" (74). The setting of the novel parallels the setting of bones, all meetings are almost meetings, as Josh the Jew wanders off to America but remembers his northern city in memos of a messenger.

Where his neurotic professor identifies himself as "Ishmael, doomed to wander the philistine earth" (88), Josh is a good deal more optimistic in his own narrative wanderings. "This unwinding skein rolls out of my hands, too far from my gray mouse. Strands of Grover, strands of war all in a rush unrolling. I would play out each segment slowly, fingerwidth by fingerwidth: I tell this tale not to line gig lamps symmetrically" (89). Although he rejects Virginia Woolf's "transparent envelopes," he narrates through window frames, yet he frequently gets caught in classical labyrinths where Hebraic wanderer turns Hellenic Ariadne or Daedalus: "A woman sat mourning a length of thread in her hand. I spoke to Ariadne, and heard a reconstructed tale" (122). Josh identifies with the myth when "Theseus's blade cut Ariadne's deheroizing thread" (123), for he has experienced both surgical cutting and heroic spinning out of his plastic cast, emerging above ground from the hospital's labyrinth. Narrative threads deconstruct the tale of Josh's filiation; messianic epiphanies occur when the narrative skein ceases to unravel. "Back in my north city I saw a messenger once ... and think of him now this skein has momentarily stopped its fated unrolling. Lights fall on space at special times. Divine sparks break out of unsuspected stony places" (90). Ludwig compares this vision to Yeats's fisherman, another apocalyptic figure who demonstrates how ordinary messengers prefigure messianic epiphanies.

More important than labyrinths, unwinding skeins, and spinning casts for Ludwig is his use of "palimpsests" — historical coverings for enigmas which, when uncovered, turn into epiphanies. Josh's friend's sister Evvie becomes insane and eventually commits suicide with her face strangely painted — a "mimeface, warmask, smeared palimpsest" (80). Josh tries to reverse her situation, to undo her insanity, but she is beyond reach in a reality he stares at but cannot see, a psychic underworld labyrinth. "Archaeological subcity. Hellcity. My feet walked a modern street but my step might echo in a dark town totally hidden. Scrubbed of lipstick, rouge, and mascara, Evvie's face sent out no messages. Unchanged outside. Belowground cronecackle mocking my seeing eye, and my happy-ending vision. Turn one knob and everything reverses" (81). Like Klein, Bellow, Cohen, and Levine, Ludwig is an urban archaeologist, unearthing memos of a ghetto, excavating Freudian messages buried under surface pavement, and reversing the onrush of time's haze. At his own wedding, Josh notices his Uncle Bim aging, heading towards death, so he tries to turn back to Bim's earlier selves, the younger man beneath "This face a palimpsest, all the earlier images erased, blurred, or harshly scrawled over" (91). Like psychoanalysis, palimpsests conceal and reveal family histories or origins, as in the case of Josh's cousin Tamara who "is the first etching on the palimpsest, which then was Aunt Reva, then was Evvie ... In time palimpsests surround us" (136). These pentimentos of the Diaspora or racial memory are remarkably akin to Derrida's paleonymics, part of textual and animal grafting which Ludwig exemplifies in his narrator-protagonist.[7] Just as his uncles and other family members form palimpsests, so Nina and his other lovers belong to the "palimpsest of failed lovers" (185).

Josh's experience of New York — the Diaspora's Canaan — is similarly palimpsestic in so far as he invokes Genesis, origins of American margins:

Astraddle the sundrenched street I felt the globe turning under my feet. Heelmarked and hoofmarked and bellymarked. Palimpsestic avenue, man-recording, creaturerecording. Space inscribed by time. Who walked here and breathed here and died here. Palimpsest of history, prehistory. Primordial. The first mark of motion. Doomcrack birthcrack ...

Step, toe, retrace the tread of all those who loved a mad girl ... It's all there, transparent spider threads weaving a palimpsestic tale.

Miracles I carry in my bones. Not when voice spoke out of whirlwind; or seas parted; or man was swallowed then spewed by a whale.

When Abraham went out was a miracle.

And Rebecca walked to the well.

And Jacob again saw Joseph. (348)

For the messenger who encodes and decodes Winnipeg's messages, signs lyrical and semiotic signatures in California's sand, and spins space in New York, Josh reads time into his walk in space. The various marks — Achilles' heel, creaturely hoof and belly — together with the cracks in his bones point to Josh's limp, which is at the core of Ludwig's obsessive palimpsest. At Peniel, Jacob wrestles with an angel, and with his wounded thigh is transformed into Israel; in Winnipeg, California, and New York, a nameless narrator struggles with surgeons and voices of authority to metamorphose into Josh, the lover of mankind and womankind. Harold Bloom's biblical exegesis applies to *Above Ground*: "Israel's limp testifies to having been crippled at a particular place, but the far more vital testimony is to the triumph of having prevailed into a time without boundaries."[8]

By the end of the novel Josh has wrestled with the angels of his parents' death, but he arrives at tentative answers for his "three-dimension palimpsest, where every motion — like a filament once glowed, now out — burned its signature" (361). In this mourner's house Josh joins sounds, makes episodes continuous, and discounts the finite. If Klein's "Portrait" defies the gape of gravity, then Ludwig's portrait of the narrator as a young man defies entropy in his "unfinishing tale, cast images in frames, of swift metamorphoses" (363). Lyrical dreams conquer "almost everything, except what's broken, here, and still unhealed" (363). The wound and the tale lack closure, for *différance* imposes itself at every turn in the heroic breach of hope above ground.

In Ludwig's last novel, *A Woman of Her Age* (1973), the setting shifts to Montreal where a series of characters revolve around the octogenarian Doba Goffman. To intermesh the various sections, Ludwig borrows techniques from Joyce's *Ulysses* and Virginia Woolf's *Mrs. Dalloway*, abandoning plot to devote his energies to style. The style consists of Yiddish words, phrases, syntax, and rhythm injected into streams of consciousness; in a sense, style itself becomes the narrator and protagonist, and like most of the other characters in the novel, style is Jewish. While comedy derives from such onomatopoeic words as *klotzy, zetz,* and *oontz,* the word *t'shuvoh* — derived from Buber — lies at the heart of much of Ludwig's fiction. Its religious meaning is "repentance," but it also means "return" and "answer," as if the correct answer were to return to God's ways as a means of repenting for one's sins. In the final chapter, "Tutti," a recapitulation of all the characters and their dreams, set at two in the morning against the sound of churchbells, some of the characters concentrate on *t'shuvoh.* One of the characters imagines the Messiah's footsteps on the roof: "the

Meshiach Meisseh, which goes on and on like one of Barney's philosophic poems ... Jacob waiting for the Messiah"[9] — an exercise in deferment, Jewish fiction as messianic diversion.

Assaulted by so many confusions and contradictions in the Diaspora, Ludwig maintains that one *must* go home again, return to one's ghetto roots. This Winnipegger reclaims the ordinary and adds a mythical dimension to the golden boy on top of the Parliament Buildings so that it may attain the Keatsian immortality of the nightingale. From the one-dimensional satire of *Confusions*, he progresses to three-dimensional *Above Ground* beyond "the 3-D color postcard City Hall"[10] where imagination discovers the real, Victorian city hall. Revolutionary archaeologists excavate a sunken fabled city rooted in the higher reality so that golden boys are aligned with Yeats's golden birds. Having wandered away from home and the familiar, Ludwig returns to his memories of Winnipeg: Bibul drowned but shining like phosphorus at the bottom of the waters which surround a northern island, eastern metropolis, or California's sandy coast. Between satire and nostalgic lyricism, he defeats the threat of paralysis and packs the void above ground. In Ludwig's transterrestrial aviary, there are indeed many ways of looking at a blackbird: lyrically and mythically, on the wings of the dove or on golden boughs; satirically, killing a mockingbird; naturalistically, sparrows in gutter-scattered ghettos, or a homing pigeon returning with its *t'shuvoh*, its message, signature, and space spun from a decentring diaspora toward a cold northern city with its warm ghetto origins. His necessary angel may be an incomplete angel, but in its sight we see earth again with its roots and its wanderers.

CHAPTER SIX

From Origins to Margins: Adele Wiseman's Immigrants

I could conceive of another Abraham for myself ...
who was prepared to satisfy the demand for a sacrifice
immediately, with the promptness of a waiter.

Kafka

The epic scope of Adele Wiseman's fiction encompasses Canadian vastness, Russian roots, and a biblical world of history and myth. Describing her Manitoban background, Wiseman sketches a Chagallian bird in flight, refers to the Noah's Ark of her childhood and Tower of Babel of her adolescence, and offers a childhood painting of the prairies:

There was the sky. Always the sky. Not just to look up to, that blue in the dominant, but to look round at, yes, down at even, from the precarious shelf of prairie to look down at an underlying horizon ... Here you hang in the sky with only the soles of your feet glued to earth, flies on the ceiling of the universe. Breadth and depth of sky, uncompromising stretch of prairie, leading on like the endless dream, the dream of becoming a writer someday ... of discovering whether, if you go far enough, sky and sod will meet and be reconciled.[1]

This dialectic, or almost meeting, of sky and sod, wings and roots, heaven and cloaca recurs in her autobiographical *Old Woman at Play* where she traces her mother's Ukrainian roots to the Bug and Sinyuha rivers near Odessa and Kiev. "You went up from the edge over vague tracts of water, on a kind of wooden stepladder to a boardwalk to the sky, and there they were, the rickety wooden houses, the cows, the peasants, the rivers, the grandparents and aunts and uncles, my mother's people, my auxiliary world."[2] With its Chagallian effect of transcendence and surrealism, Wiseman's diasporic imagination possesses this auxiliary world which links Winnipeg's "edge" to Russia's *shtetl*, an exilic home for Sholom Aleichem, Chagall, Isaac Babel, and Osip Mandelstam.

Wiseman's Winnipeg, like Bellow's New York or Chicago, fosters dreams of leaving North America to merge with Russia. Her dual longing for home and cosmic significance, for proximity to and alienation from tradition, finds its Russian counterpart in Osip Mandelstam's compassion for the earth, archaeology, etymology, Promised Land, equation of Jew and poet, and invocation of Chagall. Burdened with a heritage of sheep breeders, patriarchs, and kings, Mandelstam walks through the Kiev of Wiseman's and Klein's ancestors: "I hear some muttering just underfoot. Can it be a *cheder*? No ... a basement. A hundred venerable old men in striped *talesim* are seated like schoolchildren behind narrow yellow desks. No one pays attention to them. If only Chagall were here!"[3] Yet his emancipated imagination paradoxically distances itself from these origins: "I have not taken it into my head to justify on esthetic grounds the ghetto or village life style. Rather, I am speaking about the inner plasticity of the ghetto, about that immense artistic power which is surviving the ghetto's destruction and which shall emerge completely only after the ghetto is destroyed."[4] The Russian-Jewish-North American alliance in the plasticity of Chagall, Mandelstam, Bellow, Klein, Ludwig, and Wiseman guarantees the ghetto's survival over vague tracts. Curtailing routes and rootedness, beleaguered Ostjüden do battle with the indifferent frontiers of a new land and the outmoded world of their fathers. Across intercontinental drifts of the Diaspora, fathers sacrifice for their prodigal sons and delay meaning for another generation and a newer genesis.

Adele Wiseman's first novel, *The Sacrifice* (1956), bases its characters' names — Abraham, Sarah, Isaac, Laiah, and Moses — on the Old Testament. Her major characters lack family names, as if to suggest simultaneously their homelessness and their universality, for each of these rootless refugees may be taken as the Everyman of contemporary society. Similarly, as in Ludwig's novel, Wiseman's Winnipeg remains unnamed since it is everywhere and nowhere, universal and unique. The disorienting process from biblical archetypes to East European immigration to North American acculturation belongs to a tragic mode in *The Sacrifice* but takes a comic turn in her second novel, *Crackpot* (1974), as Jewish immigrants struggle with their own marginality and nomadism. Displacing patterns of movement and vision impose themselves on characters whose free will clashes with the deterministic forces of a disruptive universe. The auxiliary world of immigrant, orphan, and adolescent settles at best for an almost meeting with the Canadian landscape and culture.

The Sacrifice opens with Abraham in throbbing motion on a train which blindly carries him and his family across their new continent. His spontaneous decision to disembark stems from a blind rebellion to act according to an inner drive which countermands the endless locomotion. "Enough! With a sudden rush of indignation, as though he had been jerked awake, it came to Abraham that they had fled far enough. The thought took hold in his mind like a command. It came alive in his head and swept through him angrily, in a wave of energy, a rebellious movement of the blood."[5]

The frequency of similes and "as though" constructions in *The Sacrifice* points to a highly comparative mode in which immigrants adjust to new American circumstances so different from their previous European habits; in addition, the comparative mode invokes the supernatural in the otherwise ordinary lives of characters, lending a vertical, epic dimension to the novel. A Judaic note enters with the first exclamation of continuous suffering and wandering, and carries through to the "command" simile in the Mosaic tradition. Yet at the same time as the patriarch obeys God's commandments, he is also an iconoclast rebelling against certain forms of authority. In his opening decision to arrest movement, as in his later fatal decision to destroy Laiah at the novel's climax, Abraham re-enacts "the unhappy, split consciousness" of a being caught in Kierkegaard's teleological suspension of the ethical.[6]

Having wandered for fifteen months and eleven days, Abraham is determined to set down roots no matter where he is. When he addresses the conductor in Ukrainian, Yiddish, Polish, and German, exhausting his linguistic repertoire, he realizes that he is caught in a migratory Babel: "Would I have understood him even if he had understood me?" (5). Yet linguistic incompetence is only an external manifestation for a far more deep-seated psychological and existential incomprehension which overwhelms Abraham's family. "It did not really matter whether they stopped here, blindly, or went blindly on to the other city" (4). Blindness pervades *The Sacrifice* — Abraham loses sight of reality, and fate turns a blind eye from these Jewish immigrants who are dislocated in space, time, language, and vision. Isaac imitates his father's "oblivious purposefulness" (the oxymoron underlining their blind will which struggles against deterministic forces), while his mother, Sarah, finds herself "hypnotized" in visual paralysis. The young boy surveys the landscape with its double-crested hill that dominates the east: "To Isaac the land seemed like a great arrested movement, petrified in time, like his memories, and the city crawled about its surface in a counterpoint of life" (13). This nomadic immigrant seems especially sensitive to patterns of motion

and stasis, those rhythms in his own brief life where space is trans-
lated into time. While Abraham paces home over the same ground
that meets his stride firmly, as though he has just learned to walk,
Isaac watches the double-crested Mad Mountain towering in front of
them, solid, stable, rooted. "It was like the sight of his father's face
when he had opened his eyes for the first time after the fever, towering over him, claiming him" (22). In this sacrificial chain of being,
Abraham towers over his son and claims him, only to be claimed
ultimately himself by Mad Mountain — Ararat's ironic refuge, fate's
Moriah, or a displaced Sinai signifying the immigrant's maladjust-
ment to the Canadian landscape. Without the Mount Royal of
Montreal, Wiseman superimposes her magic mountain on a horizontal landscape to add a mythical dimension for surveying Old World
past and New World future.

Abraham soon finds work in Polsky's butcher shop where he meets
Chaim Knopp, the *shoichet* (ritual slaughterer), to whom he confides
his past as a butcher's apprentice. On one occasion his master decides
illegally to perform the ritual slaughter in place of the designated
shoichet, while Abraham watches, paralyzed by the blasphemy. When
his master next commands him to slaughter a cow, he feels that this
is his true initiation, his real *bar mitzvah*. "Not only did I see in that
moment the depths of baseness in a man, but when I turned, trembling, to face the beast, I approached another mystery. Who has to
take a life stands alone on the edge of creation" (37). In fear and
trembling, Abraham treads that fine line which separates life from
death, wondering, as if in biblical times, where this had happened to
him before. "I felt as though I had suddenly been taken out of
myself, as though this moment did not really exist and as though it
had existed forever, as though it had never begun and would never
end" (37). Groping for the knife and for psychological balance, the
apprentice patriarch becomes destabilized through all those "as
though" clauses that scatter his being, deferring the moment
between origin and eternity. Abraham's re-enactment of his
forefathers' sacrifices initiates him into blindness, paralysis, absence,
and the almost meeting between life and death. The "sky crowded
into my eyes piercingly, blindingly. Inside of me I could hear someone crying — so strange, so isolated. A living creature is different
from the dead meat I was used to handling. The difference
frightened me" (38). Even as the sky above blinds him, so the cow's
eyes beneath him make him dizzy; henceforth, *différance* continues to
haunt Abraham whose internal decentring parallels his diasporic
wanderings.

Losing control, Abraham also tells Chaim about the death of his sons during a pogrom in Russia. "For a few moments he moved about aimlessly, quickly, back and forth … His arms moved as though he had no longer any control over them" (58). When Isaac is seriously burned after saving the Torah from the flames of the synagogue, Abraham's split deepens into two voices, one rejoicing in his son's heroic act, the other questioning the impending tragedy. After Isaac's death, his mind increasingly wanders, the whole man dissolves like the distinctions between one object and another. "He did not even know what he looked like any more … Here his arm lay in front of him loosely on the table, his fingers drumming, a thing apart from him" (250). Having crossed so many borders, he loses sense of his internal boundaries, all of which have become burdens, especially weighty after his bitter argument with his daughter-in-law. "It was as though another vital part had been slashed away from him, and he was all contorted, trying to hold his wounded members in place and at the same time trying to fend off with his own fury the fury that threatened to dismember him entirely" (288). In this tragic dismemberment, the butcher becomes sacrificed to uncontrollable forces so that he is "unaware of direction, scarcely aware even of the piston movement of his legs" (292) which have now taken over the earlier mechanical function of the train.

Blindly and heavily he goes to visit Laiah, the ghetto's *femme fatale* who whispers to him, "like one," a false union between the two sexes, a false union between his contradictory voices, and a false union of the two halves of simile wherein Abraham has tried to comprehend the New World. "The other part of him — that was empty, unbelieving, the negation of life, the womb of death, the black shadow that was yet clothed in the warm, tantalizing flesh of life" (300). All along, Abraham has been confused by life and death, having to sacrifice far more than his biblical namesake; in this absurd universe, his mind zigzags back and forth from past to present, rebounding from the unreality of each, even as he roams the earth.

Looking at her then, he was lifted out of time and place. Lifetimes swept by, and he stood dreaming on a platform, apart, gazing at her with fear growing in his heart, and somewhere his Master, waiting. As in a dream, the knife was in his hand, the prayer was on his lips. Praying over her, at some neutral point in time, he saw her as though for the first time, and yet as though he had always seen her thus, saw her as something holy as she lay back, a willing burden, to offer, to receive, as once another. (303)

Though on the point of some revelation, Abraham remains blind to reality; though weighed down by sacrificial burdens, he is raised beyond spatial-temporal boundaries in this ecstatic moment; and though he has seen Laiah repeatedly, this seems to be the first time as Abraham cannot separate the original from its repetition. In this mystical moment, time is deferred, space dispersed, while the old apprentice waits for his master, a slaughterer of progeny. His platform is the sacrificial platform, the train platform where wanderers alight and disembark in their diasporic plight, a neutral point between the contradictions of offering and receiving, first times and their archetypal repetitions, absence and presence. The iterative "as though" in Wiseman's syntax disseminates and universalizes meaning, yet Abraham inverts the meaning of life and death when he stabs Laiah, and all prior sacrifices flash before his mind.

While Abraham's sacrificial act is both spontaneous and preordained in his contradictory life of nomadic paralysis and revelatory blindness, Isaac's life is similarly guided, by an oblivious purposefulness. He envies what he thinks is his father's steadfast, absolutist vision, but his own conflicting, relativistic mode of perception has its blind spots. "Why couldn't he be like his father, keeping his eyes fixed somewhere, at a point, so that everything he saw had to mold itself to his perspective? Instead his eyes wavered from point to point, and nothing remained fixed under his stare but, moving, changed and revealed itself as something new" (68). Isaac's wandering vision actually imitates his father's, yet, for both generations revelations are enigmatic epiphanies shifting between confusion and certainty. He tries to transmit his sense of vision and motion to his son Moses as they lie in a park watching a cloud move while the earth revolves. In turn, Moses in visionary and revisionary company blinks experimentally through his spectacles, each generation viewing the New World as empirically as Spinoza as if it were for the first time. And when Abraham teaches his grandson about biblical sacrifice, he is at once recounting the original and rehearsing his slaughter of Laiah in a unification of past, present, and future.

In that moment lay the secrets of life and death, in that closed circle with just the three of them, with Abraham offering the whole of the past and the future, and Isaac lying very still, so as not to spoil the sacrifice, and the glint of the knife and the glare of the sun and the terror of the moment burning into his eyes so that when the time came many years later when he must in turn bless his sons he is too blind to see that Jacob has again stolen the march on Esau. (177)

In his retelling of the biblical story, Abraham combines life and death, motion and stillness, clarity and blindness, and a closed circle which is broken by a decentring destiny.

Isaac's spontaneous rescue of the Torah from the flaming synagogue prefigures Abraham's sacrifice of Laiah when on the point of some wonderful revelation his arm and the Word leap. "Leaping out of the inferno, like a revelation bursting from the flaming heavens, ran Isaac" (195–6). Although all three generations respond in a vast ecstasy, Isaac's heroism proves hollow, the revelation dissolves when his action results in paralysis.

He was imprisoned in a transparent bubble of some plastic materal ... Sometimes, in a burst of energy and desire, he pushed out and outward, expanding his sphere, stretching his limbs beyond any length that they had ever achieved, so that the tips of his toes and fingers alone touched its surface, and he poised in the ecstasy of effort, certain that one final burst of strength and will would stretch the bubble to its limits and he would break through. (197)

The closed circle of Abraham's sacrifice corresponds with Isaac's spherical enclosure; the immigrant's expansion into the New World proves to be a tragic illusion in the face of fate's limitations. To break through the bubble's confinement is to die, so that the choice or individual free will has no place in a blind universe where ecstasy is sheer fantasy. Just as his father ends up on the periphery of society on Mad Mountain, so Isaac is doomed to marginality and a borderline existence. Destiny crushes: "If I broke through I'd no longer have the sphere as my boundary, but I'd lose protection too. The bubble bursts, and I burst with it, into the unknown ... Aren't the two things in the end the same, my victory and my defeat both illusory?" (199) Isaac's dilemma points up the ghetto's boundaries; sacrifice ends in absence, paralysis, blindness, and silence — an exilic circle.

After all the disintegration in *The Sacrifice*, there is a glimmer of hope or reunification at the end of the novel as Moses visits his grandfather on Mad Mountain and joins hands in a linkage of generations: "he felt not as though it merely lay superimposed on his own but that it was becoming one with his hand, nerve of his nerve, sinew of his sinew; that the distinct outlines had disappeared. It was with the strangest feeling of awakening that he saw their hands fused together — one hand, the hand of a murderer, hero, artist, the hand of a man" (345). Abraham the murderer, Isaac the hero, and Moses the artist embrace and "hand" down to one another, a tradition of vision and action, always on the threshold, platform, or margin of a new understanding threatened by blindness and paralysis. Despite the defeat of an individual, only through a larger sense of familial unification can any semblance of continuity be guaranteed; one generation sacrifices itself in order to be restored through its progeny, but when the reverse occurs, tragedy hangs in the balance. Abraham, Isaac, Jacob, and Moses lose themselves in repetition from biblical genesis to this twentieth-century tragic restaging. The novel comes full circle when the driver announces the destination and Moses repeats his grandfather's gesture; lifting hand from face, Moses looks curiously at his fellow man even as his fellow man reciprocates with a glance of estrangement. Only a trace of the auxiliary world remains between the grandfather's rigid orthodoxy and the artist grandson whose "disappearing act" leads the reader back to Klein's *The Second Scroll*: "All of him in one fluid turn would flow into the music and remain, invisible" (328). Floating sounds and unfinished stories stretch across the prairies eastward to Klein's Montreal, and further to Russia, where Hebrew violins delight in oriental notes.

Wiseman's grim vision in *The Sacrifice* changes to comedy in *Crackpot* as birth and marriage replace multiple deaths. Hoda, the comic protagonist and ghetto prostitute, strives to integrate mankind and defeat fate: out of her marginal status she creates a central position, challenging authority through her grotesqueries. Like Moses in *The Sacrifice*, Hoda is artist and magician transforming visibilities. The epigraph or anterior margin to Harold Bloom's *Kabbalah and Criticism* — "A song means filling a jug, and even more so breaking the jug. Breaking it apart. In the language of Kabbalah we perhaps might call it: Broken Vessels"[7] — seems interchangeable with the epigraph to Adele Wiseman's *Crackpot* — "He stored the Divine Light in a Vessel, but the Vessel, unable to contain the Holy Radiance, burst, and its shards, permeated with sparks of the Divine, scattered through the Universe."[8] Where structuralism deals with the metonymic relationship between container and contents, poststructuralist criticism deconstructs vessels, displaces inside and outside, and disperses meaning. Wiseman's decentring novel resembles a cracked pot whose fissures expose a grotesque universe, as do the stories of Sholom Aleichem and Isaac Bashevis Singer where samovar replaces golden bowl or grecian urn.

Crackpot opens by tracing genealogies, in biblical fashion, celebrating origins, creativity, creation, and procreation. "Out of Shem Berl and Golda came Rahel. Out of Malka and Benyamin came Danile. Out of Danile and Rahel came Hoda. Out of Hoda, Pipick came, Pipick born in secrecy and mystery and terror, for what did Hoda know?" In this parodic echo of Genesis we learn of Hoda's origins and progeny, her body being something between a divine vessel and an earthy pot — an interface between shifting insides and outsides, tops and bottoms. Hoda's mother carries a magically endless supply of food to silence her: "Things can't go in and out of the same little mouth simultaneously" (7), except, however, in a cabbalistic universe of broken vessels containing everything and nothing. Everything does go in and out of Wiseman's protagonist; hedonist, heroine, whore, golemess, container, and deconstructress, Hoda personifies simultaneity. Emerging from an "ever-so-slightly hump-backed mother," hyphenated Hoda celebrates decentring, and in all her naivete unseats authority. By invoking and updating a cabbalistic tradition, Wiseman shifts her marginal Jewish prostitute to a central position and in doing so scatters Winnipeg's ghetto and regathers the shards.

Hoda's grotesque origins stem from the graveyard: "they take the two poorest, most unfortunate, witless creatures, man and woman, who exist under the tables of the community; they dig them up, he out of his burrow in the woods, she from the heap of rags in which she crouches, and they bring them together to the field of death. It is the tradition to take the craziest and most helpless you can find" (17). Hoda emerges from these humble underground origins — the union of blind Danile and hump-backed Rahel — to save their community from a raging epidemic. Up from the ghetto, this Mary Magdalene is out to save the world. At school Hoda relates the story of this earthy salvation, much to the horror of her teacher, the inverted Miss Boltholmsup or "Bottoms-up," who "saw in disgusting detail the whole obscene picture, the wretched couple of cripples copulating in the graveyard while a bearded, black-robed, fierce-eyed rabbi stood over them, uttering God knows what blasphemies and unholy incantations" (97). Evidently, Hoda's story gains something in translation from old world to new, from graveyard to schoolyard. Uncle Nate shares the teacher's distaste for his atavistic family of three sacks: "An empty sack, a lumpy sack and an overstuffed sack" (49). While Rahel rationalizes the hump of her back as a carrier of burdens, she dies from the lump in her stomach. Later, Hoda returns to cemetery origins with her sexual escapades beside an Anglican graveyard where her dress is rolled up, where boys roll over her, and where her laughter rolls over the dark park on one side and the dark graveyard on the other. Potato peels she eats and peals of laughter displace the contiguous relationship in space and demonstrate that things do go in and out simultaneously; hedonistic comedy defies the grave.

The two remaining sacks or fragile vessels continue to learn the "ins" and "outs" of Winnipeg as we follow Hoda's education and apprenticeship. Although her grandfather had been a tinker who mended broken pots for the Czar's army, and although her father is adept at weaving baskets, Hoda does not inherit their dexterity for *bricolage*: "In the service of destiny Hoda was given two knitting needles and a blob of tightly wound wool that had been unravelled from somebody's old sweater" (31), but her work fails miserably and she must turn to other corporal talents. Hoda uses the rest of her body in the service of destiny, overcoming fate through her comic will. Education seems to be a matter of in and out — filling vessels that leak. Her Yiddish teacher rushes in and out of the classroom, and "his hands would throw you out and draw you in like a yo-yo" (30). In English school when her voice gets too loud she has "to catch the music, suddenly as it was coming out of her, and hold it back in her mouth" (33). Like her birth, her education is grotesque because of eccentric teachers like Miss Flake with her imaginary idiot brother and floating dental work. "When she spoke, if you hadn't seen them riding around out there on top of her big, knuckly gums, you would have thought that her teeth were running around loose in her mouth, and she was trying to hang on to them at the same time that she was pushing the words out past them" (36). This rhythm of pushing and pulling, insides and outsides, forwards and backwards, up and down, pervades *Crackpot* from Hoda's "upside down" book entry into North America, to the eccentric "tumbledown porch" entry to her house, to her father's Yiddish instruction to "repeat" her lessons — the Yiddish verb sounding like the word for "pig." In this comedy of errors, Hoda endlessly repeats her piggish activities, orally and genitally sowing her wild oats in a cracked pot.

Hoda's true education occurs outside school when she wanders about Winnipeg, tasting freedom, dreaming pavement into Bibleland, up to her neck in a cloaca while her brow touches the heavens: "she fancied herself walking off into the air, heavy Hoda, lighter than air. But she didn't have to walk off. Most of her was in the sky already. Only the soles of her feet kept contact with earthy things" (113). Above-ground astronomer or below-ground archaeologist, tutor or harlot, Hoda thrives on this paradoxical parade of up and down, in and out, front and back, birth and death, knowingly admitting to her dualistic split: "I may be screwing my arse off but I keep my head screwed on tight" (191). One minute she stands at the top of a snow castle higher than anybody, shouting "I'm queen of the castle!", the next minute her majesty hides under the bed, fearing her mother's death. "She tried to wriggle out again backwards, the horror of entrapment driving other fears for a moment from her head. But that part of her stomach which had managed to squeeze under the bar had somehow swelled up again on the other side" (47). Her mother's death seems to pave the way for her son's birth as the living lump replaces the killing tumour; Hoda's container seems "to contain nothing but her body, awash on her bed, a world that was her body trying to turn itself inside out," (146) for Pipick is born trailing clouds of gory Hoda with his umbilical tale of amniotic gore. Herself a product of the graveyard, the golemess out to save the world gives birth to a "Lump," another golem: "Hoda had pieced together, out of the confused shards of dream and desire and the longings of her shattered childhood, the following: TAKE GOOD CARE. A PRINCE IN DISGUISE CAN MAKE A PIECE OF PRINCE, TO SAVE THE JEWS. HE'S PAID FOR" (154). Queen of the castle breeds Prince Pipick, an ironic saviour, a different messiah emerging from mysterious conception and maculate delivery. This prince of peace is given the royal name of David Ben Zion, but his informal tag is Pipick because of his odd lump of navel — a curious knotted tail testifying to his origins and tying him to Hoda's clumsiness in knitting and knotting.

It is fitting that the final scene in *Crackpot* should take place in bed where most of the novel's dramatic moments occur, where Hoda learns and instructs. Lying beside her lover Lazar, a survivor of the Holocaust, Hoda discovers the answer to life's enigma — a wall-to-wall mattress. On ghetto walls hedonistic Hoda stretches her mattress while her somnambulant mind wanders through a subconscious diaspora. Wiseman plays on the word "reel" to emphasize the cinematic simile in Hoda's borderline state between waking and dreaming: "'*Almost a real* mother!' Lazar swam towards her. 'CONDOMS,' she affirmed with energy. 'PRURIENCE,' she held out her arms, a true bride. 'INCESTRY,' she sobbed, as she reeled him in by his umbilicus" (300). Hoda's hedonism undercuts the motto on Winnipeg's City Hall — Commerce, Prudence, Industry — replacing the Protestant work ethic with prostitutional ethnic wit; the portmanteau "incestry" provides the outcast with an answer to origins. So experienced in breaking vessels, dispersal, dissemination, crackpot Hoda is determined to reel in her past, to move in backwards, to inhabit her life in exile. The novel's final words reveal the outcast turned incast through the comic spirit: "With a magnanimous gesture she drew the magic circle around them, showing all she knew. Soon, she promised extravagantly, in the ardour of her vision, they would all be stirring the muddy waters in the brimming pot together." Once a pariah when the circle at school breaks and classmates scatter, Hoda now moves to centre stage, incorporating everything in her thaumaturgic melting pot — a cracked potpourri.

Hoda knows how to fight against her destiny. Her ghetto-wise education has taught her techniques of erasure, of reversing representation iconoclastically, of tracing and inverting origins:

> She had a crazy fantasy that kept tempting her. Suppose she were to re-enact all her movements of that long-ago night? Only backwards. Suppose she were to leave the house, walking backwards in the night; suppose she hurried backwards through the lanes and alleys and along the hedges and fences and across the lamplight islands of momentary yellow in the dark, moving jerkily and hastily backwards as though drawn against her will, retracing inside-out her steps of long ago. She might be able, that way, somehow to erase her earlier path, negating what had been, nullifying the past, rolling it up out of existence and finding at last that it had never been. (219)

In this passage of *erlebte Rede* where the narrative is suited to a comically perforated consciousness or porous crackpot, Wiseman depicts her protagonist's psychic route in physical terms, a Freudian journey backwards through time's labyrinth. She does actually put her fantasy to practice, regressing like a quadruped crawling through a gutter without a view of heaven: "seeing it from without herself, all cock-eyed, all unreal, like some grotesque vision of her own existence, severed from herself, and for one endless moment, while she hesitated in her backward movement, unable to tell for certain whether she was still inside there or standing out here staring at a separate existence that she could not comprehend and that did not comprehend her either" (220). These retrograde steps disrupt a rational, metonymic order of unity; instead, she now feels "the jagged chill of dislocation, of separation even of herself from herself."

Dissemination of broken containers or leaky vessels, and cinematic rewinding of actions lead Hoda to a deconstructive theory of language, an intersubjective phenomenological penetration, Freud's *fort* ... *da* game of disappearance and return.[9]

> What gave you that uneasy feeling that your tongue was turning around and without even knowing it was making a joke on itself? Word to word, sentence, whether you knew them to be false or felt them to be true, spun out across an abyss, with you swinging helplessly from them, blindly spinning and patching and criss-crossing the net that was to catch and hold the shape of the darkness in which your life was forming, but instead was itself contained by the chasm. And sometimes, as she scuttled about, weaving her thread and trying to attach an end of it somewhere where it would hold and be secure, Hoda felt a sudden rushing of wind, and didn't know where her threads connected and what the meaning was of webs that were attached to her own. (175)

There are two meanings in these webs, threads, or nets of endless commentary where metonymy decomposes. Hoda's comic tongue uncannily turns self-reflexive; ambiguity of words and sentences in her language is disrupted since an abyss or chasm, like Danile's bottomless baskets, can contain nothing or everything; the Jewish *comedienne* scuttles meaning; her wind breaks shapes or forms of destiny.

The sexual activities of a prostitute are metaphors for a higher level of awareness, an epistemology of sudden revelation for the dislocated and ostracized.

If that could happen between you and somebody you'd never even seen, what of the people with whom you were in actual fleshly contact, could you enter them too, and at will? Could a human being bear the pain of so much growth and such fierce illumination? Is that what God was? Poor God! Imagine comprehending everything, totally, constantly, in that way, the pain of it, and the thrill of power in it! Words and their threaded links were merely a pretty game you played compared to real knowing. And yet that was how you spent your whole life, diddling with the trinkets and sniffing around the edges of what really was. (193).

In a Copernican revolution within *Crackpot*'s universe, a bedroom philosopher pities God; an astronomer of the near-at-hand in her Hodacentric universe, the whore of babble-on theologizes ironically and diddles at the comic edges in order to retrieve cosmic centrality. Hoda addresses her questions to a second person — herself and the reader of this very free indirect style.

Could you train yourself, if you tried hard enough, to go in and out of people at will? What if she practiced with her customers, really concentrated. If you could time it right, could you manage to jump into him just as he was jumping into you, and feel exactly what it felt like to be him pumping it into you? She'd often thought it would be nice to feel what they were feeling too. If you could get it to work then you really would find out what it was like to go fuck yourself. (194)

Hoda's ironic "I-Thou" interpenetration is a parody of the immigrant's education: it confuses immediacy of immersion with the reality of a deferred intermediate status, never fully assimilated. Sexual self-abuse parodies self-reliance in response to society's abuses.

The prostitute-philosopher, socialist-queen gathers everyone into her decentring circle, mattress, net, web, or pot. Wealthy assimilated Uncle Nate with his own pots or sacks of money finds Hoda's cooking irresistible, "offal fit for a king" (187). Drawn towards Hoda's humbler origins, Nate is drawn away from his sons and their golf course, which become "not central to his existence. What was central to it Uncle no longer knew, perhaps only the inner end of the lopsided ball of twine into which his years had wound. But he knew that there were hot spots in his world, places where thread wound against thread for whatever reason, producing his multiple irritations, his occasional tenderness, and whatever other discomforts kept the whole rolling from its invisible source" (187). Sexual and social intercourse or golf course, golf balls or the lopsided ball of his sister's family, green money and grass or green immigrants and ground thread — these polarities create the discomforts along the path from invisible origins to a central mainstream which turns out to be decentred in the end.

If Uncle Nate finds Hoda's brimming pot of offal intriguing, the church ladies who come to visit Danile after Rahel's death find it revolting. To these uncomprehending evangelicals she describes in Yiddish terms the causes of her mother's death — the old tumour big as a watermelon, the possibilities of a pustulent liver, a gangrenous gall-bladder, a suppurating spleen, and a digestive system turned to stone. A surgeon of synecdoche, Hoda has an inspiration for making the women understand graphically: she drags them to the stove to demonstrate what she meant by a disintegrating spleen in a scene which also exposes the relationship between Jews and Christians. "She was unaware of the effect which the sight of the grey skinful of spongy, stringy purple stuff in the pot, well spiced-up, of which she was so proud, following hard in her medical revelations, had on her father's guests, for she was not much more than a child, after all, and was genuinely disappointed when they, even now, refused to sample her cooking" (64).

An irreverent philosopher-queen of comedy, she also learns how to topple authority through her comic sense and bastard prince. At school Hoda falls in love with the Prince of Wales, takes special pride every time she sings "God Save Our Gracious King," and, confusing "the old country" of Russia with "the dear little island," boasts about her grandfather who served in the Russian army under the Czar, "our gallant ally." After school she fantasizes about being the Queen of the (snow) Castle waiting for the Prince of Wales — a futile exercise:

And he wasn't the only one who would know what she was really like, under the spell of fat she couldn't escape and sloppiness she couldn't control, like the Frog Princess and Beauty and the Beast and the Ugly Duckling and Cinderella too. All kinds of girls who thought they were the fairest of them all would get a surprise some day, when the young prince who was ripening in his long-chinned, pale-eyed, nondescript, special kind of noble beauty who would come from over the seas and not even notice them at all. (36)

An outsider at school, Hoda uses her imagination to transport herself to the inner circle of empire where her obesity may be transformed into noble beauty. Comedy elevates her beastliness, weds transatlantic empire to diaspora, and displaces long-chinned Prince of Wales with her long-navelled prince of tails. When the Prince eventually visits Winnipeg, Hoda finds a place right at the front of the crowd, at the edge of the road where the royal car is going to pass. Here she realizes that there may be problems in the intermarriage between prince and fat girl. "But most of the time he got both his mother the Queen and his father the King to realize that she was best for him and was so nice the people wouldn't want to make civil war anymore when they got to know her, and she got Daddy to realize that she would be like Queen Esther and save the Jews her whole life long" (126). Just as the royal car passes in front of her, a policeman intervenes, eclipsing her vision. She later avenges this injustice by dismounting a mountie from his horse during the Winnipeg General Strike. The ghetto's golemess recognizes her socialist Yiddish teacher, "Mr Polonick, who'd got unravelled from the marching workers and was running back and forth like a loose end beside them" (142), and unravels the mountie who is about to attack him. Eventually, Hoda abandons her majestic jests and fantasies, but her son inherits them on his way to an incestuous encounter with her: "Inside of himself he could feel himself looking at himself respectfully too. Like the hero of a goddam book. Prince David Pipick Ben Zion Mac Fuck, the fastest trigger in the West!" (222). With his umbilical trace, the self-ironic hero returns to his ultimate source, achieving assimilation not only in the west, but in the flesh of his mother, another heroine and saviour.

In Winnipeg's ghetto, Abraham is the first murderer, Hoda the first prostitute to sleep with her son — both acts are primal transgressions against origins, yet tragedy excuses the former and comedy mitigates the latter. The dislocations from European persecution to North American assimilation may be tragically or comically traumatic in both *The Sacrifice* and *Crackpot*. Moses climbs Mad Mountain to unite with Abraham who prays eastward towards ancestral biblical origins unhinged in time and place from the centre of Canada. Hoda descends to her mattress to unite with sons and lovers in her all-embracing sense of humour; at a time of crisis, she too looks beyond her grotesque Yiddish roots towards biblical precedents to transcend her predicament:

For some reason it was that lady in the Bible that Hoda remembered now, and suddenly understood what had really happened to her. She had always felt sorry for that one, who, just for looking back, had been turned into a pillar of salt. Now she saw that when Lot's wife looked back she simply became what she had been, concentrated essence, pillar of tears. Most of the time you trail your life behind you in a constant dribble of leaking time, and if you don't look back, except maybe a glance sometimes, you hardly know it's there. (246)

Every forward motion of occidental acculturation is countered by a turn backward to oriental origins. The human container — anatomy as metonymy — may be destroyed in two ways: it may break, crack, leak to contain everything and nothing, plenitude and absence; or, through archetypal repetitions, its boundaries disappear so that container becomes contents, present becomes past, concentrated essence. Wiseman's tragicomic hero may be lost, lacunal, without status, an x in fate's tic-tac-toe. The ghetto's grotesque golem "will see himself as throwback, relict, freak, / his mother's miscarriage, his great-grandfather's ghost," one who will "come for his revenges; the unsuspected heir, with papers; the risen soul; or the chloroformed prince awaking from his flowers." [10] Having lost an auxiliary world of grandfathers' ghosts, Wiseman, like Klein, Ludwig, Cohen, and Richler, uses her dialogic imagination to explore the coming of age of adolescents, orphans, and Jewish-Canadian society.

CHAPTER SEVEN

Subverting Westmount: Leonard Cohen's New Jews

The clocks are not in unison; the inner one runs crazily
on at a devilish or demoniac or in any case inhuman
pace, the outer one limps along at its usual speed.

Kafka

In "Out of the Pulver and the Polished Lens" (1931), Klein champions Spinoza for his own nonconformist attitude towards Orthodox Jewry: "Is it a marvel, then, that he forsook the abracadabra of the synagogue, and holding with timelessness a duologue, deciphered a new scripture in the book? Is it a marvel that he left old fraud for passion intellectual of God?" After these rhetorical questions he concludes the poem with a portrait of Spinoza gathering flowers, the "ever-unwedded lover of the Lord."[1] This lyrical image of Spinoza plucking tulips in the garden of Mynheer would appeal to Leonard Cohen whose *fleurs du mal* inform such volumes as *Let Us Compare Mythologies, The Spice-Box of Earth, Flowers for Hitler,* and *Parasites of Heaven.*[2] As he abandons old fraud in his new scripture, Cohen's blasphemy and unconsummated divine marriage take a more strident turn in his fiction, culminating in the obscene exclamations of his protagonists in *The Favourite Game* and *Beautiful Losers* who avenge the sins of Westmount's *arrivistes*. While his first novel deals with modern Jewish-Canadian experience, his second thrusts towards a post-modernism grounded in Canadian history, Indian myth, and cabbalistic games.

Cohen's autobiographical protagonist, Lawrence Breavman, is an ever-unwedded flower gatherer who, rejecting family and tradition, strives to uncover his identity through dialogues with timelessness, lovers, and his friend Krantz. As a *Künstlerroman, The Favourite Game* examines the development of its artist-hero from his Montreal childhood to his continuing education in New York; in the course of his *Bildung*, Breavman learns how to emerge from his double Jewish-Canadian heritage. Where Joyce's Stephen Dedalus exchanges Jesuitical views in ironic catechisms with Cranly, so Breavman requires Krantz for talmudic dialogues to forge in the smithy of his soul the uncreated conscience of their race: "The Jews are the conscience of the world and the Breavmans are the conscience of the Jews."[3] If Lawrence Breavman considers himself the conscience of the Breavmans, then, with the help of Krantz, he learns how to displace his super-ego with his libido's favourite games. These two "Talmudists delighting in their dialectic" (40) resort to heretic hermeneutics, hedonistic dialectic, and unmediated dialogue to attack and rebel against authorities such as the Prime Minister and Rabbi Swort. In satirizing leaders of Canadian politics and formalized Jewish religion, Cohen recommends that his young hero should find other models for his apprenticeship.

The voice of the narrator joins in their questioning, irreverent dialectic: "Weren't they supposed to be a holy people consecrated to purity, service, spiritual honesty? Weren't they a nation set apart? Why had the idea of a jealously guarded sanctity degenerated into a sly contempt for the goy, empty of self-criticism?" (41–2). These questions point to the decline of Judaism into Jewishness, of ancient religion to modern sociology, devoid of the kind of self-criticism Breavman undertakes in his own rise to maturity as an individual set apart from his nation. This episode concerning their Jewishness ends in praise of their secularized talmudic skills: "Paradoxes, bafflements, problems dissolved in fascinating dialectic" (44), for ironic talmudists can solve anything by choosing to solve nothing. What ails these talmudists is the gulf between a rich past and debased present, their fall from Sinai to the golden calf and broken tablets of Westmount. As they grow older, they grow apart, Breavman accusing his confidant of breaking the dialogue, and Krantz complaining that they have to stop interpreting the world for one another. Their favourite games of dialogue and dialectic must be broken for them to grow out of boyhood; set apart, Breavman individualizes interpretation into manhood. After Krantz returns from England they reunite at the summer camp, but are unable to resume their old commentary on the universe or repair their long exile — problems that plague Breavman in his other relationships.

His exile from Krantz multiplies in his exile from many lovers who contribute to his education. Early games with Lisa are equally critical of parochial mentalities which impede a broadening *Bildung*. As part of their sexual instruction, they view "Thirty Ways to Screw," and "praise this film, which has disappeared with the maid into the Canadian wilderness" (29). While the wilderness offers natural freedom and favourite games, cities, because they inhibit creativity, must be scorned. "This tiny strip of celluloid shown widely in Canadian theatres might revitalize the tedious marriages which are reported to abound in our country" (30) — marriages which Breavman avoids in spite of his quest for conjugal covenants. The National Film Board stands in contrast to world federalism in the film's universal practice of physical love, just as the view beyond their window expands beyond Westmount to the St Lawrence River and the American mountains in the distance. In that same park in Westmount — Montreal's "green heart" for many of Breavman's epiphanies — Lisa wrestles with Breavman after Hebrew school and his prayer book falls to the ground like so many participants in *The Favourite Game.* "It was mandatory to kiss a holy book which had fallen to the ground," (34) but the humiliated Breavman refuses to kiss the prayer book just as he refuses to pay lip service to Judaism or embrace his religion. As Lisa enters womanhood, Breavman is exiled once again, never able to fulfil their contract. As book I ends, Breavman's maid Heather awakens from hypnosis to discover that her panties are missing: "'Jewish people,' she sighed. 'Education'" (55). The education of Lawrence Breavman includes hypnosis and undressing — ironic, circular games of a Jewish artist and magician involved in a heuristic education away from Jews on Westmount's Sinai.

During his artistic apprenticeship Breavman is alienated from his family, but always yearns for origins, alternating between irony and lyricism, disconnection and connection. Cohen portrays his Jewish-Canadian mother in mock-heroic fashion; like Belinda in Pope's *Rape of the Lock*, "Breavman's young mother hunted wrinkles with two hands and a magnifying mirror. When she found one she consulted a fortress of oils and creams arrayed on a glass tray and she sighed. Without faith the wrinkle was anointed" (9). In this boudoir burlesque, Cohen magnifies imperfections, unmasking an unholy alliance between true faith and cosmetic surface, between a Westmount fortress and a wilderness of wrinkles. When Mrs Breavman informs her son that her real face is in Russia, young Lawrence studies the atlas, searching for her origins. The young geographer learns not only about his homeless mother and diasporic distances, but also about distancing himself through irony from his formative experiences. This distancing often occurs through narrative lenses that blur the protagonist's vision in his surrealistic imagination; and his imagination develops to transform lost places and faces into a transcendence of absence. Just as his entry into the future contends with his retreat to origins, so his spatial development proceeds in two contrary directions: the circle and the departure from the circle.

Breavman's attitude toward his father is more complicated than his relationship to his mother. As a result of his coronary thrombosis, Mr Breavman spends most of his time in bed or in an oxygen tent in the hospital, and when he gets out to take his son to Mount Royal he lies about his condition. "Here was the ancient crater. Two iron and stone cannon rested in the gentle grassy scoop which was once a pit of boiling lava. Breavman wanted to dwell on the violence" (9). Once again the young archaelogist sifts through history towards origins, preferring to dwell on violence rather than dwell in his own home from which he becomes increasingly estranged. The wounded warrior hands down to his son a legacy of violence which intrudes on all his relationships with his lovers. Breavman tears the factual books his father bequeaths to him, destroys order and authority "to scorn the world of detail, information, precision, all the false knowledge which cannot intrude on decay" (21). In Cohen's world of black romanticism, decadence prevails over decency. After his death all that remains of Mr Breavman is a colour photograph, the largest picture on a wall of ancestors, displaying features of outmoded traditions: English suit, English reticence, Canadian legion pin, Victorian reason and decency, "though the hazel eyes are a little too soft and staring, the mouth too full, Semitic, hurt" (25). Having established these orderly traits in order to disrupt them, Cohen studies this portrait of a Jewish-Canadian father more closely: "He is one of the princes of Breavman's private religion, double-natured and arbitrary. He is the persecuted brother, the near poet, the innocent of the machine toys, the sighing judge who listens but does not sentence. Also he is heaving Authority, armoured with Divine Right, doing merciless violence to all that is weak, taboo, unBreavmanlike" (25). Since Breavman, like Hamlet, inherits all his father's violent concerns, he must come to terms with his dual nature, but in his private religion he disinherits public vows, topples princely authority or divine right, and definitely behaves unBreavmanlike.

While he does accept his father's favourite games of poetry, machine toys, and judgment without sentence, he must avenge his persecution. Breavman resents his tall, thin uncles who succeed where their fat brother fails, and he would like to destroy these pillars of the community. In one of his nocturnal epiphanies in the park, Montreal's Spinoza lies under the lilacs and questions his family's public religion that is so opposed to his own internal struggle: "Uncles, why do you look so confident when you pray? Is it because you know the words? When curtains of the Holy Ark are drawn apart and gold-crowned Torah scrolls revealed, and all the men of the altar wear white clothes, why don't your eyes let go of the ritual, why don't you succumb to raving epilepsy? Why are your confessions so easy?" (67). The confessions of Lawrence Breavman, prince of Montreal, are so difficult because, preferring nature's revelations over the synagogue's, he lacks the confidence organized religion provides. Just before he leaves Montreal for his exile in New York, he answers these pilpulistic questions, realizing that his dissent has taught him a rage for chaos his family could never know. Turning away from his city even as he turns from lovers and walks away from childhood games, this estranged traveller condemns their ignorance of Judaism's hidden lyricism and revealed scrolls. He has to leap over the shallow preceding generation to return to the moral passion of the prophets (Isaiah) and the fervour of a Hassidic tradition (Baal Shem Tov).

Richler's and Cohen's alienated heroes scorn their uncles who are hollow, shallow, complacent, self-righteous representatives of the Jewish community, observant of the letter of the Law rather than the spirit of the tree of life. Cohen combines roles of administering priest and rebellious poet: the alternating rhythm of his prose between negatives and parallel sentences creates an incantatory effect through which Cohen is able to participate in the ceremony and condemn it simultaneously. If Breavman wants to be among them but cannot be part of their brotherhood — an insider and an outsider — his denial of a vatic role does not negate his attitude as a poet-prophet who denounces false worship. Devoid of historical sensibility, his uncles fail to comprehend the origins of their devotion and fail to find transcendence or tradition beyond their orderly service. Invoking the ambiguous tragedy of a blind Samson against the temple pillars (50, 102) or these pillars of a Philistine community, Breavman tears down the walls of temples and ghettos so that leopards may enter the ceremony out of the wilderness and purify holy vessels belching miasmal smoke (214). Among commercial Jews he is a mild traitor who cannot be condemned outright because he might earn a living from his writing; the Jewish community may identify him with Disraeli or Mendelssohn "whose apostasies the Jewish regard for attainment has always overlooked. Also, writing is an essential part of the Jewish tradition" (102). The young apostate cultivates irony through his Yiddish expressions and Hassidic dances: at camp he wants to be a gentle hero like the Baal Shem Tov, an authentic Jew educated in alien experience, a "solitary man in a desert, begging for the inclination of a face" (187). Doubly estranged from his fellow Jews and the rest of society, he nevertheless uses Jewish tradition.

Having cut the strings of filiation, marginal Breavman flees his marginal city for the American metropolis. "Some say that no one ever leaves Montreal, for that city, like Canada itself, is designed to preserve the past, a past that happened somewhere else" (117). Just as the Jew has his "being elsewhere," so Canada has been bypassed in its colonial past. If "in Montreal there is no present tense" (117), then there is an absent tense reflected in Cohen's narrative strategy of alternating between two tenses that characterize a mature narrator looking back over Breavman's childhood. If there are no Canadians or no Montrealers, and if each man speaks with his father's tongue, then Breavman inhabits a void. Only by escaping to New York will he comprehend his earlier emptiness. After nullifying his Canadian identity, Breavman may turn to his Jewish past, but at summer camp he concludes, "Everybody is Canadian. The Jew's disguise won't work" (209). The ambiguities of his Jewish-Canadian identity remain unresolved: during his *Bildung*, Breavman must reclaim the past even as he steps into the future; archaeologist and astronomer, historian and prophet, must enter into a conjugal covenant with his lovers and his art.

Although *The Favourite Game* is generally considered a *Künstlerroman*, it may also be read as a long narrative poem since its author and its subject are poets, since its lyrical style is highly poetic, and since it incorporates a number of poems within its text. As a poem, it is divided into four books and ninety stanzas. Just as the "fact that the lines do not come to the edge of the page is no guarantee" (162) of poetry, so the extension of lines to the edge is no guarantee that the prose is not poetry disguised. This intertextuality is underscored by the poem from *The Spice-Box of Earth* which opens *The Favourite Game*. This poem puts into question where the book exactly begins. The line "As the mist leaves no scar" is reflected in the many "scars" of section 1, and the rest of the novel examines varieties of scars, traces, or palimpsests that linger or disappear:

> As the mist leaves no scar
> On the dark green hill,
> So my body leaves no scar
> On you, nor ever will.
>
> When wind and hawk encounter,
> What remains to keep?
> So you and I encounter
> Then turn, then fall to sleep.
>
> As many nights endure
> Without a moon or star,
> So will we endure
> When one is gone and far.

In each of these three lyrical stanzas the rhymes and parallel structures link nature in the first half to lovers in the second — a linkage present in the rest of the novel. Yet events in *The Favourite Game* do not always bear out these casual parallelisms: Breavman's body frequently scars others, and the country mist in book IV veils the tragic scar of Martin Stark's death; his encounters rarely amount to more than almost meetings between lovers who well may ask "what remains to keep"; and these relationships endure only through writing. Breavman leaves home, family, lovers, religion, Montreal, and childhood in this *Bildungsroman*, yet scars or traces remain after these departures. "What remains to keep" after so much has been thrown out or disposed of in so many encounters? Breavman considers himself the "keeper" of memories, the "sentimental dirty old man in front of a classroom of children" (69) where a novel of education reverses roles of teacher and learner.

If the beginning of the novel deals with scars and remainders, so too does the ending with its description of Lisa's favourite game. In Breavman's final vision of Montreal he feels at the "very centre of things," but his memory of the childhood game decentres him. After a heavy snowfall, Breavman remembers in this final segment of the novel, the children went into a backyard to play.

The expanse of snow would be white and unbroken. Bertha was the spinner. You held her hands while she turned on her heels, you circled her until your feet left the ground. Then she let go and you flew over the snow. You remained still in whatever position you landed. When everyone had been flung in this fashion into the fresh snow, the beautiful part of the game began. You stood up carefully, taking great pains not to disturb the impression you had made. Now the comparisons. Of course you would have done your best to land in some crazy position, arms and legs sticking out. Then we walked away, leaving a lovely white field of blossom-like shapes with footprint stems. (223)[4]

All of Breavman's outcast relationships may be examined according to the dialectics of breaking versus joining, remaining versus walking away, circular versus straight, turning versus facing. Similarly, those "footprint stems," like footnotes, signify either the origins or afterthoughts of Breavman's actions and memories and call into question the path of his development. Who circles whom when space is spun? Is the world Berthacentric or Breavman-centred? This favourite game is repeated when Bertha falls from the apple tree, when Breavman wrestles with Lisa, and when Shell's grotesque teacher Miss McTavish flings herself backwards in the snow.

While this favourite game has been variously interpreted as love, truth, or art, it also symbolizes the process of exile from origins through intermediate stems to marginality.[5] Exiled from childhood, the young man seeks to reclaim his past; exiled from society, the authentic Jew, educated in the alien experience of a solitary man in a desert, begs for bodies; and further exiled from society, the artist traces words, prints, stems, figures in a wintry ground or snowy desert. Far-flung from his family tree, the outsider has to graft his stem; disseminated, the poet traces word stems, conjugates verbs and lovers (194, 203); from stem to "stern Bertha" Cohen composes a circular novel where his protagonist makes his mark and walks away from roots.

In Cohen's field of entity the blossom-like shapes remain, yet disappear once the snow has melted. To underscore the evanescence of this permanent beauty, the paradoxical disappearance of remainders, Cohen has Breavman write his memory on a napkin — a disposable medium that covers and erases. To extol Shell's beauty, the poet-keeper had earlier written on napkins nine poems, but this temporary scribbling can be thrown out as easily as Bertha throws out bodies or Breavman throws away lovers, friends, family, religion, and city. "He shredded the napkins as he dug the pen in, and he couldn't read three-quarters of what he'd done; not that it was any good, but that had nothing to do with it" (147). Stuffing the debris into his jacket, he is caught in a double bind of keeping and discarding tradition — an ongoing displacement of continuity and rebellion. Napkins not only ironically absorb marginal discourse, but also chart the course of adolescence when nature, in the form of Lisa's "Curse," frustrates Breavman's sexual expectations. Kleenex stems also contribute to this ludicrous pseudo-transformation of Breavman when he stuffs his shoes to appear tall enough to dance with Muffin, herself rumoured to pad her bra with Kleenex. Although napkins cover and erase, the scars of adolescence remain in throw-away games on throw-away paper.

Cohen lists various scars in the opening section of his novel; his habit of cataloguing characters and events serves to distance and objectify these experiences, as if they were to be placed in a family photograph album, or mounted like insects in a collection. His narrative opens in the third-person present tense, a device intended to exploit the tension between involvement and distance that is central to the novel: "Breavman knows a girl named Shell whose ears were pierced so she could wear the long filigree earrings." He traces this ornamental filigree without beginning or end, even as he traces his own and Shell's pedigree; filigree or blossom-like shapes interconnect via stems of filiation and affiliation. Indeed, the thread of Shell's filigree earrings forms part of a much larger pattern of tracery that is repeated in her ear, her name, and Montreal's archi-texture of carved grapevines, gargoyle crevices, and cast-iron fences which claim Breavman. As in Joyce's *Portrait*, Cohen's artist threads his way through a labyrinth of experience; like Daedalus, he pierces a seashell, traces threads, but finds no exit. Shell appears not only at the beginning of the novel: she weaves through various sections to provide a distancing framework for Breavman's early experiences in the first two books before he actually meets her. His filigree narrative departs from a straight chronological line until the end of book II. Shell reappears at the very centre of *The Favourite Game* when her name concludes book II and opens book III in pivotal fashion: "Her middle name was Marshell ... but they called her Shell" (122). Her middle name at the middle of the novel serves to introduce the story of her own life as focus shifts temporarily from Breavman's self-centred world. Breavman wants to rescue a turtle and "write messages on his shell and put him in the sea, Shell, sea-shell" (160). We read and hear messages on ears, labyrinths, and shells that cover and protect.

The alternation between past and present tenses underscores anatomical lesions as well as distances between lovers; Cohen is an anatomist bent on inflicting wounds and healing them. "The punctures festered and now she has a tiny scar in each earlobe" (8). Shell's tiny scar at the beginning of the novel is connected aurally to the Wurlitzer at the end: "a giant beast, blinking in pain. It was everybody's neon wound. A suffering ventriloquist ... ready to fester all night" (223). Music, for poet and pop-singer, is the great weaver whereby source and destination interconnect; but the magic of ventriloquism, like the magic of hypnotism, exposes deceits and lies. Breavman continually throws his voice in a number of directions, scattering his identity. Atop the apple tree of torture, Bertha brandishes her flute, ready to strike Breavman, but falls instead and injures herself badly. The music at the Palais D'Or offers little hope for magic, except for the trumpeter who "could put a lingering sharp cry in the smoky air, coiling like a rope of rescue above the bobbing figures" (45) — the synaesthetic simile forming a Möbius strip of music and dancers. Book I ends with Heather tearing her fingers to pieces, while magician Breavman hypnotizes her with his pendulum and drives a needle through the lobe of her ear: "He had no interest in ears pierced by needles" (53), which seems to contradict his interest in Shell's pierced ears. While this section begins with the question "Is there anything more beautiful than a girl with a lute?" in reference to Heather's ukelele, book II opens with Breavman admiring Henri Rousseau's canvas: "The abandoned lute does not cry for fingers. It is swollen with all the music it needs" (58). Does the lute need a player? Does a message require both a sender and a receiver? Is there always something left over, the supplement between signifier and signified? Through the music of *The Favourite Game* Leonard Cohen weaves his contrapuntal narrative from section to section.[6]

Music is but one of several magical forms aimed at creating sacramental relationships between Breavman, his lovers, and his surroundings. Norma plays guitar: "She sent a minor chord through his spine and into the forest" (72), weaving lovers and landscape. Breavman in turn takes up the guitar in his affair with Tamara: "the purity of the music surprised and almost convinced him that he was creating a sacramental relationship with the girl, the outside city, and himself" (87). Yet, for all its harmony, his relationship with Tamara remains an "almost" encounter to be followed by his "crescendo" drive with Krantz through Quebec's Eastern Townships. Just before this musical episode of woven time and space, Breavman lies beside Tamara with his visions of vastness — "desert stretches so huge no Chosen People could cross them" (94) — and a Canadian wilderness that compounds his Jewish heritage — "Arctic territories and sled-track distances." Thus, his nocturnal drive through the Townships represents an attempt to overcome his bed-ridden paralysis. Over the radio, a juke-box song of rejection, a throbbing electric guitar, and Pat Boone with grinding chords of the hit parade combine to conquer time and space in a mystical moment. Similarly, at a party with Lisa, Breavman plays a Spanish guitar: the first chord is always crucial, for if it doesn't sound right, it rebukes him. "But there are those good times when the tone is deep and lingering, and he cannot believe it is himself who is strumming the strings. He watches the intricate blur of his right hand and the ballet-fingers of his left hand stepping between the frets, and he wonders what connection there is between all that movement and the music in the air, which seems to come from the wood itself" (113). Synaesthetic strings wed this audiovisual experience, blurring distinctions and weaving parts of the body in dancing rhythm; nevertheless, despite attempts at total unification, a skeptical presence lingers, questioning causal connections and the artist's role in all this beauty. He sings "minor songs of absence" which connect him with Lisa, and rediscovers, like Klein, "the poetry which had overwhelmed him years before, the easy line that gave itself carelessly away and then, before it was over, struck home" (113). Associated with this musical rhythm is a pattern of lines leading outward but always seeking "home."

In the music room of World Student House, Breavman experiences another epiphany in preparation for his union with Shell. "He had never really listened to music before. It had been a backdrop for poems and talk" (157), but now he listens to the unmediated speech of other men and his ego is diminished. Shell enters as he follows the flute in a Schubert quartet, a kind of aesthetic fallacy for their encounter. "It climbed and returned and ascended again, launched and received by low powerful strings" (157). Not only is the interplay between instruments a prelude to the foreplay between sexes, but it recapitulates a central rhythm in Cohen's quartet, the four books of *The Favourite Game*: Breavman continuously climbs and returns from the heights of Westmount to the depths of personal hells like eternal basement Bunny Hops. Indeed, much of the musical weaving is connected either ironically or lyrically to dancing, from the Bunny Hop to the violence at the Palais D'Or to the "therapeutic dance" at the Allan Memorial Hospital to Anne's beautiful dancing. Favourite musical and dancing games belong to larger patterns of interconnection — conjugal covenants between ever-unwedded lovers, accompaniment to open-endedness.

At summer camp Krantz's classical music weaves and weds all the figures in the campground's tapestry:

Mozart came loud over the PA, sewing together everything that Breavman observed. It wove, it married the two figures bending over the records, whatever the music touched, child trapped in London Bridge, mountain-top dissolving in mist, empty swing rocking like a pendulum, the row of glistening red canoes, the players clustered underneath the basket, leaping for the ball like a stroboscopic photo of a splashing drop of water — whatever it touched was frozen in an immense tapestry. He was in it, a figure by a railing. (205)

Sewing, weaving, touching, trapped child, mist, emptiness, hypnotic pendulum, players in favourite games, and photography are all recurrent images in the novel. Yet amidst all this Breavman remains isolated, an outsider beside a railing, raised on a balcony at a height from which he superciliously surveys the world and condescends to its inhabitants. Within the novel's geometry are strings of contiguity, photographic frames, frames of Brueghel's and Rousseau's paintings, circles, filigree networks, bloodlines and guidelines of affiliation: all of these are synaesthetically intertwined with Cohen's musical harmonies.

If organizing lines into photographic frames orders the chaos surrounding Cohen's protagonist, so too do the story's other cameras — the rooms or partial homes Breavman inhabits. He graduates from his magical basement to a lover's room with Tamara because he knows he is going to be with her in rooms for a long time. "Then what about rooms, wasn't every room the same, hadn't he known what it would be like, weren't all the rooms they passed exactly the same, wherever a woman was stretched out, even a forest was a glass room, wasn't it like with Lisa, under the bed and when they played the Soldier and the Whore, wasn't it the same, even to listening for enemy sounds?" (79–80). Like individual frames in a film and like interconnected lovers within them, all rooms in *The Favourite Game* are the same, yet different, and it is this difference between containers of experience that Cohen explores. In a tourist house in Virginia, Shell rearranges the bed and decor, for she is the "Carry Nation of Evil Chintzy Rooms" (128). "She had changed the room. They could lay their bodies in it. It was theirs, good enough for love and talk. It was not that she had arranged a stage on which they might sleep hand in hand, but she had made the room answer to what she believed their love asked. Breavman knew it was not his answer. He wished he could honour her home-making and hated his will to hurt her for it" (129). Shell prepares the room for the sleep of love and death, questions and answers fail to correspond, and home-breaker Breavman rejects her home-making because it reminds him of his mother's hovering fastidiousness. He prefers instead the natural debris of slum roaches to Shell's fairy-tale upbringing of goose-feather beds, mansions, and castles. He advocates the "time between" (130) when the light has just been switched on and the roaches, leaving no scar, begin to disappear. This calls to mind the time between childhood and maturity, between an instant and eternity, the history between genesis and exodus, expulsion and exile, the temporal deferment between lovers, connections and rooms.

Just as he had watched Montreal from the window of his room, so he leans his elbows on the window sill of World Student House which overlooks the Hudson. In New York, Shell is constantly connected to rooms: the sexual room she and her husband never enter, the hotel with Med "in a room like the ones Breavman built" (152), and the music room framed by the window in lyrical ecstasy. Women like Shell create beauty around them: "They break down old rules of light and cannot be interpreted or compared. They make every room original" (158). Shell attains the summit of beauty beyond all previous models; beyond origins, comparisons, and interpretations, she transcends earthly forms. Ultimately, however, Breavman has to break away from these lovers' cages be they in Montreal or New York. He runs to the window of Tamara's room, smashes his fist through the glass, and screams, "Get the car, Krantz" (216), in an effort to retrieve that liberating moment of exhilaration through a nocturnal drive.

Between the internal intimacy of rooms and the open, public arena lies the balcony, an interface for marginal man and one of Breavman's favourite places. He is attracted to balconies because of their intermediate state beyond windows and their superior location overlooking the rest of the world. After his father's death, people congregate on the balcony as Breavman and his mother descend the stairs. His friend Philip masturbates in the sun-room which is no more than an enclosed balcony attached to the back of the house. From the balcony of the Palais D'Or, the lofty artist plans mass-hypnosis on the crowd dancing beneath him: "Breavman leaned over the rail one more second and wished he were delivering a hysterical speech to the thick mob below ... and you must listen, friends, strangers, I am binding the generations one to another, o, little people of numberless streets, bark, bark, hoot, blood, your long stairways are curling around my heart like a vine" (48). The poet-prophet seeks his own level of irony from stuffed shoes to Westmount heights designed to humiliate the underprivileged. The Old Testament figure loops bloodlines and lovers, but soon smashes the scene: he "seized the pillars and brought down the temple of the Philistines" (50). From blind Samson Agonistes, Cohen switches immediately to demonic balcony visions: "He would love to have heard Hitler or Mussolini bellow from his marble balcony, to have seen partisans hang him upside down ... to see the black or yellow hordes get even with the small outposts of their colonial enemies ... to see the chalices on any altar tremble with congregational Amen" (51). A rebellious artist controverts part of his favourite game, his agon of blindness; he is a leopard entering the temple. Cohen lists his framed favourite heights of power and privilege — the marble balcony, the press box, the projection-room, the reviewing stand, the minaret, the Holy of Holies — all of which oscillate like his hypnotic pendulum, between centres and margins. Before Krantz departs for England, he and Breavman survey the city from their Stanley Street balcony; by leaving Montreal, Krantz distances himself from Breavman who, in turn, has distanced himself on balconies from everyone else. Later at summer camp, they resume their position, but on the balcony of the camp's administration building — that mediator between authority and chaos. Similarly, Breavman stays motionless on the mess hall balcony as he surveys the beauty around him. More than just halfway places between original rooms and peripheral exteriors, these balconies are also stems between *heimlich* and *unheimlich*, disappearance and return. Breavman's first sight of Shell, however, forces him to denounce these visions of power as he learns something of himself; after first seeing Shell, "he didn't want to stand on any marble balcony" (146).

Descended from balconies Breavman experiences favourite epi-phanic games at ground level in his communion with nature both in Montreal's park and at camp in the Laurentians.

He began to circle one of the playing fields. The tall pines around the field and hills gave him the impression of a bowl which contained him. There was one black hill that seemed so connected with his father that he could hardly bear to look up at it as he came round and round, stumbling like a drunk.

Then an idea crushed him — he had ancestors! His ancestors reached back and back, like daisies connected in a necklace. He completed circle after circle in the mud.

He stumbled and collapsed, tasting the ground ... Something very impor-tant was going to happen in this arena ... Not in gold, not in light, but in this mud something necessary and inevitable would take place. He had to stay to watch it unfold. (188–9)

As in Lisa's favourite game, Breavman begins his encounter with the ground in a decentring motion where nature acts as a secure metonymic container of artistic impression and expression. Like the dark green hill in the opening poem and the black hills from Westmount park, this black hill enters the game of metaleptic connec-tion through its association with a buried father. The pathetic fallacy of the rain and isolated lights prepares for Breavman's sudden illumi-nation about death and origins: his ancestral revelation in the mud represents both an evolutionary regression of a Caliban towards rats, turtles, frogs, and cats, and, through Prospero's thaumaturgy, a paradoxical transcendence beyond the Laurentian hills.

The inevitable tragedy about to unfold in this muddy arena is the death of Martin Stark, the divine idiot crushed not by an idea but by a tractor in the marsh — that missing part of Shell's name. Out of the mud, ground, pavement, garbage river, or cloaca, the Jewish artist-magician-photographer zooms to heaven beyond rooms, balconies, and mazes: "I think that if Elijah's chariot, or Apollo's, or any mythi-cal boat of the sky, should pull up at my doorstep, I would know exactly where to sit, and as we flew I'd recall with delicious familiarity all the clouds and mysteries we passed" (80). Hitching his wagon to apocalyptic, Chagallian visions, a Jewish Daedalus sublimates mire into miracle. Martin's death, however, has been prepared for well in advance. All those instances of scars, wounds, torture, broken bodies, and deaths culminate in the squashing of this "incoherent oracle," himself a gleeful squasher of thousands of mosquitoes. Scars, muti-lated bodies in the family film, the rat skeleton buried under the pansies, Bertha's torture tree, Lisa's imitation Nazi torture, the corpse-heap of men who smiled at Mrs Breavman, Mr Breavman's swollen body lowered by a pulley system, the message in the bowtie buried under the lilies-of-the-valley, Rousseau's "no guts on the sand" compared to Martin's mouth full of guts — all of these adumbrate the violence of Martin's death. More fully developed is Krantz's and Breavman's dissection of a frog. At the foot of Montreal's war memorial, Breavman announces that they are in charge of torture as he smacks the head against the inscribed stone and proceeds to remove all the organs. Its "heart, which already looked weary and ancient, the colour of old man's saliva, first heart of the world" (61), continues to beat in salt water. This episode, in turn, anticipates the death of a cat outside Breavman's and Tamara's window of love. Animal deaths prepare for the stabbing of a man in New York; Breavman cannot decide how to react to the body with the slit throat: "Two years ago he would have dipped the jacket, made the gesture, connected himself with the accident. Was the ritual dissolving?" (143). His education seems to be moving in the direction of disconnection of commitments and relationships; eviscerated rituals dissolve in saline solutions. At the same time, his mind branches from this personal event to broader historical tragedy which involves him even in his detachment: "A vision of Nazi youth presented itself. Rows and rows of gold heads filing past the assassinated soldier. They lowered their company flags into the wound and promised. Breavman swallowed bile" (143). Having previously disdained crowds, he now follows the rest of the crowd, an individual *artiste manqué* who reacts by vomiting just as he had done with the rat in his basement and just as Tamara had responded to the dead cat.

"Puking clears the soul," Breavman repeats in his narrative refrain or litany, rendering him clean, empty, free. Through this catharsis he feels as if he can begin again: "every free deep breath was a beginning" (144) towards origins as he remembers his Montreal childhood. (He expresses this same desire to begin again in his final letter to Shell, the only letter without a carbon copy. The original, the "clean slate," *tabula rasa*, Freud's mystical writing pad constitute traces of illusions on napkins, paper tigers.)[7] Circular imagery informs his memory, linking past and present in strange loops, and retarding his progressive development: the "new school year coiled like a dragon," while compasses "containing millions of circles, too sharp and substantial for the cardboard box that contained them" make and break circles into Möbius strips. From ten-year-old neatness, perfection, and eradicable mistakes, Breavman returns to New York as the bad juices of imagination reimpose metaphor on everything: "New York got lost in Breavman's private city. Gauze grew on everything and as usual he had to imagine the real shape of things" (145). The mimetic child has grown into a Romantic poet projecting a "gauze of melancholy" and "therapeutic stockings" through a kind of magic realism; in Breavman's private Canadian city, Tamara's thighs fill the streets, while buildings press blossom-like shapes through the therapeutic stockings which cover her footprint stems.

An anatomist who purges his soul, dissects frogs and other creatures, and covers cities with gauze and therapeutic stockings, is also a doctor who heals bodies by sewing them together through art and love. "Meanwhile, back at the Montreal poem factory, Breavman is interning, training to become her Compleat Physician" (136). His medical training begins at a young age — scars, wounds, pimples, his father in an oxygen-tent in the hospital, Dr Farley the cardiologist, a hypnotist or militant Saint Francis commanding the world. During the dissection of the frog, he suggests that thread could repair the animals. By the end of the novel, as he climbs the mountain and lists all of his lovers' bodies, he realizes that he is in the very centre of things: "The heart of the city wasn't down there among the new buildings and widened streets. It was right over there at the Allan, which, with drugs and electricity, was keeping the businessmen sane and their wives from suicide and their children free from hatred. The hospital was the true heart, pumping stability and erections and orgasms and sleep into all the withering commercial limbs" (222). An ironic urban cardiologist, Dr Breavman keeps that heart beating with his saline solution — a grain of salt for limbs and stems, not the pastoral green heart of his park.

In addition to his healing powers, the young poet acts as archaeologist, geologist, and astronomer cataloguing the universe in his museum. Examining Shell's scars, Breavman describes himself as "the original archaeologist of earlobes" (22), combining history with anatomy above and below ground. When he undresses Tamara and she immediately puts her clothes back on, he feels "like an archaeologist watching the sand blow back" (78), as if history were to reverse its directions. From his childhood interest in the atlas that displayed his mother's Russia, to his love of volcanic violence on Mount Royal's ancient crater, to his eternal country drive "showing all the layers like a geologist's sample" (97), Breavman indulges in an archaeology of the frivolous. The adolescent historian seeks all the layers of meaning at eighty miles an hour, but he also interprets the world as a museum or container of the muses' evidence. Kitchen drawers are friendly museums (17,40), Shell's library quadrangle is a museum of bones (133), Breavman sits on the steps of Montreal's museum and breathes a historical sigh, and the perfect drive is "the eternal case in the astral museum" (98). Increasingly, the archaeologist turns astronomer in his planetary growth. Book IV opens with a list of Breavman's lost bodies — a rat, a frog, a girl sleeping, a man on the mountain, and the moon — which burn to become "faint constellations." Mr Breavman's planet or cannibal galaxy is controlled by a hebraic code: "It might be said they were eaten by the Mosaic bush each of us grows in our heart but few of us cares to ignite" (176). At camp, the keeper observes the stars and although he "didn't know the names of the constellations, [he] judged confusion to be an aspect of their beauty" (181); and when he spies a falling star, he judges it to be a "contract of cosmic significance" (182). Favourite games of contracts and covenants range throughout a diasporic cosmos.

As a keeper of museums from cloaca *ad astra*, Breavman has to catalogue experience, framing, containing, and connecting straight or filigree lines. When his mother lists their Westmount cornucopia, Breavman thinks ironically to himself, "Try and see the poem, Breavman, the beautiful catalogue" (65). In one of their innumerable dialogues, he asks Krantz, "Do you know what I am?", and Krantz responds, "Yes, and don't recite the catalogue" (103). But he cannot refrain from reciting the parts of female beauty that he has celebrated throughout *The Favourite Game*: "Krantz, the arms, the bosoms, the buttocks, O lovely catalogue!" (106). This apostrophe to catalogues reveals Breavman's poetic need to catalogue, to order his parallel lines, lists of scars, bodies, repetitions, connections. About to leave his Montreal family behind, he reviews his past in parallel structure: "when he stood among his uncles and bowed with them and joined his voice to theirs in the responses; when he followed in the prayer book the catalogue of magnificence ... " (118). If his family catalogue reflects the style of biblical and liturgical parallelisms, he soon breaks with this joining of voices, negating false values within tradition, substituting his own heretic hermeneutic as part of his *bildung*, subverting hierarchies until tangled into blossoms and stems. Like Klein's Spinoza, Cohen's brave, brief, or bereaved boy holds a dialogue with timelessness to become a Breavman who humanizes catalogue into dialogue.[8]

Lawrence Breavman's apprenticeship, education, or *Bildung* belongs to a Jewish-Canadian tradition that includes Richler's Duddy Kravitz and Noah Adler, Ludwig's Josh in *Above Ground*, and Wiseman's Hoda in *Crackpot*. The development of these characters as individuals reflects the formation of a young culture within North American society, and their teachers are often grotesque, instructing their charges in the ways of estrangement. In their progress above ground, these skeptical protagonists develop an ironic awareness of their surroundings as they experiment with forms of connection and disconnection — strings of lovers educating their bodies and minds beyond normal schooling. By deconstructing these multiple relationships and meanings, these young heroes and unwedded lovers perfect their favourite games of irony, paradox, self-reflexivity and tangled hierarchies. Out of their multiple roles, crackpots, confusions, music, and painting, they reconstruct eternal golden braids. Like Hoda's, Josh's, Noah's, and Duddy's, Breavman's coming of age coincides with a maturity beyond modernism in Jewish-Canadian literature. Out of Montreal's streets, Cohen's and Richler's childhoods almost meet to follow Klein's Torah-escorting band, with Cohen's western guitar strings returning eastern notes to Klein's Hebrew violins.

If Cohen's first novel portrays his emergence from Westmount's "ghetto" into a larger world, his second novel escapes the boundaries of any "garrison" mentality in its postmodern penetration of a historic Canadian wilderness. Klein attempted empathy with Canada's native people in "Indian Reservation: Caughnawaga": "This is a grassy ghetto, and no home."[9] Cohen develops Klein's short poem into a full-length experimental documentary about a homeless lost tribe. The narrator, a folklorist or anthropologist with a savage mind and keen interest in raw and cooked experience, would nevertheless part ways with Lévi-Strauss's structuralism, for he seeks to undo systems in his poststructural perversity. His fascination with the tribe of "A — s" and his best friend F, bring to mind Kafka's initialed antiheroes. Similarly, Cohen's System Theatre and Telephone Dance metamorphose from Kafka's Penal Colony; and just as "The Hunter Gracchus" and "Josephine the Singer, or the Mouse Folk" are, and are not, about the Jews, so *Beautiful Losers* is about a lost Jewish folk. Perhaps the A's are the "All" in "The History of Them All," the Everyman in Joyce's HCE or "here comes everybody." But these chains go against the grain of F's warning to "connect nothing," even if the constipated narrator strives "Te-kak-with-a" in his erotic fantasy.

Nevertheless the reader must fly in the face of F's desire merely to "place things side by side," for metonymic juxtapositions yield to the metaphoric flights of the narrator's needle which sews the world together. Cohen's needle of unity and meaninglessness pierces "the disparates of the world, the different wings of the paradox, coin-faces of problem, petal-pulling questions ... all the polarities."[10] Lodged in his Huysmansesque sub-basement and subversions, he needles his reader, simultaneously combining and separating, suspending "all" in an elevator shaft of alienation. The Iroquois or *hiro-koué* with their Buberesque dialogue "essayed to pierce the mysteri-ous curtain which hangs between all talking men: at the end of every utterance a man stepped back, so to speak, and attempted to inter-pret his words to the listener, attempted to subvert the beguiling intellect with the noise of true emotion" (8). "Pierce" means itself and its opposite, a contradiction not unlike Catherine's virginity (some-thing she gives up) or her apocalyptic veil.

The word apocalyptic has interesting origins. It comes from the Greek *apokalupsis*, which means revelation. This derives from the Greek *apokalup-tein*, meaning uncover or disclose. *Apo* is a Greek prefix meaning from, derived from. *Kaluptein* means to cover. This is cognate with *kalube* which is cabin, and *kalumma* which means woman's veil. Therefore apocalyptic describes that which is revealed when the woman's veil is lifted. What have I done, what have I not done, to lift your veil? (98)

This Hebraic and Hellenic etymologist hunts origins: what he does, he undoes, posing and exposing, covering names from their floating signifiers or prefixes to their apocalyptic endings or suffixes of *hiro* and *koué*.

   Between prefix and postmodern, who comes first? The narrator begins his quest and questions: "Do I have any right to come after you?" Searching for origins, for A — s, Cohen confronts his burden of the past from his epigraph's "bale" to the veil of influence to the meaning of Tekakwitha: she who puts things in order ... someone who proceeds in shadows, her arms held before her (44). Catherine is someone advancing, arranging the shadows neatly; Cohen comes to her in the same mystical fashion that stops bravely at the surface. Since the narrator wants to write well about the Jews (20) — his cab-balistic precursors who denied esoteric study to citizens under seventy — F invents the New Jew, a beautiful loser who plays favourite games and "loses his mind gracefully":

He applies finance to abstraction resulting in successful messianic politics, colorful showers of meteorites and other symbolic weather. He has induced amnesia by a repetitious study of history, his very forgetfulness caressed by facts which he accepts with visible enthusiasm. He changes for a thousand years the value of stigma, causing men of all nations to pursue it as superior sexual talisman. The New Jew is the founder of Magic Canada, Magic French Québec, and Magic America. He demonstrates that yearning brings sur-prises. He uses regret as a bulwark of originality ... He confirms tradition through amnesia, tempting the whole world with rebirth. He dissolves history and ritual by accepting unconditionally the complete heritage. He travels without passport because powers consider him harmless. His penetration into jails enforces his supranationality, and flatters his legalistic disposition. Sometimes he is Jewish but always he is American. (161)

Cohen's new lost tribe has wandered a great distance from Klein's ghetto streets, but his New Jew still practices heretic hermeneutics, tradition as adventure and discontinuity. Despite all the fragmentation, Cohen's broken vessels display an insistent Whitmanesque biblical parallelism throughout his surrealistic mindscapes. Messianic millenarianism, memory, and nostalgic theories of Black supremacy force the New Jew to invoke balefully Ray Charles' version of "Ol' Man River." The New Jew disseminates language in his masturbatory, Portnoyesque lust as he carries his iconoclasm to the limits, smashing through walls in his abusive automobile or breaking cinematic and generic barriers by letting the newsreel escape to merge in "aweful originality."

Having witnessed conversions all their lives, New Jews convert established structures such as factories into playgrounds and indulge in the free play of names. Section 14 of book I plunges us "into the world of names" which "preserve the dignity of Appearance," yet another A. The narrator inherits his grandfather's view as well as F's factory. When he and F visit their Jewish clothing factory, F addresses the Jewish ghost, "Larry!" — Lawrence Breavman or Leonard of earlier fiction and biography. In this onomastic and onanistic game, Larry Breavman metamorphoses and inverts into a beautiful loser with F as his favourite. As a child, F worked among the Jews, but later the "nameless" narrator owns the factory. Bound by the old laws of suffering and obscurity, the narrator is a New Jew for, as Derrida puts it, "anyone or no one may be Jewish."[11]

Because of the aniconic impulse of the Second Commandment, the New Jew suffers from "aweful originality" in his picturing of Catherine Tekakwitha from a Technicolor postcard to a stamped-out crucifix. Secret cabbals break the System Theatre into a stem, an origin. Cabbalists turn letters into numbers in their system of astrology or *gematria*. The narrator fails and passes his "second-to-last test" (123), and he explores the meaning of the number six across certain historic dates, recalling a line from the Cabbala (which is from the sixth part of the Beard of Macroprosopus) (126). In this neo-Gnostic universe the sixth day is the last day of creation when man first appeared, but six is also the numerical equivalent of F. The beautiful loser is the nth Adam wrapped in his second-to-last scroll, naming origins of genesis, expulsion, exile, exodus, desert, numbers, and a repetitious deuteronomy. As he traces Indian history back to 1675, he discovers that Spinoza was making sunglasses thirty years before the Jews re-entered France. Surrounded by religious medals of all kinds, the writer addresses his reader apostrophically: "In arctic isolation a man is writing this, a man who hates his memory and remembers everything, who was once as proud as you, who loved society as only an orphan can, who loved it as a spy in the milk and honey" (102). The new Jewish-Canadian entertains a dialogue between north and south, history and anamnesis. He wants thirteen-year-olds in his life, thirteen being the age of *bar mitzvah*, the *rite de passage* whose ceremony must not be completed and old magic must not be honored (51). Comparative mythologies of the Promised Land and the American Dream, Old and New Testaments, Jew and Jesuit, connect incompletely in beautiful, oxymoronic loss.

Crowds gather at the end of the novel for a "second chance," but they are denied this opportunity in favour of "All Chances at Once." *Beautiful Losers* combines a "History of Them Chances at Once" in the "split second" it takes for sand in an hourglass to be compressed in the stem between the two flasks. This mystical and metaphysical transformation leads to the "trip to the end" of the novel where apocalyptic and demonic are frequently indistinguishable. "The end of this book has been rented to the Jesuits" (242) by a sub-basement tenant, an orphaned Gerontion with a dry brain in a dry season, in a dangerous and finite house. Beautiful losers also rent the mysterious curtain hanging between all talking and writing men: the New Jew talks to the Jesuits, and Everyman carries on a hermeneutic dialogue. Leonard Cohen, tragicomedian as the letter c, begins Breavman bound and ends by deconstructing his aboriginal Everyman and the abracadabra of synagogue in this new scripture for a New Jew.

Barely fifteen years separate *The Second Scroll* from *Beautiful Losers*, yet Klein's synthesis of tradition and modernism remains worlds apart from Cohen's postmodern New Jew. The crowd that gathers at Melech Davidson's funeral differs markedly from the crowd that watches the old man's performance in the Epilogue of Cohen's novel. Where Klein's "Deuteronomy" reveals Israel's rebirth, "An Epilogue in the Third Person" depicts Montreal's springtime reawakening. Cohen's narrative lens sweeps the continent to trace warm Japanese currents responsible for Montreal's short-lived spring before his range narrows to "the beautiful waist of the hourglass" (241) — the shape assumed by a reeking Tiresias of Montreal's waste land. The old man sets out from the threshold of his treehouse where his memory represents no incident, to mythologize the change of season. He arrives at the System Theatre to watch an invisible movie on a black screen. Across the way at the Main Shooting and Game Alley, the narrator examines pinball machines with flippers that offer the player a "second chance": "Flippers represent the first totalitarian assault against Crime; by incorporating it into the game mechanically they subvert its old thrill and challenge" (237). Amidst mechanical debris, Cohen chooses his metaphors for a metaphysics of fate and essential criminal ideas: second chances challenge the first assault on the first night of spring. Out of Order signs over machines indicate the extent of subversion, apathetic anarchy, and the complexity of favourite Wurlitzer games.

The crowd of second chancers lift the "noble heap" and whisper in their hearts, "At Last," for the artists and magicians rush in for their last and second chance. Even as pinball machines offer a second chance, so the crowd of flippers, or revolutionaries, get an opportunity to watch the old man's performance: he disintegrates slowly, dissolves from the inside out, and reassembles himself. That the narrator prefaces this description with the parenthetic "which I do not intend to describe," further undercuts the deconstructive transformation of old man into hourglass, an appropriate vehicle for chiastic interchange. "And that point where he was most absent, that's when the gasps started, because the future streams through the point, going both ways. That is the beautiful waist of the hourglass! That is the point of Clear Light! Let it change forever what we do not know!" (241). Mystical revelation or ironic pose—Cohen's chiasmus goes both ways, reversing past and future order through climactic or anticlimactic metalepsis. If the old man reassembles himself into a Ray Charles movie (hence a movie of blindness), then the Epilogue's "trip to the end" returns transumptively to the beginning epigraph. The last spoken words in the novel belong to a New Jew, labouring on the lever of the broken strength test: "Hey. Somebody's making it!" The reader participates in the process of Cohen making it new, of the New Jew struggling with the agon of precursors and of poor men who have fled (243). The first item in a revived testimonial of treehouse stems and blossoms, origins and margins, reverses directions. When the old man metamorphoses into "Ol' Man River" the reader barely follows from source to mouth the course and discourse of the St Lawrence River, the Mohawk, and the Mississippi pleasure boat. Cohen writes a history of all lost tribes in first, second, and third persons. He resists graven images ("eye-con" or I-Cohen) with black pencil marks on a white napkin, throwaway figures in melting snow, and distorted mythologies on a blank screen. His New Jew, Montreal's ephebe, labours against the burden of the past as he beholds almost meetings through an hourglass darkly, a scroll, or a movie reel. Cohen's New Jew is Everyman, a "nude you," the reader stripped of all pretense. For common and ideal readers of an intertextual, metafictional diaspora, allegories of the New Jew keep and cancel tradition, question a nameless, faceless history, and master paradoxical ceremonies instead of grand narratives.

CHAPTER EIGHT

Richler's Runners: Decentauring St Urbain Street

> They were offered the choice between becoming kings or the couriers of kings. The way children would, they all wanted to be couriers. Therefore there are only couriers who hurry about the world, shouting to each other ... messages that have become meaningless.
>
> Kafka

Annie Kriegel, who watches the Jewish-American literary scene from her home in France, discerns a progression from one generation of novelists — Cahan, Gold, and Schulberg — preoccupied with the question "Où courent-ils?" to the next generation — Bellow, Malamud, and Roth — who ask instead "Pourquoi courir?"[1] Both questions seem especially pertinent to many of Mordecai Richler's protagonists who often run a frenzied race away from origins towards elusive goals, while their antagonists meet with accidents that may cause temporary or permanent paralysis. This running motif represents an accelerated version or parody of the Wandering Jew who must "make it" in a hurry in a newly found land of opportunity, who yearns for a speedy transition from immigrant margins to mainstream status. Denied recognition by New York's cultural yeshiva and by London's imperial hum and buzz, Richler's Jewish-Canadian anti-heroic sons of immigrants emerge from a double ghetto to avenge lost time and a lost place by trespassing on foreign landscapes and histories.

In *The Acrobats*, Richler's first novel, and another Jewish-Canadian *Künstlerroman*, Pepe tells André Bennett, the painter-protagonist, "In your pictures you are running away."[2] Pepe's observation points not only to the transatlantic flights of Richler and his characters, but also to the existential plights of those characters of Canadian origins who search Europe for their artistic selves. In his nightmare, André "took to flight, racing across oceans and world" (151), away from Canada in the company of Klein, Levine, and Kreisel. Furthermore, an ironic dimension emerges from Pepe's remark since the subject of one of André's paintings is a crippled beggar whose reappearance throughout the novel suggests the poverty and decadence of postwar Europe. On a physical level, this opposition between free and handicapped movement manifests itself in the contrast between the crippled beggar and parades, dancing, and acrobatics. On a religious level, Richler explores this tension when he alludes to Maimonides' reference in the *Guide for the Perplexed* to evil as "paralysis of the limbs" (55), and when he includes the story of an urgent education with Hillel and Shamai: "Teach me to be a Jew on one foot" (137). The existential choice between speedy confrontation or evasion appears in the question "WHO AM I AND WHY AM I HERE? Ask yourself this daily for you are running away" (86), and in Chaim's answer to André, "There are the times to fight and the times to run" (140). With the *Guide for the Perplexed* in one hand and a paint brush in the other, André Bennett, Richler's earliest runner, participates in a race of self-definition from rejection to affirmation.

In *Son of a Smaller Hero*, Noah Adler runs away from home when he is seven and again at ten, and when his grandfather slaps him, he runs off across the coal yard into the dusk. One summer in the Laurentians, after Noah steals a sign which reads This Beach is Restricted to Gentiles, "He ran and ran and ran."[3] Henceforth this triple repetition will form a rhythmic pattern in Richler's fiction creating a narrative pace to match much of his rapid dialogue. Noah's lover Miriam, "who had run and run and run ... felt, now that she had arrived, a tremendous need to rest" (103), for both lovers are torn between security and adventure. These characters rarely run the straight race from home and origins since they never know when they have arrived. Once again, crippling accidents and deformations stand in contrast to the strains of running: "Aaron Panofsky's Baron Byng apprenticeship had led to the loss of his legs" (84). The apprenticeships of so many of Richler's characters involve a discovery of positive directions to which they can run despite the deforming countercurrent of history.

Melech, one of Noah Adler's grandfathers, is a "fallen" king of coal yards, his other grandfather was a Hassid, but Noah is "sort of between things," neither fully Canadian nor Jewish in any traditional sense. In Europe, Noah's maternal grandfather was a poet; in Canada, just a "character" who taught his grandson about Rabbi Levi Yitzhok of Berditchev:

Man is the crown of creation. And when the Messiah comes all souls will flow together and return to be united with the Universal Soul, which is God. For the Evil One will be conquered and a New World will be established. Israel Baal Shem Tov, who was the founder of the chassidic movement, taught that it is man's highest idea to become the clear manifestation of God on earth. So he created the ideal of the Zaddik, of which he was the first. The Zaddik, or chassidic saint, fuses his soul with the Oversoul. He contains the largest number of sparks of divinity, and God, who is forever with him, illuminates not only his spiritual life but even his most trivial conversation. (89)

On the other side of the family, Melech is the king who has lost the crown of creation, and after two generations Noah laments the dwindled sparks and trivialized conversations. He runs away from vulgarities, but secular breezes rekindle a lost Hassidism and replace the crown of creation. "All their threats, all of Melech's laws, were like autumn leaves that, once flung into the wind, scattered and turned to dust. He had not done anything special with that afternoon of freedom. He had walked, but not in beautiful places. Yet somehow the whole city had seemed to be illuminated by the fire that burned within him" (74). The pace of Richler's walk increases to a run as his characters desperately seek replacements for those lost sparks and laws in a cold pastoral of city streets. Noah goes out during a storm, and, singing the prayers of his boyhood, manages to harmonize nature and culture in an aesthetic epiphany. Just before Noah leaves for Europe he takes one of his grandfather's scrolls, just as Leonard Cohen borrows lines from his grandfather's journal: the scrolls that Melech Davidson and Melech Adler leave behind influence the canon of Jewish-Canadian literature.

Nowhere does this obsession with running become more pronounced than in *The Apprenticeship of Duddy Kravitz*. The verb first appears when Duddy runs the French-Canadian chip man off the street, the verb form denoting territorial possession, Duddy's *idée fixe*. To attain his goal of land he constantly runs a race. But Duddy also runs when his father slaps his face for discovering the truth about his pimping. Yvette remarks, "You're always running or jumping or scratching,"[4] and "You almost killed yourself running after that land" (283). A representative of an American firm advises him, "You can't run before you learn how to walk" (113). Similarly, Uncle Benjy watches Duddy: "Run, run, always running, he thought, he can't even walk to his car" (245). When Yvette threatens to leave him if he starts running again, he replies: "Running doesn't give you cancer" (284). On the one hand, running takes on a sinister, escapist note when juxtaposed with illness as in the episode involving Virgil's final epileptic fit: "Duddy ran, he ran, he ran" (309); on the other hand, running can be more hopeful when associated with his promised land: "Duddy was always ahead of them, running, walking backwards, jumping, hurrying them, leaping to reach for a tree branch" (311), seizing at dizzying space, but unwittingly sawing off the branch on which he is sitting.[5]

In contrast, two characters in the novel exhibit an inability to run because of their physical handicaps — Virgil in his wheelchair and Jerry Dingleman with his crutches. Feeling superior to his earlier model, the Boy Wonder, Duddy shouts towards the end of the novel, "FASTER, YOU BASTARD. RUN, DINGLEMAN. LET'S SEE YOU RUN ON THOSE STICKS" (314). Duddy's demonic nature becomes all the more apparent when set against these two foils and when, as "chief rabbi of the underworld," he engages in dope-running. A possessive, outlandish landowner without a land, Duddy notices traces, footprint stems on his property: "The man had used a cane. Maybe two canes. The cane or crutch points dug deep near the water" (281). At once a metonymic substitute for an antagonistic Dingleman and an intrusive semiotic landmark, "cane" also carries homonymic overtones. For his cinematic role, Duddy chooses the pseudonym Dudley Kane, the allusion to *Citizen Kane* reminding the reader of Duddy's capitalistic aggressiveness. Furthermore, immediately before Duddy selects his new name, Mr Friar, his cinematic double, warns him: "I'm a vagabond, Kravitz. I've got the mark of Cain on my forehead" (118). Duddy later applies the phrase to himself in his dream (257). Duddy resembles Friar because he is a vagabond, a Wandering Jew, and because of his own mark of Cain, received when he scratches his forehead after plunging to the bottom of his lake, or, when his father's "Finger-marks had been burnt red into the boy's cheeks" (29) so indelibly that Duddy's cheeks burn red even at the close of the novel. Moreover, just as Cain's brother reminds him of his guilt, so Bradley, an imaginary brother, and Lenny, Duddy's brother at medical school whose claim that "anatomy's the big killer" is realized when he performs an illegal abortion, remind Duddy of his own failures and insecurities.

Mark, march, margin — even without Derrida's juxtapositions, one sees the connections in Duddy's step-by-step apprenticeship of running to and away from marginality, in putting his mark on experience and, in turn, being marked by it. At the very end of the novel, Max Kravitz reviews his son's past "way back there before he had begun to make his mark," but Duddy as usual refuses to smile for his father. But when the waiter accepts his credit and recognizes him, "We'll mark it," Duddy laughs, for the roles have been reversed, the tables turned, for this one-time waiter — the quickest and youngest at Rubin's.

If Dingleman's cane is his metonymic mark or substitute, the telephone is the causal instrument and substitute for Duddy's guilt in Virgil's final fit. "Above him the telephone receiver dangled loosely"

(309). This paralytic telephone, both in its cause and its effect, echoes the earlier death of Mrs MacPherson: "The receiver dangled idiotically from the hook above her" (33). Subconsciously, cane (Kane) and telephone, two instruments or double hooks in Duddy's guilt, converge in his film office, for he wants "to get a phone number that spelt MOVIES and then he could advertise 'Dial MOVIES' in all the newspapers" (118). His guilt surfaces in a surrealistic nightmare collocating Virgil and MacPherson: "A leering Mr MacPherson waited round every corner. 'You'll go far, Kravitz. I told you you'd go far.' He tried to run, he wept for trying so hard, but his legs wouldn't work" (258). Guilt, fear of paralysis, and a need to prove to the MacPhersons of the world that he will indeed go far — these, and other factors, all compel the young fugitive to run frantically. Ironically, he awakes from his nightmare to discover that he cannot get his toes unstuck. Fear of running-paralysis overtakes Duddy when he visits his land in the winter and plays his favourite game with the Laurentian wilderness. "He circled round and round, his teeth chattered, and twice he began to run. He ran and ran to no purpose until he collapsed panting in the snow ... He tripped, he fell time and again, his nostrils stuck together" (212). When with blind purpose Duddy trudges up and down the glittering scalp of ice covering his land, he repeats the identical situation and phrasing of an effete MacPherson who struggles through winter on the first page of the novel. Mac intrudes on the St Dominique ghetto, Max's son interlopes on Lac St Pierre; these parallels heighten Duddy's guilt and contribute to the reader's inability to judge Richler's central character, a picaresque *pusherke*.[6]

What makes Duddy run? His grandfather's phrase, "a man without land is nobody," acts as a catalyst for his quest to possess land and self. Since his apprenticeship must be as short-lived as possible, Duddy never has the opportunity to experience childhood in his rush toward becoming an adult. At fifteen he already has dark circles around his eyes and shaves twice a day to encourage a beard; time becomes an obsession for the chain-smoker who holds down several jobs: "ideas are ticking over like bombs in his head. Tick-tock, tick-tock" (282). Driven by this time-bomb of *différance*, Duddy is so busy doing so many things and emulating so many people that he has no time left for being a child, or if he has any traces of boyhood, they result from an identity taken from many other individuals. Uncle Benjy's final advice that a boy can be two, three, four potential people, but a man is only one, comes too late for Duddy. Scattered in time, place, and personality, Duddy cannot see that the race is not to the swift; his inheritance from his grandfather is a blind spot making his final words in the novel, "You see," all the more ambiguous.

The notable absence of femininity in the novel marks Duddy's missing boyhood and insecurity;[7] this, as well, compels him to run. A lack of girls at FFHS, Mac's dead wife, and, most importantly, Duddy's dead mother (Max's dead wife) contribute to Richler's overwhelmingly male world: "Minnie had died nine years ago and that, Max figured, was why Duddy was such a puzzle" (27). The rare enigmatic occasions depicting Duddy's sensitivity and mitigating his exploitative behaviour occur in relation to his missing mother — an absent origin for his homelessness. Upset that his father does not answer his letters from Ste Agathe (whereas Lennie used to receive mail weekly), Duddy breaks down: "Max had only been gone a moment when Duddy began to cry. Maybe it was the fever, maybe it was his bed and the room he shared with Lennie again, but Duddy wept long and brokenly before he finally fell asleep" (107). Richler indulges in sentimentalism and nostalgia:

There was a picture in the living-room of Max and Minnie on their wedding day. He wore a top hat and her face was in the shadow of a white veil. But her smile was tender, forgiving. It looked to Duddy as if she had probably used to laugh a lot. He could remember her laugh, come to think of it. Something rolling, turning over dark and deep and endless, and with it hugs and gooey kisses and a whiff of onions ... Once more Duddy was tempted to ask his father if Minnie had liked him, but he couldn't bring himself to risk it. (129)

Although the motherless child does not inherit Minnie's ability to smile, he does assume a maternal role when he prepares omelettes for the rest of his family. Aunt Ida's oedipal remark, "Your mother was taken from you when you were young and all your life you will be searching for her" (241), is only slightly amiss because Duddy searches for the lost child in himself to replace his mother. At the cemetery, Duddy lingers to take a last look at his mother's grave: "We're supposed to come here once a year, aren't we? This year let's try. We could come together" (257).

To compensate for the mother missing in his life, Duddy turns to the land, an illusory Mother Earth, for a sense of security and rootedness. Each of his seasonal visits to Lac St Pierre involves the relation between Duddy and women. In summer, he is more interested in the land than in sexual intercourse with Yvette who has guided him there; in winter, he promises to "give up screwing for two weeks" if God helps him find his way. In the autumn, he imagines his land transformed into a casino: "Outside, the stars don't care. They shine on and on. Midnight, the monkey-business hour. Bears prowl the woods, a wolf howls for its mate. Somewhere a wee babe is screaming for its mommy ... The waiters and office girls are banging away for dear life on the beach: nature" (282). Duddy is possessed by the idea of possession: just as the land transforms him, he must transform the land from its natural state to a commercial venture. His autumnal vision displays unusual fertility in its sexual association with mother nature which must be destroyed to make way for more adventurous schemes. In his attempt to regain paradise, lost innocence, and childhood, as he revolves on fate's roulette wheel and runs simultaneously towards and away from himself, is Duddy still the baby screaming for Minnie Kravitz? His loss at roulette leads him accidentally to his property; this wheel remains an appropriate emblem for a whirligig caught in strange loops: "Round and round she goes, where she stops nobody knows. It's up to fate. Kismet, as they say" (282).

Duddy's commercial destruction of nature seems inevitable given his grandfather's relationship to the land. He provides the catalyst for Duddy's search for land, security, *anima*, and self, but Simcha's frustration and failure may be found in his own land: "outside in the gritty hostile soil of his back yard, Simcha planted corn and radishes, peas, carrots and cucumbers. Each year the corn came up scrawnier and the cucumbers yellowed before they ripened, but Simcha persisted with his planting" (46). Agricultural sterility determines the character of the ghetto's inhabitants, because from where Duddy sprung the boys grew up dirty, sad, and spiky like grass beside the railroad tracks. Montreal's *pusherke* must traverse those tracks, traces, and origins on his way up from the ghetto to dream pavement into buy-more land. No sooner does Simcha teach his grandson how to plant and fertilise and eradicate the killing weeds, than Richler mentions sterile Aunt Ida who, like the land, adds to family misery. As though retaliating against his family's poverty, Duddy proceeds immediately to the Halpirins' garden in Westmount where he and his anti-pastoral gang destroy all the tuiips.

An ironic *coureur de bois*, Duddy is doomed to fail in any relationship to land or humanity. His hectic pace blinds him to any vision beyond his immediate pursuit; similarly, he is deafened by the slogans he repeats: they predetermine his course of action and thwart free will. Uncle Benjy's posthumous letter contains some conflicting advice. It claims to have no advice for Duddy, yet, Benjy's "Experience doesn't teach; it deforms" seems appropriate in view of the deformed, grotesque characters and in view of an unnatural deformation of the land. Benjy's definition of a man as one who murders four potential people differs from his own father's formula. Duddy errs in his apprenticeship towards manhood: dispossessed, he mis-possesses land, and instead of murdering conflicting drives within himself, he destroys other characters, his alter egos. Faced with two generational definitions, Duddy cannot be a *mensch*, for he never first experienced childhood; his apprenticeship lacks closure at the end of this novel and when he resurfaces in *St. Urbain's Horseman*. When Duddy repeats to Dingleman his grandfather's saying, the latter grasps immediately that the boy is reiterating somebody else's platitude. As in Jacob Two-Two's propensity for repetition, language freezes into clichés of *God's Little Acre*, the painter of interiors or exteriors, "anatomy's the big killer," and visual advertisements of ghetto commerce. When Hersh, the outsider, interrupts Duddy's dream of Parisian women with "That's a cliché. It isn't true" (225), he falls into the same linguistic trap in his belief that he has succeeded in purging himself of the ghetto mentality. Duddy's ungrammatical iteration "like they say" serves to introduce clichés, overused opinions of a collective body that includes Friar, Calder, Cohen, Cuckoo Kaplan, and other minor figures who reflect different aspects of Duddy's character — figures whose cumulative *paroles* amount to the ghetto's *langue*.[8]

With its cinematic inserts, grotesque newspaper clippings about paralysis and other infirmities, themes of running, commercial signs or slogans, and vulgar Hersh cousins who could be interchanged with many of the Kravitzes, *St Urbain's Horseman* fits well with Richler's other works. Yet despite the reappearance of Duddy Kravitz in this later novel, *St Urbain's Horseman* demonstrates a number of technical advances over the earlier fiction. Temporally, instead of Duddy's frenetic running, Jake Hersh examines time from a more internalized perspective. Spatially, instead of Duddy's limitations within Montreal's parochial ghetto, Jake Hersh widens his horizons throughout the Diaspora. Morally, instead of the reader judging Duddy's character, Jake Hersh now judges himself as a protagonist prone to introspection. And structurally, in place of earlier linear chronology, Richler now employs a circular frame which plunges the reader into the narrative *in medias res*. Section 2 opens with Jake recalling "the true beginning," while at the outset of section 3 Ormsby-Fletcher exhorts Jake, "Perhaps if you began at the beginning," to which he replies "I simply wouldn't know where to begin."[9] Jake Hersh's quest involves a search for literary and religious origins — from *The Quest for Corvo* to *Search the Scriptures* — in between composing a nightmare journal and a daydream trial.

The first two chapters reveal Jake's obsession with time as he follows the clock from 3:45 A.M. when he is awakened by his recurrent horseman nightmare to 6:30 A.M., "Stock-taking time." As the almost three-hour period unfolds, Jake shifts time in his mind and around the world: 3:45 A.M. is 10:45 P.M. in Paraguay, the *Doktor*'s time; 4:00 A.M., a three-hour wait for the morning papers; 4:15 A.M. is 11:15 A.M. in Toronto, "Tomorrow country then, tomorrow country now" as opposed to "Still yesterday ... Or was that the night before?" Before 5:30 he recalls Spain, "Ten years ago, when time had not yet begun to count" (12). Against this chaotic randomness of estranged chronological loops, Jake seeks "circles completed," a "meaningful symmetry." His father tells him that life is a circle, a little *kikeleh*,[10] but cookies may crumble or be eaten: "Eight years swallowed whole" (56). Where Duddy runs in circles, eccentric, expatriate Jake thinks in circles whose centres shift and elude the pursuer. "Escaping, escaping" (138). Like his mixed-marriage children, he "belonged everywhere. With a stake in Jehovah and a claim on Christ" (281), but the film director has difficulty directing his own life and seems to be most successful with the eccentrics of Jacob Hersh's Continuing Rep. With his dual testament he belongs everywhere and nowhere, an Ishmael of utopia.

When Jake goes to the old country to make it new, he seeks colonial and racial roots, an "other" home. Comfortably ensconced in Hampstead, he fondly recalls Toronto's Park Plaza Roof Bar, "enjoying being at home. At ease in Canada. The homeland he had shed" (5). Jake exchanges platitudes with the postman about blizzards "at home," yet at the same time he feels "boorish, but at home" (72) in London. He heads for New York, his "spiritual home," while as a Labor-Zionist he despises the British "because they stood between him and his homeland" (189). On a personal level, his parents divorced, Jake comes from a broken home; as a diasporic Jew, his home remains "elsewhere" — *heimlich* and *unheimlich*. "My life seems to function in compartments ... When I'm in Montreal, I don't believe in my life here with you and the children. In court, it seems I was born in the dock, there was no life before and there will be nothing after. But lying here with you, I can't even believe that I'm expected to turn up in court again in the morning" (443). He regards himself as a contradictory character born in the wrong place at the wrong time, unable to adjust to the codes of society because of an underlying aggressiveness directed against authority. The *pusherke* in him wants to conquer the rest of the world while the comic *schlemiel* is thwarted by society.

For Jake, home is above all his aerie, an inner sanctum, which alternates with the dock of the Old Bailey as a setting for the present narrative tense. But an aerie also serves as a nest for a bird of prey, both Jake and Cousin Joey being predators intent on revenge. Racked by guilt, Jake is not simply on trial: he puts the rest of mankind on trial and decides on revenge. When he first meets Nancy, he carries on the conversation like a duel: "Vengefully, he countered" (50). Like Joey, "demanding vengeance" (71), and like the black fanatics of his imagination, the concentration camp survivors, and the starving millions, this injustice-collector will "live only for vengeance" (89), demanding justice from predecessors and contemporaries alike. Like Oscar Hoffman in his tiny cell, Jake spends "vengeful days" (220) in a world where *The Avengers* bombard the media. Even when he speaks to his dying father about film and television stars, he answers "vengefully." One of the attributes Jake shares with loveless Duddy, friendless Harry Stein, and messianic Cousin Joey is vengefulness. On a physical level Jake's revenge of spraying a murdering lime solution on his neighbour's rhododendrons resembles Duddy's destruction of Westmount tulips, Harry's slashing a Silver Cloud Rolls Royce with his knife, or Joey's fight at the Palais d'Or. Sexually Jake the Ripper and his cast of doubles are torn between hedonism and puritanism. But most importantly, Jake's revenge aims at history — the immediate history of the Holocaust and a longer history plaguing him with an anxiety of influence.[11]

Jake's revenge against the Nazis takes the form of a mythical projection in which victim and victimizer become almost indistinguishable; he imagines his cousin Joey as a horseman slowly extracting teeth from the *Doktor* Joseph Mengele, the torture contrasting with the horseman's usual galloping speed. He records this episode in his journal which remains incomplete because the exact dates of Joey's birth and death are unknown. He includes a list of Joey's aliases: the Golem, Jesse Hope, Jacob Hersh as descendant of the House of David, and the multiple doubles of Harry Stein, Duddy Kravitz, Luke Scott, and Thomas Neill Cream. Even Peregrine Pound serves as an avenging double wanderer: "Mr Pound tried to skewer Jake on the stand." Jake meanwhile feels guilty towards his gardener Tom: "He thinks I only sit out here to demand my pound of flesh." Just as Jake alters time through his messianic second coming at the end of the novel, and just as he disperses space through his peregrinations, so the central character fragments himself through doubling emanations or projections of the fantasy-spinner: "Jake was not surprised that out of his obsession with the Horseman he had been delivered Ruthy. / Who had sent him Harry. / Who had served him Ingrid" (89). If the injustice-collectors seek him out, he will retaliate vicariously against history through his journal where the pen overpowers the sword, righting tangled hierarchies.

Another section of Jake's journal, "Jews and Horses," also remains incomplete, waiting for the reader to fill in the blanks. The first entry belongs to Isaac Babel, always a touchstone for Richler, and a standard for Jake and Nancy who possess a copy of his short stories. Babel's cavalryman remarks that "When a Jew gets on a horse he stops being a Jew": once mounted he transcends his former inferior status, a reversal echoed in F. Scott Fitzgerald's allusion to the Jews overtaking the Cossacks on horseback. "The web of messengers," whom Richler revises, might also include Swift, a fellow satirist devoted to Yahoos and Houyhnhnms; Cervantes, a fellow traveller in Spain; and Spenser, whose Red Crosse Knight rides through *The Faerie Queene*. If Spenser seems remote, one need only remember The Sword of Justice (1563) in Number One Court: "*a very fayer and goodly sword well and workmanly wrought and gylded*" (74), not totally alien to Jake's "aerie-fayerie" sphere of influence. Furthermore, in Jake's reconstructed allegory Cousin Joey (a reversal of J.C.) rides a red MG that "could have been a magnificent stallion and Cousin Joey a knight returned from a foreign crusade" (129). The sword of justice jousts with the pen of revenge: an eye for an eye, a gold tooth for a gold tooth, synecdoche for mythology, Jake's trial for Mengele's. After Babel, the ghetto's Pegasus wings its way through the Diaspora.

In addition to his revenge on anti-semitism Jake also retaliates against a literary past. Once again Harry and Duddy, his alter egos, epitomize this revenge at the physical level: during the war Harry "exacted retribution by slipping into the library and tearing pages out of the reactionary old bastard's collections of first editions" (22), and Jake even admires Harry when he deliberately burns a hole in his couch. Duddy's literary exploitation of history consists of his Canadian Jewish Who's Who, bringing "modern marketing knowhow and sales savvy to hitherto underdeveloped but colorful *coureurs-de-bois*" (166). But Jake's relationship to literary history is far more complex as he struggles to overcome the burden of the past: "the bookshelves filled him with weariness. Books bought in Montreal. Books bought in Toronto. Books bought in London ... Books lugged from country to country, flat to flat, across the ocean, crated and uncrated, and still largely unread" (11–12). Like the Jews in history, literature is dispersed and deferred: "Proust put off for so many seasons would now have to be read or discarded" (293). Jake judges Nancy by her bookshelves, and as he waits in his car envious of Luke and Nancy, he reviews his unaccomplished goals which include killing a Nazi, meeting Evelyn Waugh, reading Proust; he recalls that at his age "Dostoevski had written *Crime and Punishment*, Mozart had done his best work. Shelley, dead." He would also like to reject a knighthood: "It was never my wish / To be Sir Bysshe" (55). In such visionary company the anxiety of influence becomes unbearable; Auden is by no means the only judge of Jake: Samuel Johnson and a mainstream of other literary figures have also set standards for Richler and his artistic protagonists. New York may be represented by the *Partisan Review* and *New Republic*, while England may claim *The New Statesman* and *Encounter*. Jenny, whom Jake reveres for escaping from the ghetto, reads Keats, the *Saturday Review of Literature*, *Nana*, *The Shropshire Lad*, Emily Dickinson, and Kenneth Patchen, as allusions multiply. At school in Montreal, England meant Tennyson, Scott, and the exquisite novels of Jane Austen. "A literary experience" (190) denied later in life: "Literature, once his consolation, was no longer enough" (302).

Richler's satire often fuses literary and Jewish traditions. Nancy may be successful in the garden, but she doesn't know the Holy One's secret name, the sayings of Rabbi Akiva, or how to exorcise a *dybbuk*, but she has mastered the Orangeman's Talmud and the Protocols of the Elders of the Compost Heap. Jake's Jewish allsorts bag contains the thirty-six just men, Maimonides, the Golem, Trumpeldor, and Leon Trotsky, the affirming flames of his Jewishness. He even appropriates the 1777 diary of Reb Shmul Johnson: "When I survey my past life, I discover nothing but a barren waste of time, with some disorders of the body and disturbances of the mind very near to madness, which I hope He that made me will suffer to extenuate many faults and exercise many deficiencies" (91). Jake traces his criminal ancestry to Lord George Gordon (in Dickens' *Barnaby Rudge*): "Once Lord, now Reb, Gordon lingered on in Newgate for some years ... keeping a kosher cell" (43), the converse of Father Hoffman's accounting cell.

Jake's revenge against his family partakes of his revenge against cultural history and anti-semitism. He gleefully salvages a splinter of satisfaction from his American rejection knowing that he will cause more Hersh border trouble, depriving his uncles and aunts the delights of Miami. Yet his sense of remorse surfaces at Christmas in London. "His forebears hadn't fled the *shtetl*, surviving the Czar, so that the windows of the second generation should glitter on Christmas Eve like those of the Black Hundreds of accursed memory" (286). On seeing Irwin after Uncle Abe's socio-historical lecture, Jake retorts in the same vein: "My grandfather didn't come here steerage, Baruch didn't die in penury, Joey wasn't driven out of town, so that this jelly, this nose-picker, this sports nut, this lump of shit, your son, should inherit the earth" (412). On the surface, many of Abe's avuncular values appear acceptable, but they are all undercut by the absurd figure of Irwin at the end of his speech. Jewish children "can't sleep, they feel guilty about the Indians" (408) while Abe would feel guilty masturbating; the centripetal uncle has both feet on *terra firma* while the centrifugal nephew steps on quicksand everywhere he goes. "Yankel, this is our home. We live here, you don't ... I am not one of your bitten Hershes, a wanderer, coming home only to poke snide fun and stir up trouble. A shit-disturber" (409). As a "pile of shit," Irwin justifies Jake's "shit-disturbing." Yet even Jake himself is astonished at the Hershes' values that prevent him from properly mourning for his father; despite the vulgarity of his family who fail to learn from history, "within their self-contained world, there was order. It worked" (396). "We're all becoming our fathers" (288) summarizes Jake's anxiety for origins in exactly the same manner as Lawrence Breavman regards his Montreal family; with their Jewish allsorts bag of anarchy, Breavman and Hersh cause border troubles and destroy orderly, self-contained worlds.

Even in his latest novel, *Joshua Then and Now,* Richler has not entirely abandoned his theme of running. "Run, Joshua, run" contrasts with the closing image of Joshua leaning on his cane.[12] What binds this later novel to Richler's first is the passage referring to Maimonides' description of evil. All of Richler's perplexed runners seek guidance to endure a race which has no end in sight: even if they overcome paralysis of the will, they are condemned to run in circular repetition within and without the ghetto walls.

The first half of the novel's title, "Joshua then," refers to the 1940s childhood of Joshua Shapiro who, like Duddy and Jake, attended Fletcher's Field High School in Montreal's ghetto; Joshua "now" refers to a later generation looking back at the earlier period. Where Jake Hersh is a media director and private historian of the horseman, Josh Shapiro is a television personality and social historian who has passed through his diaspora phase to return to his Montreal homeland. Within one generation, the outsider-turned-insider has made it up from the St Urbain ghetto to the gilded garrison of Westmount — from immigrant marginality to Canadian centrality. This dichotomy between "then" and "now," not only in Joshua's personal history but in Canadian and Jewish history, plagues him wherever he turns. Loping, sloping, and interloping, this grotesque golem in search of a soul wanders through the Diaspora, laughable because lopsided, split between two legacies — one defying death, the other powerless to be born. To overcome his comically divided self — mindbody, upper-lower, Jewish-Canadian, cloacal-heavenly, archaeology-astronomy, tradition-adventure — Joshua tries to recapture a sense of wholeness and balance through anyone concealing the past. With Maimonides' *Guide for the Perplexed* as his Baedeker through the labyrinths of history, Joshua struggles against his own confusions and unmasks those characters hiding behind the superficial veneer of a present that conceals their modest roots.

Like Ludwig's Josh in *Above Ground*, Richler's Joshua emerges from hospital pulleys that were placed to heal his fractures. Removed to his cottage in Quebec's Eastern Townships to mend his fractures if not his ways, Joshua is carefully guarded against intruders by his father, an ex-boxer, and his father-in-law, a senator. Ironically, though, the WASP villagers on Lake Memphremagog regard Shapiro as an outsider, "and it was Joshua who was taken for an interloper. A tall, loping, bushy-haired stranger, obviously street-wise; a lean, middle-aged hawk with a hooked nose, a pockmarked face, who, practising God knows what necromancy in depraved Europe years ago, had seduced their Trout and might yet poison the wells or abscond with one of their babes, its blood required for his Passover rituals. Beware" (30). Since the displaced person trespasses wherever he steps or runs across the Diaspora's invisible borders, he turns to irony, comic revenge, or heretic humour as a first and last resort. Richler inverts a tradition of anti-semitic stereotypes into purposeful comedy.

Joshua has inherited a comic genetic code from both of his parents. His *bar mitzvah*, a "then" episode, marks the pseudo-transition from boy to man as his mother ceremoniously performs a striptease much to the delight and embarrassment of the boys. Shedding her garments, Esther Shapiro simultaneously strips away conventional decency so highly prized by other Jewish mothers. The more she is socially scorned, the greater her defiance in displaying her underwear on the ghetto's laundry line where a middlebrow visual community may be raised. Richler flaunts his Queen Esther, moving her out of the closet and onto the clothesline, from embarrassing underworld of taboo to front row; turning *bar mitzvah* into burlesque, he shows what happens when religion becomes sociology — Judaism changed into vulgar Jewishness. In the face of convention she flies through bedroom windows.

Josh's pugilistic father hands him an equally aggressive comic tradition in which a hypertrophied body comes to terms with its atrophied intellectual powers. A Bible in one hand and a glass of ale in the other, Reuben Shapiro mixes high and low brow when he teaches his son about sex and Jewish tradition. The Shapiros' muscular Judaism has little patience with a quiet *mentschlechkeit*, and their

attempts to integrate the two extremes into a unified society meet
with inevitably comic results. Reuben opens his Bible for a lesson in
humorous hermeneutics that parallels his pugilistic instruction.
"Quote, Thou shalt have no other gods before me, unquote. You see
there were lots of contenders, other gods, mostly no-account idols,
bums-of-the-month, before our God, Jehovah, took the title outright,
and made a covenant with our forefathers who he had helped out of
Egypt. A covenant is a contract" (81). Even Shapiro quotes scripture:
this heretic humour derives from the disjunction between sacred
history "then," and its Reubenical exegesis "now." Reuben inherits a
comic covenant that permits him freedom of interpretation to use
his low-brow vernacular as a vehicle for instructing his son in the ways
of monotheism. Ironically, his own vulgar approach with its body
language parallels his forefathers' iconoclasm: where Abraham
smashed idols, Reuben breaks the fists of those who fail to adhere to
their part of the contract, whether in gangsterism or pretentious
religious affiliation. In the examples of the Shapiros, we see how the
mighty of "then" have fallen into the commonplace of "now," how
material progress becomes a façade for spiritual regression. Through
these Jewish jokes we regain paradise, not for eternity, but for an
instant of laughter that bridges "then" and "now," and retrieves historical loss. To counteract the Fall and the Expulsion, comedy raises
the spirit and reintegrates the outsider into society. Richler employs
slapstick, practical jokes, running laughter and running commentary
in his marathon.

Josh's comic inheritance helps bridge the distance between low and
high brow, between ghetto poverty and the *arriviste*'s affluence, for
Richler's satire exposes the gap between origins and margins of Jews
who deny "then" in favour of "now." One of these is the psychiatrist
in the novel.

The esteemed Dr. Jonathan Cole, author of *My Kind, Your Kind, Mankind*, a
rotund man, brown eyes mournful, turned out to be Yossel Kugelman, of all
people. When they had been kids together on St. Urbain Street, Yossel had
already catalogued his library of Big Little Books ... And now, Joshua could
see, Yossel was still a collector. From salvage he had graduated to art.
Canadiana. A Pellan hung on one wall, a William Ronald on another. (71)

These transformations from junk to art, from origin to margin, from
kind to man to universal mankind — Joshua exposes all of these as he
assaults psychiatric authority, trying to remember whether Yossel had
been the one to turn up at Bea Rosen's sweet-sixteen wearing a fedora
hat. During their hostile reminiscence, the distance between them

shrinks, and, by the end of their meeting, Josh has Yossel worried about his wife Bessie and his own health. Later, when the Coles are on vacation, Joshua enters their home and defaces one of their paintings, a valuable A.Y. Jackson landscape, by erasing the signature and signing, *sous rature*, "this copy by Hershl Sugarman." An interloper and a vandal, Josh rewrites history for those who seek to forget.

What Joshua enjoys most of all is baiting old classmates — St Urbain urchins who had struck it rich. Try as hard as they will, they cannot erase embarrassing traces of their ghetto upbringing that clings to them in their climb up the vertical mosaic to the heights of urbanity — Montreal's Westmount district. Irving Pinsky, now a dentist, lives on Summit Circle, drives a Mercedes 450SL, travels around the world, belongs to a gourmet club, and collects vintage wines. "They passed through a laundry room, with its twin tubs, into the sanctuary, its up-to-date thermostat set at thirteen degrees Celsius. And here a glowing Pinsky allowed a fulminating Joshua to fondle, warning him not to shake unduly, his cherished bottles of Château Mouton Rothschild '61 and Château Lafite '66" (127). Pinsky's "now" exaggerated fastidiousness is deflated by his "then" "celebrated … sneakers he let rip in Room 42, FFHS," flatulence that must still be washed out in the twin laundry tubs. He remains blind to the two people he really is: the young stinker who once forced others to sniff, and the man who now sniffs the best wines. The contrast between an "up-to-date" thermostat and the historical 1961 and 1966 points to the broader comic incongruity of a "with-it" Pinsky who relies on labels alone, those outer superficial trappings of success. But beneath his air of success, his body still communicates with the world through its celebrated sneakers, the oenophile debased by the coprophile. Josh takes his revenge on Pinsky's historical amnesia by stealing into his mansion, invading the "inner sanctum," removing all the labels from his bottles, and rearranging them on the racks. Where once his father had broken dentist's fingers for the mob, Josh discovers a subtler method of retribution: Pinsky will now have to rely on his well-trained nose instead of his blind eyes to discover the truth in taste.

Even wealthier, the Montreal tycoon Izzy Singer finally receives the Order of Canada. This forces Joshua to laugh aloud as he remembers him from Room 42 and his twelfth birthday when he played violin and was betrayed by a "stream of hot piss darkening Izzy's trousers, spreading in a tell-tale puddle round his shiny new pair of shoes." And now he owns an empire that sprawls from Los Angeles to Nova Scotia — a more extensive puddle than that which surrounded him as a child. As some Jews commit the genetic fallacy of forgetting their humble origins in their drive toward American expansion, Richler's satire serves as a reminder that the past deflates all pretensions to superiority. "Ostensibly, the perfect prosperity package. But his onyx cufflinks were just a mite too large, and the initials woven into the breast pocket of his shirt too prominent. Izzy, of St Urbain born, was still pissing in his pants as he played" (317). The emperor's clothes do not quite fit his body, his body does not quite fit his soul, and his present circumstances do not fit his past. For every centrifugal force of achievement and recognition, there is a comic centripetal force returning the assimilated to the provincial ghetto: Izzy's mainstream status is contradicted by a stream of hot piss that accompanies him from one end of the continent to the other. The external Order of Canada is denied by the internal disorders of his body, his past, and his make-believe world. Despite the opulence of his Westmount home, everything is in conflict — the conflicts of "now" and "then," living room artifacts and kitchen delights, a veritable delicatessen tempting Izzy for a midnight snack that sets off his entire alarm system. Trespassing and pissing on his own property, the *parvenu* can never really be at home, for he is betrayed by his bodily needs and his roots. Comedy, which leaps over boundaries between ghettos and empires, and shifts margins, may be his true home: the tell-tale told by an idiot joy.

But there is a darker side to Joshua's comic revenge against history once he abandons his Montreal childhood and its demarcated ghetto. In his attempt to retrieve history in Spain at the age of twenty-one, Joshua encounters Dr Mueller, a menacing antagonist who forms part of his recurrent Ibiza nightmare evoking Nazi atrocities and uncovering his Jewish identity. While his *bar mitzvah* marked a ludicrous transition, his true entry into manhood occurs in his confrontation with Mueller. "If you think you can rob me of my manhood, you're out of your mind. I'm not running, Mueller ... I'm a man, not a mouse" (185). Conversations between Mueller and Joshua are not so much dialogue as debate in which each accuses the other of weaknesses in their respective heritages or personal histories; victor and victim spar, the German accusing the young Canadian of cowardice. The lie dice that they roll symbolize their tangled, perverse relationship to one another, to fate, and to history, with Joshua having to establish himself not merely as a Canadian or a Jew but, more importantly, as a man rather than a mouse. Joshua humiliates Mueller when he steals a beautiful woman from him: "He had taken on a Nazi *mano a mano* and demonstrated to Mr Hemingway that he did not lack for *cojones*" (336). But comic revelations soon dispel these sinister events, for the opposition between working-class Jew and aristocratic

German is too pat: Josh's victory proves illusory since the woman's preference was based on the size of Josh's ears, nose, and toes — parts that promise equally large sexual gratification. Josh has confused the literal meaning of testicles with the figurative sense of courage, just as he misinterprets Mueller, who turns out to be Gus McCabe, the celebrated author of westerns. The entire episode then turns into a parody of Hemingway in which a Jewish-Canadian poses as a tough American challenging European civilization.

In pursuit of this comedy of errors, Joshua returns to Ibiza twenty-five years later to find out what happened to its various inhabitants after his departure. With Mueller's death and innocence, he realizes his mistake "and laughed until he almost cried" (396). Those ambivalent tragicomic tears deconstruct his labour of avenging history: since nothing can undo the tragedy of the Holocaust, Josh comes to terms with his limitations, but instead of despairing he resorts to laughter as catharsis. He resigns himself to his fate, but rises above his own condition through a humour that bypasses the obstacles of history and its persecutions. "*You did. You didn't. Ancient history.* But *my* ancient history, damn it. He paused to set his wristwatch to Montreal time. Home time. Family time" (397). The comic Jewish historian, or Hemingway-hero *manqué*, who doesn't possess ultimate answers overcomes the universality of ancient history and the Diaspora by a subjective gesture — he does not set time according to general cosmic history, but to a personalized version which can be controlled. Like so many other wanderers in the Diaspora, Richler's comic hero domesticates Jewish humour by returning to his native ghetto, regressing from marginal manhood to original childhood. Powerless to change the grand designs of history, he can at least cultivate his Montreal garden and set his home in order through a comic spirit that triumphs over past tragedies. When the *pusherke* grows up, he continues pushing upward and outward beyond ghetto horizons toward a wider world that offers no answers. The prodigal son returns home without answers, but with the right comic questions; his St Urbain street savvy broadens into worldly wisdom and wit, those comic weapons that slay hostile dragons of the Diaspora.

Duddy Kravitz, Jake Hersh, and Joshua Shapiro originate in Montreal's ghetto and FFHS where they precociously learn comic tactics to rebel against the authority of the right side of the tracks. Duddy traverses those tracks that lead eventually to Lac St Pierre, but in doing so he drags behind him street values that clash with his pastoral vision. Jake Hersh moves further afield, but even in London he carries his St Urban apprenticeship that collides with his status as adult, as British resident, and as successful member of the bourgeoisie. Joshua Shapiro completes the cycle, returning from European margins to Montreal origins, having reconciled possession of land in the Eastern Townships with his experience in England, France, and Spain. Duddy circles round and round his land recalling Moses from *Bible Comics*; Jake thinks of his Laurentian past as "circles completed" and life in general as a "circle. A little *kikeleh*," diminutive, homey, comic; Joshua seems to reach his promised land, but this proves to be an illusion, hence comic, for the diasporic Canadian Jew is decentred among Montreal, New York, Hollywood, London, Paris, Ibiza. Richler's aggressive triumvirate — dirty duty Kravitz, jakes Hersh, josher Shapiro — take comic revenge on this decentred world and all Dickensian caricatures and multiple doppelgängers who attempt to impede their progress. Mounted on their hobbyhorses, these Jewish-Canadian rakes and rogues cross borders from a "then" apprenticeship to a "now" fulfilment, from a grudging smile to full-blown laughter. Those existential choices between boy and man, man or mouse, are mediated by an avenging horseman, a grotesque golem who emerges from Montreal's ghetto to stalk through the Diaspora, Everyman's land for every landsman. Richler's journals, like Klein's, chronicle these journeys between and beyond "then" and "now" — the twilight zones of *différance*.

CHAPTER NINE

The French Disconnection: Monique Bosco en abyme

One of Monique Bosco's volumes of poetry, *Schabbat 70–77*, opens with a section entitled "Voyages d'exil" and ends with a prose poem: "La loi de la dispersion est respectée aux quatre coins de la terre. On honore l'héritage du juif errant."[1] Born in Vienna (like Henry Kreisel), educated in France and, after the war, in Montreal, Bosco abides by the laws of the Diaspora in most of her writing, expressing her displacement in forms of almost meetings, loss, and absence. In an exchange with Derrida she complains about the loss of her mother tongue, German, and citing the example of Kafka and his translator Milena, relates translation to feminism and exile.[2] In Bosco's linguistic prison-house, woman, writer, Canadian, and Jew experience exile on the margins of an abyss where not quite all is lost in translation.

Poststructuralist criticism has eagerly seized upon Gide's concept of *mise en abyme*, a phrase borrowed from heraldry referring to an inner design of a shield in which the shield's overall pattern is repeated. Modern critics have extended this synecdoche to include the image of two parallel mirrors which create infinite reflection, repetition, or vertigo such as might be experienced on the edge of an abyss. This sense of vertigo appears as an important characteristic of Quebec fiction in general, and although it takes on various forms in her writing, this *mise en abyme* is central to the novels of Monique Bosco.[3] While her characters lose themselves in bewildering labyrinths of obsessive repetition, from which they emerge only to find themselves reeling on the brink of an abyss, her protagonists and narrators are preoccupied with repetitive thoughts, actions, and language — a preoccupation that reflects the dilemmas of the author's origins.

Un Amour maladroit (1961), winner of an American first-novel award, begins with:

Je suis devant le mur
Le long mur
Le mur des lamentations
Le mur des ancêtres qui,
La face couverte de cendres,
Venaient pour s'y lamenter
Se lamenter
La seule chose gratuite
Suprême consolation permise.[4]

In these lines Bosco announces her obsession with lamentation: repetitive tears in front of repetitive walls that connect her to her ancestors. In her claustral universe "walls" play a central role. These walls are occasionally pierced by windows or mirrors that intensify a sense of endless repetition and incarceration rather than offer relief or escape. Immediately following this poem about Jerusalem's Wailing Wall and psychological ghetto walls, the narrator "reflects" upon her existence: "image fuyante, miroir infidèle. Miroir, dis-moi qui je suis: ni la plus belle ni la plus laide." Through her looking-glass the Wandering Jewess perceives a doubling confirmation of her internalized identity, a vision confounded by domestic labyrinths of absence: "Longs corridors sans fin où j'erre, interminablement qui ne donnent que sur des chambres désertes, désespérément vides. À l'intérieur, tout n'est que noirceur. Dans chaque pièce, un miroir dont je n'aperçois que l'envers" (202). By the end of the novel, she has resolved the question posed at the outset of how to grasp her life as she returns to her mirror: "Dans la glace, j'accepte que mon reflet me paraisse enfin familier et inévitable. Je n'espère plus de transformations miraculeuses pour mon visage" (213). Where earlier she had sought "le miracle d'une métamorphose," she now resigns herself to confronting a reality unchanged by flattering mirrors.

Like her self-reflexive mirrors, the windows in *Un Amour maladroit* offer no outward escape, for they serve only to isolate Bosco's young protagonist from society. She addresses a shop window which separates a little girl from toys: "Un même mur, invisible comme une paroi de verre, se dressait toujours entre la vie et moi" (170). This self-proclaimed masochist finds no outlet at her window which reminds her only of the happiness of others: "Chacun se hâte vers le but qu'il s'est choisi; quant à moi, je m'efforce de ne penser à rien, penchée à cette fenêtre qui ne débouche que sur la joie des autres" (184). While others rush forward, she remains alone, static, petrified at her window: "J'aime cette insidieuse maladie qui me transforme lentement, inexorablement, en une statue de sel" (207). Not unlike

Anne Hébert's heroines, Monique Bosco's protagonists find themselves stationed at windows peering into vacant external worlds, or
surrounded by walls that enclose an equally internalized emptiness.

Confined within *huis clos*, the narrator eventually succumbs to a
dizziness caused either by the contraction of walls on her psyche or
by a labyrinthine branching of endless corridors which perplex her
divided ego. Her reaction to her psychiatrist places her on the brink
of an abyss: "Un jour qu'il avait réussi à me pousser plus loin de
coutume, j'eus la sensation d'être perdue dans le corridor sombre et
désert d'une mine abandonnée. Un pas plus avant et j'étais certaine
de tomber dans le noir absolu d'un précipice sans fond" (148).
Though ashamed of her excessive egocentricity, she cannot renounce
her martyrdom, her quest for identity fails because the walls of her
ego block her entry into the lives of others. "Je vais, je viens, je tourne
en rond, sans fièvre et sans caprice, de façon inéluctable ... Je ne puis
même pas prendre place parmi les pleureuses du mur des lamentations" (187). The misery of her awkward love knows no company, for
Bosco's obsession with walls merely accentuates the whirligig's com-
pulsive *abyme*, shelter, and invisibility: "De cet échafaudage est né le
long mur qui bientôt m'encerclera étroitement, refusant l'entrée de
ce domaine à quiconque. Derrière son enceinte ... Là sera mon arche,
à l'abri des regards, où je serai invisible pour l'œil même de Dieu"
(207). Walls protect her against decentring forces of an internalized
diaspora where she joins the invisible company of Jewish-Canadians.

While she fails to establish contact with mankind at large, she is no
more successful in relationships involving women, her family, and
her Jewish religion. Just as she is surrounded by walls, so is she
enclosed by a feminine family of mother, sister, aunt, and grandmother, for she was born fatherless "en une gynécée." Where her
younger sister Elizabeth (whom she considers her double) has a
name, she remains "la Petite," an anonymous narrator whose patro-
nym, the sole inheritance from her father, embarrasses her at school.
Her grandmother recalls the family's flight from Poland to Paris, and
her mother instructs her in the ways of religion: "Tremble, m'a-t-elle
dit, fille digne de moi, / Le cruel dieu des Juifs l'emporte aussi sur
toi" (10). From this simple rhyme she graduates later in life to Sartre's
Réflexions sur la question juive and a masochistic Jewishness: "Pour
m'en punir, je reprendrai la route, la longue route sans fin du Juif
errant" (185). But her Wandering Jew turns inward to repeat her
intramural role: "Je demeurais prisonnière de mon infernal ghetto
individuel ... Nulle issue. Nulle sortie vers le monde" (198). Thus, the
externals of the plot — hiding in Marseilles during Word War II and
later emigrating to Montreal — complement the wanderings of a cen-

tral consciousness paralyzed *en abyme* where family and religion do not help in a quest for self-identity and the world at large.

La Femme de Loth (1970) picks up where *Un Amour maladroit* leaves off with the emphasis once again on obsessive repetition, enclosure, and infinite, abysmal doublings. Structurally the division into 240 short sections furthers the atmosphere of enclosure as one section echoes another. "Toi" and "tu" reverberate throughout the novel as the first-person narrator, Hélène, addresses her departed lover, Pierre, in a refrain of bitterness. This speech is bracketed within interwoven narrative and chronological sequences encompassing biblical history, family history, the immediate past, and the present that fluctuates between Montreal and Venice, scene of an earlier novel *Les Infusoires* (1965). *La Femme de Loth* begins and ends in circular fashion with Hélène contemplating suicide: the walls and mirrors of the first novel turn to a window in this later work which seems to have been influenced by Diane Giguère's *Le Temps des jeux* (1961). In Giguère's novel the young heroine experiences vertigo from her window overlooking an existential abyss: "ouvrit la fenêtre, se pencha sur le seuil et ferma les yeux. Son corps oscilla dans la lumière. Il y avait longtemps qu'elle songeait à cette issue, mais elle perdait toujours courage au dernier moment … Prise de vertige, la nausée l'envahit et elle appuya ses coudes à la croisée."[5] Bosco begins comparably: "Il y a la fenêtre. Un bond. Et on échappe à l'horrible son d'une voix. Douce voix, soudain transformée en voix ennemie … Dans ce dur pays de froid, les fenêtres ne s'ouvrent pas sur le vide."[5] To the windows, transformations, claustral emptiness, and suicidal depression of the earlier novel is added the image of "voice" — whether her lover's or her own that echoes in obsessive litany. As a child, she suffers from vertigo near her window: "Je restais près de la fenêtre à relire interminablement mes nouveaux livres. Je les savais déjà par cœur. Je n'osais regarder au sol, à cause du vertige" (56). The window separates the internal world of literature from external reality — a central theme in *La Femme de Loth*.

Hélène's soliloquy or interior monologue heightens the claustral reverberatory effect. The auditory equivalent to parallel mirrors in *mise en abyme* would be a continuous echo, the voice and name of Pierre resounding through section after section. "Tu te moquais de mes 'litanies,' de ce besoin de répéter ton nom, à l'infini" (256). Excluded from the world at large by her closed window and by her rejection at the hands of Pierre, Hélène repeatedly defines herself through a series of negatives that deny the possibility of human contact or relationship. She remains an outsider even to her parents, whom she regards as an ideal couple. When she asks for a baby brother her parents reply, "Il y a des maladresses qu'on ne peut répéter" (26). Their refusal to repeat their error takes on a more poignant note as the child recalls voices that wonder why she fails to resemble her mother and father: "Et la même voix, ou une autre, différente, ou mille autres, réparties au long des années, reprenait en écho, en leur passage: 'Le beau couple ... C'est fou comme ils se complètent'" (27). Ironically, her Parisian accent distinguishes her at school in Montreal, and later in life she is complimented for her voice alone, the rest of her body relegated to an inferior status.

Instead of resembling her parents, Hélène discovers that she looks more like her grandmother, who is the link to her Jewish background extending from the Bible to the Holocaust. The narrator regards herself as a latter-day wife of Lot, for she must learn to define herself independently of Pierre with an eye to the unknown future rather than a failed past. "En laissant la ville en flammes se consumer. Sans se retourner ... Il faut aller de l'avant. Sans un regard pour le passé. Pourtant quand Yahvé voulut sauver Loth, il l'autorisa à partir avec sa femme, ses filles. Et malgré la présence de Loth, le réconfort des enfants nées de sa chair, elle se retourne, malgré la défense formelle, la vieille femme folle regrettant ce qui a été" (21). The cumulative "re" prefixes stamp Hélène's perverse predicament indelibly upon the archetype to form a palimpsest or statue of salt. This memory of her personal past and her archetypal past causes a feeling of nausea in Hélène who is constantly torn between the demands of past and future, the former somewhat less painful than what awaits her. "J'aimerais comprendre pourquoi Dieu voulut sauver Loth et sa famille s'ils ne retournaient pas sur la ville en flammes. Je comprends si aisément la femme de Loth. Moi aussi, à la fin de cet été, je me serai peut-être transformée — à force de répandre des larmes sur le passé — en une autre statue de sel" (65). As Bosco's narrators survey their past, they appropriate the myth of Lot's wife with its emphasis on the transformation of tears into a saline statue; this biblical leitmotiv reappears towards the end of the novel:

Loth et sa famille. Les filles sont jeunes, avec l'avenir devant elles. Pour la vieille femme, c'est tout son passé qui s'engloutit. Alors elle tourne la tête, cherchant à distinguer ce qui se passe, ce qui s'est passé. Elle se retourne, malgré la défense expresse. Pauvre vieille femme. Dans la Bible, tu n'as pas de nom. La femme Loth, cela suffit ... Une statue de sel. La belle image. L'admirable symbole. Une statue de larmes pétrifiées ... Je me retourne, moi aussi, sur ce passé dévasté. (268–9)

Review, return, repeat — these constitute the static actions within *Un Amour maladroit* and *La Femme de Loth*, the retrogressive pull inhibiting any future progress; moreover, these "re" prefixes, which mean "back" and "again," focus on forms of doubling in the novels.

Hélène's solitary existence defines itself in contrast to forms of doubling including the ideal couple that her parents represent or the other young couples who meet and marry while she remains alone. For her, this pattern extends back to the biblical archetype: "On accepte seulement les 'couples' comme dans l'Arche de Noé" (159). So, like other masochistic heroines with whom she identifies, she looks into her mirror for a doubling, narcissistic illusion: "Miroir, miroir, dis-moi que, pour lui, je suis celle qui compte" (240). When the flattering mirror fails, she turns to her window only to be reminded once again of her separation from any communion or community, and the impossibility of substituting "romantic" dreams in place of harsh realities: "J'ai passé des années à faire du lèchevitrine aux étalages du bonheur conjugal. L'Amérique entière affichait ses richesses aux fenêtres panoramiques de toutes les belles banlieues peuplées de couples amoureux. Il me convient de pleurer sur mon ersatz de rêve d'arrière-cour" (240–1). Faced with the claustral reality of four walls, a room of her own, Hélène gains some comfort from literature — from reading and writing — where she can find some doubling fulfilment not offered by society. "J'ai toujours été étonnée de voir mon ombre se profiler sur un mur, sur le sol. J'avais donc une ombre. Des empreintes digitales uniques au monde ... J'essaie de les nommer, de les cerner, sur ce papier ... En cessant d'exister, je ferai mon premier choix de vivante. Exit Hélène" (147). Hélène projects her shadow on a wall and a dramatic role upon herself thereby splitting herself into an acting self and a recording, observing self.

Caught between past and future, Hélène recognizes her dual personality: "Vieillarde prématurée. Fausse jeune fille prolongée. Voilà mes deux faces" (180). Her destiny lies *en abyme*: "Je serai double jusqu'à la fin. J'hésite entre l'amour et la haine. L'Ancien et le Nouveau Testament. Parjure aux deux." Even her marriage to Claude, a homosexual, thwarts any desired fulfilment; instead it provides her with another doubling role: "Il incarnait un rôle. Volontairement, je donnais ma réplique dans cette mauvaise pièce de boulevard" (144). Her awareness of this replication and role-playing occurs at the very centre of the novel in a series of short sections, "cette farce que je répétais" and "mon simulacre de rôle." "Le passé est passé. J'ai tort de m'acharner envers ce double d'autrefois, ma sœur d'hier ... On ne se refait pas" (145). Abundant references to novels within the narrative further contribute to the *mise en abyme*;

Proust, Kafka, Dostoyevsky, Sartre, and de Beauvoir provide Hélène with examples "d'y retrouver le reflet de mes angoisses." Literature, books, words, transform life and reality for her as she depicts her own metamorphosis from girl to woman; contrasting life and art, she states her purpose in creating *La Femme de Loth*: "Je n'écris ce roman que pour éloigner l'échéance de la vérité" (42). Writing alone saves her from committing suicide by the end of the novel: "Pauvres pages. Preuve dérisoire qu'en fin de compte tout est littérature ... Simulacre et dérision" (281). Through parody, she deconstructs her own portrait; in her voyages of exile, a Jewish-Canadian writer awaits a parody of despair. Like Wiseman's Hoda, Bosco's Hélène turns back to survey her past, revise biblical myths, and tangle hierarchies.

Bosco transforms Pierre, the doctor, in *La Femme de Loth* into the protagonist in *Charles Lévy, m.d.* (1977), and continues her earlier preoccupations, only now she portrays a bleak world through male eyes instead of from a feminine perspective. Dying of cancer, Dr Lévy laments his past failures through first-person narrative and interior monologue. Gloria Escomel has noted "un effet d'écho" between Hélène and Charles: "ce chassé-croisé de personnages produit un effet de mise en abyme des deux romans."[7] In other words, the *mise en abyme* found in individual novels may be carried over to Bosco's work as a whole marking a central preoccupation in her fiction. In this latest novel, however, she carries thematic *dédoublement* and repetition one step further by adding an obsessive, stylistic double entendre.

Like David Canaan in *The Mountain and the Valley*, Charles Lévy has an incestuous relationship with his twin sister Sarah which is more satisfying than his marriage. Bosco introduces the doppelgänger motif near the beginning: "Ma moitié. Ombre de notre ombre. Double cruel d'Edgar Poe ... la sœur perdue, le vrai double, ma précieuse jumelle."[8] Twin phonemes echo each other and stress thematic and imagistic concerns at all stages. Like Bosco's other Jewish protagonists, Charles complains about his racial identity: "Libre Lévy, sauf de la vie. O les vies non vécues de tous ces gens de ma race. Lévites. Toujours plus vites" (10). He places orthodox Jews *en abyme*, "ghetto dans le ghetto," and regards his personal past in similar terms, ontogeny recapitulating phylogeny: "Je ne suis jamais vraiment sorti du ghetto d'enfance" (128).

Paronomasia pervades every aspect of his life as linguistic and existential elements fuse. The moribund physician of language diagnoses his condition *en abyme*: "ces mots creux qui prolifèrent comme mon cancer. Un mal, des maux. J'ai des maux à l'infini. Et des mots aussi" (19). Sexual distinctions also proliferate through echoing homonyms in clipped sentences with absences of verbs: "La maleheure. L'heure des mâles. Du mal" (19), "Femme. *Fame*, faim en italien. *Fame*, en anglais" (16), "Ombre. Ombre. Hombre! Voie des voyages. Voix. Vois. Vois l'âge" (15). The surgeon who dissects language to this extreme ultimately loses his way and his voice in a never-ending labyrinth, "L'énorme grotte ... Tuyaux d'orgue à l'infini ... Un vide sans écho" (55). Words turn upon themselves in imitation of the egos of introverted narrators and protagonists who stare into a series of shattered mirrors. In Derridean fashion, Lévy disseminates language.

Thus, each of Bosco's novels reveals her preoccupation with various forms of doubling, echoing, and repetition *en abyme*. Bosco seeks shelter behind cloistered walls pierced by windows, mirrors, shadows, and the echoes of ancestral voices which haunt her prose and pull her back from the brink of a contemporary abyss. The same notes, incidentally, resound in her prose poem "Jéricho" (1971): "Je n'irai jamais à Jéricho. Je renonce à l'héritage. J'accepte qu'au bruit de ma voix, nul écho ne réponde. Que les autres entonnent leurs trompettes, faisant crouler les murs humains. Je reste sagement à l'abri d'un pauvre présent. Le passé est mort. Et je récuse, d'avance, l'absurde futur incohérent."[9] And as the walls of an individual ghetto close in on Charles or Hélène, so the four corners of the earth disseminate and encompass the Diaspora.

Monique Bosco, Adele Wiseman, and Miriam Waddington have been attracted to the myth of Lot's wife because it symbolizes the tension between exile and a return to origins — women's defiance against paralyzing structures of walls or pillars in desert, northern wilderness, or ghetto. Waddington's poem, "Lot's wife," echoes Bosco in its conclusion of retrospection and iconization — the same techniques used by Wiseman's Hoda.

> In your eyes
> I saw suffering,
> it was my own suffering.

> Through your lips
> I felt kisses,
> they were my own kisses.

My hope reached
tall as the world,
it was your world.

The pillar broke,
light crumbled,
my heart turned
and turned to salt.[10]

In their backward glances, Bosco and Waddington review burdens of the past through an adventurous tradition. As their intertextual diaspora swerves between departures and meetings with the past, Lot's wives inevitably suffer from paralysis and vertigo. Empathetic doubles haunt their labyrinths, pointing both toward their schizoid solitude, and to the universality of their condition. Like Klein — another translator from ancient Mediterranean testaments to *Ultima Thule*'s inventions — Bosco curtails routes through an odyssey of revision. Like Richler's prodigal sons of smaller heroes, Bosco's daughters of diminished heroines inveigh against Montreal. Her writing reconfirms that Nietzschean equation of woman, Jew, and artistic translator of displacement.[11]

At first glance Bosco would seem to have little in common with Klein, but a second, more telling, look at Lot's wife reveals shared traits. Klein's portrait of the poet as a shadow's shadow staring at a mirror recurs in the "shivering vacuums" Bosco's absence leaves. For if Klein, the first solitary poet in the Jewish-Canadian landscape, had increasingly to go it alone in later life, then Bosco's isolation as the only female francophone Jewish writer in North America places her in his company. Moreover, just as Klein gave voice to his isolation through the monologic tradition of Browning, Sholom Aleichem, and Isaac Bashevis Singer, so does Bosco exploit the monologue to exorcise the demons of her loneliness. With her absent lovers, and madness just around the corner, she seeks out doubles in her monologues: equivalent biblical myths, doppelgängers from a Romantic tradition, and *dybbuks* from a nineteenth-century Yiddish tradition. Where Klein's narrator stalks a vanishing messianic uncle, Bosco's solipsistic narrators turn inward to follow their haunting demons. As ominous as Singer's satanic recreations of *shtetl* life and Klein's dramatic monologues ultimately silenced, Bosco's "demonologues" bridge the abyss of her several solitudes — woman, Jew, Canadian, francophone, writer. Through these "demonologues" she internalizes a ghetto populated by the *dybbuks* of a mythological past carried into the present by the enigmatic fictions of Kafka, Freud, and Malamud. Divorced from lovers and reality, these Jews remarry in language, mythology, and fantasy. In contrast to the festive dialogic humour of Richler, Roth, or stand-up comedians, the tragic Jewish soliloquy — Bosco's complaint — gropes for a hermeneutic audience. Like Kreisel and Kattan, she has lost one language to find her voice on the edge of another, where Rabbi Levi Yitschak's "where shall I find Thee?" resonates from Babylon to Berdichev.

But if Bosco still seems remote from the Kleinian tradition, then perhaps Miriam Waddington might serve as a mediator between the two. Waddington, who has written extensively on Klein and whose second volume of poetry, *The Second Silence* (1955), echoes Klein, has also written an autobiographical essay, "Exile: A Woman and a Stranger Living out the Canadian Paradox," which would certainly apply to Bosco. Indeed, the works of one complement the other's. Waddington's lyrics tend toward a slim, columnar verticality on the page, while Bosco's prose poems fill the centre of the page leaving blank spaces above and below these verse paragraphs. Bosco moves predominantly in a novelistic direction, while Waddington has attempted some short stories, but has developed mostly as a lyrical poet. Where Bosco turns inward, Waddington proceeds with an outward empathy toward nature and humanity: love, for one, is fission, for the other, fusion. Under Bosco's negations lies Waddington's passion to say the yes of Molly Bloom. In her essay, Waddington discusses the invention of the Jewish-Canadian: "These two cultural aspects — Yiddish and English-Canadian — did not come together in me for many long years. They simply existed side by side and I devised two codes of behavior, one to fit each world. That's why I also had to create a third world which was my own invented one, where I could include the elements I chose from the two other worlds."[12] These solitudes almost meet through opposite ends of their dream telescopes where Bosco and Waddington create second images of silence, negating multitudes and nothingness. Waddington's numbers unite Bosco and Klein:

We are not one but two
we are not two but four
we are not four but many
sometimes we are not any

where single
is double
and the double
is neither.[13]

Of Klein's later development Miriam Waddington remarks that as he shifted from purely Jewish subjects to broader Canadian concerns in *The Rocking Chair* so he moved away from archaism toward metaphor. The "double time" of archaism gives way to "double meaning."[14] Whatever overlapping vision Klein saw between Jewish- and French-Canadian identities in their threatened survivals, his bifocal sense of time and meaning was appropriately conditioned for bridging the "bilinguefact." His English, French, Yiddish, and Hebrew traces merge into a Canadian portrait, and beyond to a universal text like the one described by Jabès in *Le livre d'Aely*: "C'est pourquoi j'ai rêvé d'une œuvre qui n'entrerait dans aucune catégorie, qui n'appartiendrait à aucun genre, mais qui les contiendrait tous ... un livre enfin qui ne se livrerait que par fragments dont chacun serait le commencement d'un livre."[15] If these words serve as an apt description of *The Second Scroll*, they also depict Klein's aesthetic in *The Rocking Chair* with Montreal's "double-melodied vocabulaire" joining Klein to Bosco. Enigmatically Waddington joins them to "together make an ambiguous form, / like a folded loneliness / or like mirrors that reflect only each other." The ambiguous *abyme* continues the dialectic, but Lot's wife synthesizes into finality. Expert in exile, and distrustful of master narratives, the other solitude translates Canada's "bilinguefact," "double-melodied vocabulaire," and dual code of behaviour into intertextual scrolls.

CHAPTER TEN

Invisible Borders: Naim Kattan's Internationalism

For Judaism and writing are but the same waiting,
the same hope, the same wearing out.

Edmond Jabès

In an appreciative article, "A.M. Klein: Modernité et Loyauté," Naim Kattan outlines Klein's peripheral position with respect to English and Jewish literary traditions. James Joyce, who introduced Klein to modernism, showed him resemblances between the Irish and Jewish situation: "marginal à la puissance britannique, de filiation extra-territoriale, il donnait l'exemple de l'adhésion au grand tout mais une adhésion à ses propres conditions, une adhésion dont il établis-sait lui-même les termes. Les moments d'exaltation alternent avec des haltes de réflexion, de retour sur soi."[1] While Joyce and Klein share self-reflexiveness and exile from the mainstream of English culture and the metropolis, their approaches to empire differ: the former challenged the great tradition in *Ulysses*; the latter adhered to tradi-tion in his fidelity to Britain and the Bible in *The Second Scroll*. Kattan sees Klein's *The Second Scroll* as an open-ended modern reading of the world and he regards Klein's final silence as a fulfillment of Kafka's dream of becoming a "petit Juif de l'Est." Kattan, whose name shares with Klein's the meaning "little," demonstrates in his own fiction the impact of another kind of "petit Juif de l'Est." Against the *pintele yid*'s lack of status, the *lamed vavnek*'s halo of anonymity, and the drowning instant of the Diaspora, the writerly ego marks time.

The diasporic trajectories of Kattan and Derrida bear a striking resemblance: the former left Baghdad, the latter Algiers, to study in Paris after World War II. Their double sense of exile derives from their minority Jewish status within a Moslem majority and their colo-nial marginality with respect to the French metropolis. Their *diffé-rance* (or what Klein might have labelled anti-*mellah* mentality) may account for similarities in their hermeneutic readings of spatial signs and dispersions. Derrida's categories parallel the antitheses developed by Kattan throughout his essays: "When a Jew or a poet proclaims the Site, he is not declaring war. For this site, this land, calling to us from beyond memory, is always elsewhere. The site is not the empirical and national Here of a territory. It is immemorial, and thus also a future. Better: it is tradition as adventure. Freedom is granted to the nonpagan Land only if it is separated from freedom by the Desert of the Promise. That is, by the Poem."[2] Kattan employs similar terminology in his dissemination of spatial and temporal categories that apply to the Jews in his essays, novels, and short stories: le lieu et l'espace, terre promise et terre de promesses, le désert et la ville. "Vivre dans l'éternité c'est nier le moment. Le judaïsme aurait été réduit à une abstraction s'il n'avait pas placé le moment au cœur de sa démarche, mais le moment ne peut être vécu qu'épuisé par le lieu. Si le lieu devient temple, il égare le moment et le nie; et s'il est désert, il le situe dans l'attente. Les juifs ont pérégriné entre le désert et le temple."[3] Like Derrida, Jabès, and Memmi, Kattan focuses on *différance*, *désert*, waiting, "in-betweenness," and almost meetings. In that dialectic between moments of waiting and settling, leopards enter the temple and unsettle resolutions.

To achieve his "I-Thou" dialectic, Kattan relies on the mediation of "thresholds," a liminal poetics where, according to Derrida and Jabès, the centre is the threshold. Mary Ann Caws aptly summarizes this condition of modernist and postmodernist perception with its shifting of margins: "This broad threshold includes at once the multiple notions of border, hinge, and articulation — Jacques Derrida's concept of *brisure* or the joining break neatly resuming those meanings — of beginning and exit, of the place for crossing-over, and of the link between inside and out. Any serious mention of liminality has to take into account the anthropological notions of passage and its rites."[4] In his essays and fiction, Kattan often situates himself at various thresholds for meditation and mediation of *rites of passage* from oriental spontaneity to occidental dialectics. The charisma of chiasmus attracts him because it frees him to represent shifting points of view above an otherwise vertiginous chasm. Against the cross-eyed and the myopic, Kattan's spectators hinge on Buber's "in-between," a swinging space between the long distances of horizon and Diaspora.

In several genres — essays, plays, short stories, novels — Kattan (like his namesake Klein) addresses himself exhaustively to such polarities as occident and orient, north and south, Arabic and French, male and female, artist and administrator, particular and universal, reality and theatre, memory and promise (or Derrida's tradition and adventure). At times, these binary oppositions branch to form tripartite categories in discussions of Islam, Judaism, and Christianity, reflected in the setting of the works in Baghdad, Paris, or Montreal, that is, the Orient, Europe, and North America. He advocates a kind of phenomenology of simultaneous participation and detachment where man is dialogically himself and the other, he is actor and spectator. These internal splits permit immersion in a multiplicity of roles: "I am irresistibly drawn to this magnetic universe with its seductive multiplicity, but just at the point of being absorbed and swallowed by it I draw back: the actor doubles his function, I become a spectator. I have one foot in each world, I have only to shift and it is the East that becomes a spectacle for me. This movement to and fro, this perpetual change of viewpoint, is ... uncomfortable, unless I recognize in it ... a secular heritage."[5] Within this decentring magnet, Kattan doubles as Sephardic tight-rope walker and acrobat whose unique perspective affords insights in a world where certainties crumble and the frontiers between reality and theatre blur. Oscillating between perpetual nostalgia and a loss of some portion of himself, the voluntary exile finds in his distress a new balance of energy greater than the blindness of a rooted existence.

Kattan's first novel, *Farewell, Babylon*, covers his childhood and adolescence in Baghdad up to World War II. The nameless first-person narrator of this apprenticeship novel traces his self-ironic development towards personal and national emancipation, leaving behind Iraqi repression for educational possibilities in France. Before bidding farewell to his native land, Kattan has to cross a number of boundaries. From his rooftop vantage point behind a white iron enclosure affording privacy, the child addresses visiting Bedouins across the street: "I would shout with the secret satisfaction of crossing boundaries that adults would not have the audacity to transgress."[6] In the world of childhood he is neither Jew nor Muslim, so he may speak to a Bedouin without running any risk — one nomad almost meets another. Similarly, from a small crack in the shutters of a cousin's house (another marginal vantage point), he observes Shiite flagellation, a ritual of total release, and precursor of the *Farhoud*, the notorious pogrom of 1941 which forced many Jews to emigrate.

Other boundaries must be crossed on the boy's road to adolescence. Invisible boundaries separate poor Jewish neighbourhoods from the others, and, traversing the barrier, the boy becomes aware of his own wealth in relation to those who are crowded five or six to a room. The protagonist knows even less of the forbidden Muslim territory, but during an emergency he has to go to a Muslim to heal his elbow. "Holding my father's hand, I felt as though I were leaving on a trip, and secretly prepared myself to cross the boundaries of my own country" (41). Invisible boundaries disappear in the world of work where fellow workers are Moslems or Christians; that Jews are employed as interpreters in the civil service because of their linguistic training further accentuates their roles as intermediaries stationed at the crossroads of language. Within an Iraqi mosaic, Jews lead a double life: "Our origins had more to do with geography than beliefs. In this conglomeration, each of us possessed his territory which extended beyond walls and invisible boundaries" (51), but most parents prefer to barricade themselves behind the walls of their own neighbourhoods and states of mind.

Literary publication and sex — pleasures of the text — are the two crossroads of the narrator's initiation into the adult world where he passes beyond parochial boundaries. When his stories appear in print, he discovers a new identity with the external world revealed anew: "With the book under my arm, the streets seemed different ... I felt I was seeing the people in the street for the first time!" (64). On the way to a Muslim editor, the fourteen-year-old Jew moving through enemy territory passes through the red-light district where his short pants prevent him from being initiated into manhood before seeing the editor-in-chief. The boy is equally fascinated by the veiled oriental female as he is by the western woman revealed and exposed in the cinema and literature. "We were continuing to discover western literature but our true occupation, a painful one that secretly underlay all our conversations, was woman" (128) — a discovery so prevalent among *Bildungsromane*. Veils establish sexual boundaries, almost meetings, and erasure; under her veils Sarah embodies the mysteries of feminine beauty: "Once she was washed and made up, properly dressed, she would triumph over the fabulous heroines of western novels" (129). Through *écriture*, Kattan's narrator crosses sexual and cultural boundaries, and dreams of studying in Paris, a metropolis beyond ghetto regionalism where "woman" symbolizes cultural mediation.

His visit to a brothel adjacent to the synagogue has all the trappings of a *rite de passage* found in Joyce's *Portrait* and *Ulysses*. Nessim, his friend and confidant, acts as a guide in this theatrical adventure, rehearsing accent, threshold, and identity. The pimp "did not give up his Muslim accent even though no one had any illusions about it. We were all Jewish. But as soon as we crossed the threshold of the house, we changed our identities. In this exotic land, the Jewish accent would seem out of place ... With our new faces, we would become unknown" (135–6). Displaced in their Babylonian exile and captivity, *kawad* (pimp) and *dellah* (matchmaker) serve as comic and conventional mediators of boundaries for this clandestine clan. The next encounter or social penetration with prostitutes goes one step further in Maydane, the red-light district in the Muslim part of the city where total freedom of sexual exhibition contrasts sharply with the hidden, mysterious, sheltered women of the city's other quarters. All of the prostitutes, however, display grotesque infirmities; one of them, for instance, has only one eye. "The boundaries between what was real and what was dreamed became evanescent" (169). Reality and imagination fuse into nightmare in this inferno where the adolescent envisions corpses walking through music and coarse laughter.

Having crossed sexual and literary thresholds, the narrator has one more boundary to face — the national margin of emigration. After the disruptive *Farhoud*, Jews throng Baghdad's passport office where they become aware of their place in the Diaspora. "We had cousins in Indonesia who were claiming us, brothers in Calcutta who offered their hospitality, uncles who had made their fortune in Mandalay and were now inviting us to share their prosperity. And like titles of nobility, we recited our prospects for new lives" (28). Again, after the war, the noble narrator imagines himself in Paris even though he mingles in Baghdad with Muslims and Christians. "We had deliberately crossed boundaries to join the opposite camp" (149). An underground Zionist movement helps Jews cross the Iraqi frontier illegally, while others await legal documents for emigration. "We often walked a tightrope, under the threat of touching the boundaries that separated us, and we tacitly sought to conceal the fact that we were Jews" (163). Even a Syrian official in the visa office preparing to go to the United States "belonged to the two worlds which in my mind resembled two waves" (185). The final departure scene repeats images of a threshold existence: "the pain of separation was mixed with relief at leaving these walls which were being covered with shadows" (190), and "sand was enclosing us, extending a curtain, cutting us off from the city which moved farther away in a fog that was ominous and dark" (191). Emigration becomes an "almost departure" from origins since shadows of memory, traces and curtains of nostalgia linger in the process of dispersion.

Kattan's second novel, *Les fruits arrachés* (1977), picks up where the first Babylonian exile leaves off: Nessim reappears, the narration remains in the first person, and Méir is the protagonist who, in Paris, falls in love with three European women. The "torn fruits" in the title of this Parisian interlude refer to Méir's uprooted existence in Europe away from his origins in Baghdad; a deracinated postwar Europe, and his torn love with three women. By the end of this novel, Méir prepares to leave for Montreal, the third stage of his life's journey. Unlike his first novel which contains many narrative and descriptive passages, *Les fruits arrachés* relies mainly on dialogue to convey cultural exchanges. Méir's lovers represent entries into various European societies for the oriental outsider, a lover who loses in these almost meetings. Kattan cultivates an ironic distance from his self-ironic *schlemiel* who stumbles among the unexpected absurdities in human relationships — experiences plucked from a double mosaic. The Camus-like sparseness of the prose may be attributable not only to Kattan's colonial past, but to his sense of biblical chronicle — what Erich Auerbach calls "background" in the Old Testament.

The third part of the trilogy, *La fiancée promise* (1983), opens with Méir sharing a compartment in a Canadian train with a Jewish refugee from Poland, the two of them discussing their transatlantic voyage. Essentially a *roman à clef*, *La fiancée promise* depicts French-Canadian society around the middle of the century. Once again, women symbolize society — this time the promised land of America. The novel ends with Méir's repeated dream of himself walking on a tight-rope towards his lover Claudia, neither of them afraid of the surrounding void. Kattan's autobiographical trilogy traces the fortunes of a traveller and tight-rope walker crossing invisible international boundaries, the radius of decentring diaspora from origins to margins.

Kattan's short stories focus less on the Jewish aspects of his past than do the novels; instead, they share American experiences with European and Arabic settings and hence lend an international impression to the overall collection. Like his essays and novels, the short stories explore two sides of a borderline existence, as well as the need to be able to renew one's life at any time. The stories encompass a variety of cultural situations — Arabic, Jewish, European, North and South American — each characterized by a sense of absence which is either spatial, temporal, or existential. While the title of the first volume, *Dans le désert*, seems to locate spatially or existentially in an arid waste-land setting, the introductory "En bordure du désert" shifts the frame of reference to the borderline. Indeed, the titles of the five volumes of stories suggest diasporic boundaries or borderlines between space and non-space: in the desert, the crossing, the river's edge, and the island's sand.[7] This marginality of space through the Diaspora is matched by Kattan's diachronic base of biblical history that emphasizes themes of waiting, expectation, memory, and renewal — boundaries between time and no-time. "Le récit marque la halte entre la mort et la vie nouvelle."[8] Kattan analyzes the spatial title, *Dans le désert*, from temporal and existential perspectives: historically, the title is a literal translation of the Hebrew title of *Numbers*, the fourth book of the Old Testament, which chronicles the forty years the Jews spent wandering in the desert before reaching the Promised Land. Kattan poses a series of rhetorical questions in the introductory "En bordure du désert" that bear directly on the themes within the stories themselves. His characters, at turning points in their lives, judge their past performances: Have they lived a full life? Or have they lived a false existence? Will memory be a source of energy and renewal or will it dissipate into nostalgia that blocks future achievement? Like the children of Israel, the protagonists of these short stories inhabit a desert while looking forward to a new life; like Klein, Kattan revises scripture and observes tradition as adventure.

The first story, "Le Tableau," contrasts the eternity of a large Corot canvas in the Frick Gallery with the transitory rendezvous between the narrator and his absent lover. Effusive in his interior monologue, the narrator repeats his lover's "sourire d'éternité," her synecdochic representation played off against the immortal canvas.[9] The story interweaves three points in time: the past, their meeting in San Francisco two years before the story opens; the present, the narrator's description of the canvas and the tourists who pass by to examine it; and the future, the expectations for the reunion of the two lovers which occurs in the last paragraph. All of the characters remain nameless, suspended between ghost-like evanescence and eternity; the name and the canvas of Corot serve as a focal point for the reunion, the passing tourists, and the narrator's Browningesque musings about love and art. "Tu n'étais plus qu'un tableau" (18) fully identifies woman and painting, yet all we learn of her is that she has left her husband and has one son who is very ill in hospital. The story begins and ends with questions: What will they do now that they are reunited? Can they reclaim their past passion? "Le Tableau" seems very much a phenomenological study examining responses of characters to each other and to the Corot canvas that is the common, immortal ground for international tourists. Despite the painting's vast horizon, there are weighty limits everywhere, just as freedom has its own boundaries. "Peut-on enfermer l'espace pour que son étendue ne brise pas notre imagination, ne la réduise pas à la répétition perpétuelle d'une image affadie de notre soif?" (12). Can the narrator recover his past emotions as Corot has managed to do throughout the ages?

Jamesian in its subject rather than in its style, "Le Tableau" explores different cultures, nationalities, and genres as it wavers between essayistic speculation and lyrical evocation. Corot's picture within Kattan's verbal tableau, a reading and receding scene, acts as a medium for cultural interpenetration and aesthetic interpretation. The closing words of the story resist closure, for we do not know what the lovers will do in the present, what form their dialogue will assume in its repetition. Is the second tableau of reunion a palimpsest or pentimento superimposed on the original in this repetitive game of numbers and mysteries? Kattan's pictures are framed on two sides by characters, on a third side by the reader, while the fourth border remains open. Cultural convergence remains an illusion, the lack of closure at the story's end indicates an incomplete dialectic to be filled by the reader who is engaged in a hermeneutic haunt of Kattan's "fraught background" — a background that inhibits representation.

Yet Kattan's story reveals his method of misrepresentation, of facing the faceless. The lover's nameless smile is timeless because it lasted only one day before taking on the eternal quality of art and illusion. The verbal painter observes that nothing is precise, details are effaced in an impressionistic blur. If Corot's trees are a superficial delusion, then his lover's (sur)face poses a problem of representation that can only be overcome through a *via negativa* of absence, departure, distance, dispersal, disarray, waiting, and mystery. Passersby observing the landscape reveal an emptiness in their expressionless faces, their lost gazes. San Francisco's pervasive fog reinforces the mystery within: "Nous passons et nous ne laissons pas de trace dans la brume" — an echo of Leonard Cohen's lyricism. Sudden transitions from past to present also create an impressionistic mist, a veil over Corot's pastoral landscape. "Les arbres sont transfigurés dans un espace qu'il faut briser, en forcer l'entrée pour que nous y soyons. Comme il a dû ressentir la douleur d'être constamment dehors, toujours à l'extérieur" (13). Kattan's outsider wedges a hermeneutic space to gain access to the pleasures of the text, the enigmas of representation where distortions and disfigurations are all. By the end of the story, the pre-Impressionist Corot has turned surrealist, producing mirror-like pictures and paintings of empty chairs. Like Magritte, Kattan's mimesis informs us that while a pipe is not a pipe, neither is the smile that holds the pipe eternal.

The somewhat surreal blending of different chronological sequences recurs in "Rue Abou Nouas" with the Dijla River measuring time and emotion in the objective-correlative manner of the Corot canvas. As the opening paragraph is in the third person, it acts as a frame for the narrator who, as the Dijla's waters flow by him, is seized by nostalgia for his past in Baghdad. The rest of the story switches to first-person narration, and alternates between the oriental past in Baghdad and the occidental present in Ottawa. Towards the end, the paragraphs become shorter, the alternations more lyrical. While the Iraqi scenes with Hassan and Hind are filled with love, nature, and the out of doors, the Ottawa scenes are predominantly indoors as the narrator is isolated for the weekend in his friend's apartment. The first transition epitomizes the difference; the natural rhythm of love and the river changes to the new, yet already decrepit mechanical elevator. He further contrasts the two streets — Rideau and Abou Nouas — until the end of the story when he comes to the clock, the pendulum oscillating between two hemispheres: "Voici l'horloge. C'est la Porte de l'Est. Ici commence la rue Abou Nouas" (35). Simultaneously, this gateway to the east both returns to primitive origins and welcomes the dawn of a personal renaissance. The gateway — also a threshold, or Levantine chiasmus — forms the almost-meeting point for cultural dialogue, for a "quête d'une improbable rencontre" (34) between reality and theatre.

The third story, "Sur le balcon," also has a double spatial-temporal frame of reference between Blois of the past and Rio in the present. The balcony setting points to the interface between internal privacy and the public which is admired by the narrator but feared by his paranoid friend Julio. On the balcony which overlooks the beach — the setting for the pleasures with which the hedonistic narrator identifies — Julio reminisces about their escapade twenty years earlier with a young woman in Blois, the illuminated château being contrasted with the Rio highrise. The contrapuntal rhythm of the memories of French youth, combined with the domesticated actions of his Brasilian neighbours highlights Julio's Kafkaesque vision of a world which pursues him as he decays in his own paranoia. The narrator cannot comprehend who is persecuting Julio, but the latter's reference to Gogol's *Dead Souls* provides a clue. Like Julio, this Russian novelist was a tortured man whose soul is enslaved to *thanatos*; and Julio, like Chichikov, collects souls from the past. Julio's final words, "you cannot understand," are addressed to the reader as well as the narrator as they share a quest on the unenclosed balcony of otherness and psychological penetration. Like several other stories in this volume, "Sur le balcon" dramatizes the transience of travellers only partly settled in a culture that is midway between a nomadic orient and theatrical occident.

Once again, Kattan's characters find themselves in the desert or on its fringes in his second collection, *La Traversée*. So many of the characters are emigrants, travellers, or transients visiting friends, family, or lovers before pursuing another destination. They are on a threshold traversing two modes of being, and, in this intermediate state, a gap always remains between characters separated by age, geography, and sex. Having crossed the Atlantic in *La Traversée*, Kattan relies on Canadian settings far more than in the earlier stories. In "La Fin du voyage" a young couple, recently married, return to Montreal from Africa to stay with the wife's parents. They soon grow tired, however, of the parents' routine and decide to move into their own apartment. After their extensive travelling, the end of their voyage presumably coincides with the end of the story when they are about to settle down to a new life in which "Peut-être allait-elle se remettre à aimer son mari."[10] But the flat, neutral tone of the story's last line, "Il n'y avait dans sa voix ni colère ni amertume," provides no guarantee that the future will prove promising; experience ends one stage of life only to be followed by the unknown in the next stage. Liminal perception resists closure.

The title of the second story, "Les Bagages," also implies some kind of journey: this time, a female narrator recounts her love for and marriage with Edouard. "Et maintenant que tout est fini, je cherche à reprendre le fil afin de comprendre" (23). The clash between the anglophone South African husband and his bourgeois, francophone wife reaches a crisis after they move to the east end of Montreal. At first the marriage ceremony had been "un départ, une reprise. Elle traça une frontière, marqua un passage d'un état à un autre" (28). But soon after they settle into a routine which includes Edouard's insistent courting of the lower-class neighbours, she decides to leave him. "Qui était-il, lui qui connaissait si bien mes origines? Soudain, il m'est apparu, tel que je l'imaginais: un homme qui me voulait, que je désirais et dont je ne savais rien" (32). So she crosses the city to her parents' home where she realizes that she has forgotten to bring her luggage with her. "Il fallait retraverser la ville, seule, pour aller chercher mes bagages" (33). Exiled in her own home, having traversed Montreal and an important stage in her life's cycle, the narrator compresses her existence into portable baggage to start a new life or resume her pre-Edouardian origins. Repressing their past, uncanny travellers forget their cultural luggage, but it returns to haunt them along the three stages of their *rite de passage*: preliminary, liminary, and postliminary. New beginnings are simultaneously a kind of recapturing, a crossing over borderlines from an ancient past to a postmodern present, from order to disorder reduced to the synecdoche of suitcase for one's (be)longings.

The stories in Kattan's third collection, *Le Rivage*, demonstrate a continuing preoccupation with themes of departures, waiting, absences, repetition, and expectations in beginning a new life. If the desert remains sterile and the river offers potential fertility, then the river's edge represents another transitional image of a flowing borderline between desert's memory and river's promise of possible fulfilment. Completion of a "nouvelle" implies renewal: the short story serves as the bank of a river that can overflow its borders to renew a desert.[12]

Kattan's fourth volume of short stories, *Le Sable de l'île*, opens with "Les Yeux fermés." The title of this story refers at once to the literal physical reaction of one of the major characters, the figurative condition of ignorance shared by the two major characters, and a mode of representation. Ruth and Mordecai, two former concentration camp inmates, rendezvous at the bar of Montreal's Ritz-Carlton Hotel furnished with "les dames d'un chic suranné dans le décor insolite du début du siècle."[12] Mort's name, Ruth's "air d'absence," and the absence of their respective spouses contribute to the disjunction between their past tragedy united by memories of the Holocaust, and present love united sexually in a motel room after they have left the Ritz. By keeping her eyes closed and repeating Mordecai's name during their lovemaking, Ruth manages to obliterate the past through total immersion in the present. "Ruth fermait les yeux, l'entourant de tout son corps, cherchant avec acharnement un abri, le lieu où, au-delà de l'oubli, elle découvrirait enfin une immobile sécurité" (13–14). Then, one day she opens her eyes and a double shock results: the expression in her eyes recalls the past for Mort, while Ruth cannot bear his discovery of her innermost self. "Ces yeux le renvoyaient à son monde, au malheur de toujours. Lui, qui voulait être une armure et une protection, n'était qu'un fragile résidu, si foncièrement, si fatalement vulnérable." And once he has invaded her privacy, "elle ne pouvait plus subir Mort sans étouffer" (15). After such knowledge, what forgiveness? Departure is inevitable: "il partait en voyage" while she hangs up the phone "sans dire un mot" in contrast to her former repetition of Mort's name. To unface, envisage, or disregard the past, history's survivors close their eyes and stare indirectly.

La reprise, Kattan's fifth collection of short stories, resumes his fictional enterprise announced at the beginning of *Dans le désert*: "Le récit, marque la halte entre la mort et la vie nouvelle." Indeed, the very title, like "cleave" and "bound," means both itself and its opposite, a palindrome of the signified rather than signifier: "reprise" is both repetition and fresh start. This built-in contradiction invites a deconstructive reading, for how can something be both a repetition and a new beginning? Each short story and each collection of short stories constitute a repetition as well as a new beginning, a continuation of archetypes and a repudiation of past burdens. "*Reprise*" has a third meaning: it refers to mending or sewing in the tailor's trade.

Kattan's tales stitch time in the foul sweatshop of the heart, they bind texts and textiles, mend invisible borders, and seam covenants. History, literature, and the lives of characters demand readerly reprisal. Similarly, the endings of these stories present a double bind in their lack of closure. And, in-between beginnings and endings, there is an epiphany, a halting spot of time between death and a new life. Kattan's belated scrolls second the emotions attendant upon emancipation into modernism; they depict personal conquests of self and past, of borderline acculturation from east to west, from Jew to Canadian.

The title story describes the retirement of an Ottawa secretary, Julie, who has worked in the same office ever since her husband's death twenty years earlier. Her life is a series of routines: office work followed by domestic habits of feeding her birds and fish. A farewell luncheon in her honour marks the only break in that routine, but soon all will return to their typewriters and telephones, "stèles immuables sur une route infinie. Et c'est elle qui disloquait, pour un moment, l'écoulement constant des instants".[13] Mute and immutable, these steles signify the paralysis of routine and infinite routes in this naturalistic slice of life. Julie's speech, which opens the story, dislocates (or dis-loquates) the flux of time, breaks a routine of stelar silence en route to the end of the story when the protagonist finds her own voice. But whatever freedom attends her retirement soon dissipates, for Julie remains a prisoner of her deterministic past, trapped by the habits and limitations of her working class. Devotion to domestic routine also proves illusory when her fish die and the two birds fly out the window, their flight symbolizing the absence in Julie's life and her need to escape the confines of her small apartment. But her decision to move is also fraught with ambiguity: will a change entail simply another repetition or will she discover a new life? Without closure, fragile birds and windows may meet with destruction in the broader world, a double bind that applies to so many of Kattan's stories where the circumscribed borders and routines of a naturalistic universe define an individual's existence.

If finding one's voice serves as synecdoche for individual identity, so too does naming, as so many of the protagonists in these stories possess no more than their first names. The omission of surnames indicates both the dissolution of family ties for widowed and divorced characters as well as the limitations of their development within the genre of shorter fiction. The first story, "Les mémoires," revolves on the widowhood of Esther who has to decide whether to publish the memoirs of her philanthropic husband whose public life barely coincides with her own private perceptions of him. The final story, "Mon nom est Esther," similarly focuses on the relationship of naming to identity. The first Jew to arrive in Canada is out of place, for she appears too soon in an empty northern refuge forbidden to Jews. Kattan describes the various guises of his historical character, Esther Brandeau, who disguises her religious and sexual identity: "je porte un nom antique: Esther ... Femme et juive" (223). She carries a fate as ancient as her name — the fate of the persecuted wandering Jewess of Portuguese origin who travels from Bayonne to Amsterdam to meet her fiancé, but meets with misfortune instead. Having survived a shipwreck, Esther awakens in Biarritz where she unwittingly eats pork and becomes as nauseous as she was earlier with seasickness. Overwhelmed by guilt at this transgression and the sexual advances of some sailors, she feels unworthy of her parents and fiancé, and decides to escape, disguised as a Catholic boy, Pierre Alansiette. This chameleon has to adjust her sexual and religious identities wherever she goes: "temps de m'habituer à mon apparence, d'en vivre la réalité et c'est à nouveau la routine et l'ennui. En route" (228). If Jewish identity involves breaking routes and routines, it also means departures for the New World where Esther may recover her name and be reborn. In Québec she rediscovers her true voice, body, soul, and identity: she will return to her origins and her true faith. Unlike Robinson Crusoe who may begin anew in isolation, Esther must emerge from history's shipwrecks to rejoin her community.

In a more contemporary setting the narrator of "Le pacte" traverses the Atlantic to come to terms with his Jewish identity. A Montreal Jew visiting Munich uses his knowledge of Yiddish to orient himself in this German city. "Soudain, une stèle, semblable à une grande pierre tombale, me frappa. Des lettres hébraïques me fouettèrent en plein visage" (95). Obstacle and epiphany, the Hebrew and German letters signify the memory of a synagogue and a civilization destroyed. In a Bavarian beer parlour the anonymous Jewish-Canadian stranger becomes disoriented: "Mon nom était ma possession" (100). As if to atone for his drinking, he decides to visit Dachau to confront yet another stele: "Une masse lourde pesait sur mes épaules" (103). The burden of the past, a tragic spot of time, impinges on his historical consciousness. Whether at the site of a destroyed synagogue, a Bavarian bar, or Dachau, the nameless narrator almost encounters the past, each episode heightening his dislocation. At Dachau, he meets a young American Christian who shares with him the tragic memories of World War II and promises to write, "comme pour sceller un pacte." These concluding words of the story turn stele to seal, burden to bond, and epitaph to covenant even as the photograph of the narrator's young son holds promise for the future — repetition combined with rejuvenation. But the sights have discomposed his son's face.

Most of Kattan's short stories explore separations, divorce, widowhood, retirement, exile, and travel through various cultures which put into question individual identity; and this particular genre seems appropriate for dramatizing and isolating the moment of crisis. "Les murs transparents," a lyrical essay on the phenomenology of a modern traveller alone in different hotels, uses a third-person refrain, "il dit," to distance Kattan from autobiographical experience and to suggest the repetitive sameness in hotels in Québec, Toronto, San Francisco, Vancouver, Lima, and Copacabana. "Dans cette alternance de l'attente et du passage, il aménage le lieu. Le lieu multiple qui n'est demeure que dans la répétition. L'espace se découpe en arrêt et reprise; attente et recommencement" (45). From these rooms he studies different bodies of water to accentuate his own stream of consciousness: rivers represent time's flux; the ocean, that infinite space between Europe and America; and the lake, that mirror wherein his weightless body becomes one with space. From the water's transparency, he dreams of a glass house whose transparent walls protect yet offer unlimited visual freedom so that all those transient hotel rooms might be fixed in a permanent dwelling. Permanence with renewal where he may learn the words, "la première phrase ... Il dit" (48) — the open-ended conclusion of the short story and the nomadic turn of mind. Those transparent walls belong to Kattan's invisible and international borders of perception; he opens the windows of his house of fiction to admit his secularized heritage.

CHAPTER ELEVEN

Matt Cohen's Jeru-Salem

Matt Cohen has been generally recognized for his series of Salem novels which explore the life of agrarian, Protestant families living in the area around Kingston, Ontario. More recently, however, he has turned to his Jewish roots, *The Colours of War* (1977) being a pivotal novel as it treats Salem from a peripheral, Jewish perspective. Theodore Beam, whose lover remarks, "Theodore Beam. What a name for a Jew."[1], narrates this story from the attic of an old stone church in Salem. In the words of his father, Jacob Beam, who speaks in "Talmudic fashion" (223), this is "an excellent place for a Jew to begin his married life" (208). But, despite his father's comments, most of this novel is set inside a train travelling from Vancouver to Ontario during an imaginary Canadian civil war. Between the locomotion of a trans-Canadian train and the stasis of Salem's church, Beam searches for his voice, the sound of past and future in his bones. "Old words flood through me. This hand records them — my hand, my father's hand" (234). Old worlds and fears generate Matt Cohen, adding an extra dimension to his regional isolation: "Even though I had been born here, as had my mother and her mother, there was some part of me that recognized what he was saying — that the mixed-up set of European races had eaten away at their own history, at their own imagination, so that finally they belonged nowhere at all" (158). Where do the solemn, eccentric Beams feel at home? In the old outpost of Salem, a diminished town in the centre of Ontario? In Vancouver? In a train suspended between the two? "In all my years here I had been waiting to feel at home, truly rooted" (27), not only in Salem's soil but in Jewish history.

I can remember the first time my father took me inside a synagogue. They were singing, a strange humming chant that seemed infinitely sad and familiar, like all the funerals I had ever imagined moved into one place, the different voices swaying and diverging from each other, some of the old men turned into their own corners, each faced in his own mysterious direction, towards his own Jerusalem ... bits of old history clinging to them. (45–6)

His experience within the synagogue epitomizes the ambivalent alienation of a secular Jew: strange, yet familiar, Jewish voices swerve to and from tradition. Cornered old men with history and mystery transmit to the young man from Salem the sobbed oriental note of Jerusalem, relentlessly reverberating in eastbound trains.

Cohen's mixed colours and divided voices seek fusion within the family. When Theodore visits his grandfather in an old-age home in Toronto, he realizes that in possessing the same name, they are different versions of the same person. His grandfather's gift of a gold watch cements their union and highlights Theodore's feeling that his eyes are a thousand years old. Against this millennial vision, more recent history intrudes uncannily in the form of twentieth-century wars inside and outside trains. As the train violently fights its way through the Canadian landscape, one cannot help but think of cattle cars transporting Jews across Europe in a war within a war. Beam reduces his moustache "to a small Hitler-style decoration. We Jews have a weakness about Hitler ... Who wants to be Hitler?" (138). The prodigal son returns to a home that is simultaneously *heimlich* and *unheimlich*; the beam of light fades, the beams of Salem's oldest house burn even as its inhabitants sing "Keep the Home-fires burning" (226). History haunts these attics, inflaming frozen dwellings of fiction. Cohen finds his voice between Salem's regionalism and historical cosmopolitanism through a war of words, waiting, wandering across the demilitarized zone of the Diaspora.

One of Cohen's earliest short stories, "The Watchmaker," depicts a forty-year-old who relates his European past to the young narrator, everyone remaining nameless in a kind of Kafkaesque temporal suspension. The opening picture of the watchmaker's gold wallet with its picture of the village green, and the red satin cushion in his pocket soon fades into a colourless vignette of his life. "At times I think he has no face. There is bone and flesh. There are networks of nerves, veins and arteries that lace through the surfaces. But sometimes he seems to have transformed himself into a blank, a man who sits in the corner and talks to the grandfather clock."[2] As faceless as Melville's Bartleby or Klein's persona, he represents Everyman, every survivor of the twentieth century. Cohen's blank, laconic prose in this story maps the surfaces, but underneath that network of nerves he conceals an entire history, for the watchmaker talks not only to the older clock but to the younger narrator as well. Like so many other Jewish fiddlers, he frets with time as the huge pendulum of the grandfather clock ticks off the seconds. Cohen's vagueness pursues this unbeliever through timelessness. "It would be easy for him to do certain things. He could set all the clocks in his shop to different times. He could grow a beard ... But he restrains himself. He fears that he will reduce his options, lose the mornings under the awning, earn the enmity of his grandfather clock" (13). Like a Malamudian shopkeeper measuring out his life with coffee spoons, he pretends to work at his trade, but, all the while preoccupied with something else, he disappears into history. Even the young narrator feels that he has wasted some seconds, "some in which I should have been doing something else. I fabricate my mortality. I ask him if he ever feels like that, if what he is doing is sitting by the grandfather clock letting his life escape" (14).

A maker of instruments of time and an instrument of time himself, he puts his hand on the clock and recounts his European childhood to the narrator, lost on a sunken, century-flicking pendulum. Before his parents were killed by the Nazis, they placed him in another family where he escaped their fate. Here he learned to fix clocks and watches, yet when he repairs the Germans' watches, they are never quite right. After the watchmaker tells his story in the past tense, the outer narrative frame reasserts itself in the present, concluding with a repetition of his disappearing face which, with its networks of nerves, veins and arteries, watches the movement of the pendulum. "Sometimes it took forever to go from one side to the other. Sometimes it moved so fast that it was almost invisible. Sometimes it stopped altogether" (19). History's oscillations and transatlantic nomadism haunt "The Watchmaker" which ends with the narrator playing chess with the violinist. The narrator wraps his hands delicately around the pawns, which are symbols of fate wherein the Jew has been checkmated. "He says he has told me all his secrets; but still he tolerates me. I am patient." Only time will tell these secrets, these hermeneutic codes of the Holocaust, a vigil of victims and survivors.

If the grandfather (clock) represents a generation lost to the Nazis, then Cohen explores that generation further in "The Universal Miracle," from his collection of short stories entitled *Night Flights*. In "The Universal Miracle," Cohen investigates the death of a grandfather, not in the Holocaust but in the cancer ward of Toronto's Princess Margaret Hospital. Alienated from his own tradition, Harvey Zackman has to come to terms with his grandfather's death and the arrangements for the funeral. The title refers to the grandfather's faith in science as he searches for a method of keeping automobile oil perpetually clean so that filter changes would be unnecessary. Science fails him not only in this design, but also in his cliché that everything ends in the stomach, precisely where his cancer ends, "the exploded particles and mutant cells following inside him the voyage his planetary crust had taken years before."[3] Indeed, this story revolves around the tension between a genetic code and the Great Code, that biblical tradition inherited by Cohen and Zackman. Zackman's science and faith are on the point of exploding: while radioactive particles bombard his grandfather's chest, "there gathered a tension just beneath the surface of his skin, and by morning he could sense black focal points creating themselves, galvanic nodes of fear and betrayal that would eventually become tumors" (113). Grandfather had told grandson that his son was a "mutant" and that he would not turn out to be like his father, but after the funeral Harvey feels one generation closer to the grave. At the cemetery, he pictures his grandfather — "wing-headed, stocky and muscular, The Universal Miracle printed into his genes" (121) — the white wings of hair contrasting with the rocks and clods of earth raining upon the coffin. By the end of the story, Zackman remains alone drinking: "With each sip, he felt new radioactive particles invent themselves and explode beneath his skin" (123). Holding his scotch in one hand and a wax-filled mourner's glass in the other, Harvey tries to reconcile the polarities of his Jewish-Canadian life as he kneels to utter a blessing.

As he repeated that over and over to himself, the sound of the words melted into the earth and rocks homing into the coffin; and the sight of his own praying dissolved into old men's faces, drunk and delighted to be paid in two-dollar bills to stand and kibbitz during a funeral, old men's faces laughing at these crazy Jews so lost from themselves they needed professionals to stone a cheap coffin down to the grave. (123)

Despite verbal and generational repetitions, homing rocks and unhoming memories, Cohen's lost tribes of Jews try to find themselves amidst a surrealistic blur.

During his eulogy, the rabbi extols grandfather Zackman for knowing where his own universe ended and God's began, but nothing is further from the truth: "his universe never ended, not for other people or for God" (120). Cohen reduces the universal miracle to a particular miracle of Jewish survival, even on the fringe of identity where modern science and ancient faith threaten to explode through genetic fallacies: "the wonderful perfect way in which the whole universe was made up of billiard balls, each set assembled in a tiny replica of the solar system, tricky billiard balls which could themselves break apart into an infinity of fragments and in doing so, according to Albert Einstein and others, possibly blow up the whole world" (119). In that delicate balance between science and religion, universals and particulars, Matt Cohen develops his own theory of relativity, otherness, limited fragmentation, and imperfect reconciliation.

If "The Universal Miracle," because it ends at night, belongs in this collection of short stories, so does "Vogel," for it focuses on a particular kind of flight. Sam Vogel, the protagonist (whose name means "bird"), feels "his own body in flight, running" (45). What makes Sam run is his doctor's warning about his deteriorating health: "your body's on a one-way trip." So he runs to reverse this aging process, to recapture an earlier self before he became an atavistic Jewish haberdasher on Toronto's Spadina Avenue. Ironically, during one of his five-mile runs he suffers a heart attack, caused not only by his attempt at fitness, but also by the effects of fitness in his affair with a student, young enough to be his daughter, who works for him mornings. Generational split appears in the opening sentence: "Sam Vogel carried, between his social- and medical-insurance cards, a picture of his high school graduation class." Sandwiched syntactically and existentially between his social-being (sexual affair) and well-being (healthy body), his former self acts as a reminder that one of the "two Sam Vogels" has yet to graduate from a belated apprenticeship with his assistant, Emily Gathers — a name which contrasts with the final bursting of Vogel's heart. If the picture in his wallet is "his first image of himself," then the second, more recent, exists solely in his mind, surrealistically superimposed like an existential palimpsest covering twenty-five years of marriage. The "image of himself running became almost abstract: a moment frozen out of a grainy black-and-white movie ... he felt himself running through the middle of his own life, running into darkness" (51). By the end of the story, the two pictures of himself melt together, only to be "burst open" in the last sentence. When his heart does burst, he curls up "like a baby" on the track, reverting to a more primitive foetal form, even as he imagines himself transformed into a horse, then a monkey, during his lovemaking with Emily. His straight back and perfect stride contrast with his bent body and imperfect life which is overburdened with too many selves. Vogel's night flight collapses, for he is

on the wrong track, a misfit as well as a haberdasher, a Jewish jogger
returning from a one-way memorial trip.

The groundwork for Cohen's two Jewish novels, *The Spanish Doctor*
and *Nadine*, is laid in two short stories from *Café Le Dog*, "The Sins
of Tomas Benares" and "Sentimental Meetings," which trace
genealogical roots back through generations and centuries. "The
Sins of Tomas Benares" explores different generations within one
family to determine whether the sins of fathers shall be visited upon
their sons. Fleeing Franco's Spain the Benares family arrive in
Toronto in 1936 where Dr Tomas Benares opens his practice and
prospers until his ninety-fourth birthday almost fifty years later.
While Cohen's temporal weaving covers events through the middle
of this century, his historical telescope in Benares' memory returns
to Toledo at the time of the Spanish Inquisition. Remembering his
grandfather who was born in 1780, Tomas realizes "suddenly that he
was holding two hundred years in his mind," shifting from Kiev to
Toledo, the cradle of his ancestors.[4] Methuselahs of the Diaspora, the
Benares's have been blessed and cursed with the burden of longevity:
"the Benares men were long-lived relics whose minds sent arrows
back into the swamp of the past, so deep into the swamp that the lives
they recalled were clamped together in a formless gasping mass, waiting to be shaped by those who remembered" (80). Cohen's fictive
memory shapes and forms that mass from primitive swamps to the
new Jerusalem in Toledo to a prosperous city in the New World.

From his grandfather he learned to be "stubborn as a donkey,"
stiff-necked from pride and the burdens of persecution. He imagines
ancient Spain: "a vast, sandy expanse where Jews had been persecuted and in revenge had hidden their religion under prayer shawls
and been stubborn as donkeys" (80). Against all that repressed
Judaism, Tomas Benares cultivates his own garden in Toronto, keeps
a diary, and heals the ruptures of history, as Cohen stitches together
temporal threads of filiation. He has a vision of himself as an old-
fashioned movie: in each frame he lives a different life, and only
accelerating the reel can make the crowd into one person. This
cinematic foreshortening lies at the heart of Cohen's technique,
which at times verges on magical realism, shaping through memory
yet deforming his gasping mass of narration. As the aging doctor
watches shadows flickering across his ceiling, he recalls his younger
self, a "distant twin" who lived in Madrid forty years earlier, while
another part of his memory focuses on his son who died in an accident. When he makes love to his widowed daughter-in-law, he feels

something inside of him break even as the night breaks open, and, like "a gigantic black and dreamless mouth, it swallowed them both" (95). Earlier, Tomas had compared the daughter-in-law to an ant teetering at the lip of a honey pot, and both of them now enter the abyss of history in their union and separation, the incest and taboo of a family romance. At the end of the story, Tomas senses Death turned trickster and spits in Its face, for the stubborn sin has defied the rupture of filiation by returning to the past. In his dream, Benares (son of cedar) transforms himself into a philosopher who spends his life thinking about oak trees; racial roots take hold in Cohen's swamp where they branch out to family trees and forests of history.

"Sentimental Meetings" presents another episode in the Benares saga. Joseph Benares, Tomas' grandson, travels to Paris to visit a relative, Hanna Santangel, and to Spain to recover ancestral roots. The "sentimental meeting" of relatives is announced in the opening sentence. In the view from the airplane, "Planet and sky met in a long curved strip of light" (119), as if Cohen were implying some cosmic or metaphysical significance to this family meeting. On the airplane Joseph thinks about Christopher Columbus returning with his savages to the Spanish court. In Spain, Hannah recounts history from 1391 until 1492 when Ferdinand and Isabella reconquered Spain from the Muslims: "To celebrate they expelled all the remaining Jews and sent Columbus off to discover the New World" (131). Cohen regards Columbus symbolically as a historical pivot and framework both for the end of a Jewish golden age in Spain and the beginning of life in America where another utopia beckons. Cohen plays off the medieval against the modern hemispheric split, for Joseph Benares is divorced from Judith, yet hopes for some "cosmic reconciliation" to match that opening meeting between planet and sky. To complicate these irreconcilable differences, Joseph and Hannah encounter a German film crew entering the Synagoga del Transito; when these leopards enter this temple, Joseph drinks chalices dry until everything is "out-of-focus" in the haze of Hannah's nightmares and war experiences of the Nazis overrunning France. Just as Joseph can no longer remember where "home" is, so Hannah keeps forgetting the difference between Canadians and Americans, but she downplays that part of his identity in favour of his international Jewish discovery of himself. Touching Joseph's naked chest at the end of the story, the German film director has the last word — "Welcome home" — as if meetings and reconciliations are possible after Europe's treatment of its Jews.

Cohen's interest in a Jewish golden age in medieval Spain continues in *The Spanish Doctor*, which opens with an account of fourteenth-century Toledo and a description of the luxurious temple built by Prince Samuel Halevi. Part historical romance in the manner of Walter Scott, and part magical realism in the manner of Gabriel García Márquez's *One Hundred Years of Solitude*, *The Spanish Doctor* is epical in scope as it moves from Toledo in 1391 via Montpellier and Bologna to Kiev in 1445. Through the sentimental meetings of Benares and Hannah in the twentieth century, we are able to trace Cohen's medieval tapestry and historical sweep back to Dr Avram Halevi, the protagonist of *The Spanish Doctor*, and Gabriela Santangel, his lover. At the novel's opening, Avram surveys Toledo from his perch on the stone wall, an appropriate refuge for this forcibly converted Marrano who inhabits a "no-man's-land," concealing his faith, even from himself.[5] He decides to pursue a career in medicine to pare away superstition, while with his sword he also parries persecution. A new man for a new age, Avram cuts the bonds of Toledo's barrio and begins his journey away from militarized and demilitarized zones.

Cohen describes Toledo repeatedly as a beast preying upon its Jews in the jungle of medieval history. When Avram and Gabriela first make love they defy their tormentors "until by desire and wanting alone they could shoot free of the shadow of the beast" (85). But after this momentary transcendence the beast continues to pursue them until their combined death in Kiev at the end of the novel. Cohen also establishes an opposition between beast and breast (86), not only between hatred and love, but also between death and birth, for Avram's surgical dexterity saves the lives of mother and child reunited in nursing. A saviour of the womb, he saves himself by performing these miracles on the prominent Velásquez family who are able to protect him from insurmountable tyranny. Over and against sexual and medical forms of union and separation, the religious background of the Spanish Inquisition comes to the fore. The Roman Catholic Church blames the Papal schism on the Jewish scapegoat stubbornly persisting in its otherness: "To unite, to become one: the great community of man linked heart-to-heart, soul-to-soul, God-to-God" (89). Until Church and state are twins, Cardinal Rodrigo Velásquez will not rest; what his adversary wishes to unite, Avram seeks to untie. An explanantion for this separateness appears in Avram's climactic revelation at the end of book I. He dreams that he is standing naked in the desert, not the barren land between Toledo and Barcelona, but the ancient Sinai outside the kingdom of Canaan. As the sky turns a deep scarlet, God's unseeable presence confronts him, and even after he awakens, he finds God in the room: "the dream was over but God's presence filled the room like a giant predatory hawk" (155). Jewish predator supplants Christian beast, the sky with "the deep new red of the inside of a baby's mouth" (154) gives way to the revelation of Gabriela's breasts; the golden sun, Gabriela's golden skin, and the golden calf of the Bible culminate in the gold chain of the star of David "that hung in the valley between" (156). Colourful but contrived, dazzling but deceiving, Cohen's Romantic epiphany with its Keatsian and Tennysonian excess mars the design of its medieval tapestry.

Speaking on behalf of his brother, Juan Velásquez tells his doctor that Rodrigo is the face of history that has gone against the Jews, even as the Jews have gone against history. More flexible than his fanatical brother, Juan shifts with the tides of mercantile history away from ownership of land toward movement and trade. And if the merchant of Toledo undergoes a sea change, then the miraculous Marrano prefigures the Renaissance in his desire to invent himself in the face of history (255). Janus-faced history confronts the Spanish doctor, neither and both Christian and Jew; in Gabriela's words, he has hidden himself in a trunk (along with his anatomical drawings) while presenting to the world a puppet of his own invention. Fate does find him out by the time he emerges from his diasporic trunk in Kiev, which is repeatedly described as the edge of the world, a place out of the sight of God's eye. On one side of the Dnieper, a massive cliff or gigantic rock fortress rises up to greet the refugees; Gabriela understands this cliff to be "the unbreachable barrier" (425) between herself and the world she had left behind, exchanging one barrio for another. The novel opens with Toledo's flames and ends with Kiev's furnace: the "firebox was like the stories of Hell that had been described by the old men of Toledo" (440). Ramming the log into the "womb," Avram feeds the fires of history, those fateful conflagrations that consume his descendants exactly five hundred years later.

The rational man of science bent on mapping human anatomy forms only one side of Avram Halevi's character. On his deathbed he is presented with a copy of drawings of dissections made by his students, and their dedication refers to him and his work as "Guide to the Unknown Country of Man," (470) for the resident alien inhabits a perplexing diaspora of dissolving borders. Even Velásquez discerns that unknown country where the irrational peels back layers of history and consciousness: "he is the dancer, dancing among the demons, dancing out our dreams. And so mad is his dance, so mad his separation from man and God, that when he dances we want to dance with him; and when he falls, we all fall down" (381). Larger than life, this mad man, who had been the most heretical young Jew in Toledo, stands apart, separate from the homogenizing tendencies of the majority. An ancestor to Spinoza and Freud in his glass work and anatomizing of unknown countries, Halevi studies the Cabbala in prison, turning Hebrew letters into numbers, a semiotics of the sublime. The letters of his own name guarantee, according to the old cabbalist who shares his cell, that he will be transformed into pure spirit. After the cabbalist's death, his body is replaced with an oak table; in his memory, Avram stares at the surface of the table, trying to turn his contemplation of God's work (the once-living grain of the wood) into the contemplation of God. Yet, after nine years of mystical imprisonment, of staring at the oak fibres that prepare for his future in lumber and link him to Dr Tomas Benares, he cannot quell his skepticism: "for all those hundreds of days that he had watched the sun make its way across the worn surface, that he had dulled his eye staring at the light's invasion of each solitary fibre, had God truly entered his soul and transformed his being?" (389). Blinded by surfaces, Avram dissects to the depths, past layers of rationality, from opaque oak to translucent glass.

In Kiev, a fellow Jew, Viladestes, advises Avram to "let the past fly free" (465), a prescription he follows as he abandons his need to escape it. (This Freudian formula applies equally to Cohen's muse of history — Clio of *The Spanish Doctor*.) But Viladestes also teaches Avram the Zohar, the holy book of the Cabbala, where each letter contains a light that leads to the end of history. Torn between these pages and his guide to anatomy, the mystical skeptic or scientific cabbalist can assume many forms. One minute "a crazed and backward Moses" (468), the next a "slayer of superstition" (491), Avram is indeed a slayer of Moses wielding the cutting edge of heretic hermeneutics. *El Gato* (the Cat) leaping from barriers metamorphoses into "a fancy bird who knew how to change his plumage with the season" (469), for he is a chameleon who destroys a cardinal and sires Joseph the dreamer. Gabriela also lets the past fly free when she unites with Avram, their passion transcending the prison house of history. "Avram, Léon, Juan Velásquez, Carlos — all merged together into one insatiable man-stallion, a mindless and murderous beast" (434). Gabriela internalizes that outward Spanish beast and unifies what the Church has been unable to accomplish, but her merger leads to ecstasy: "she was blown out of this frozen skin-heaven and into the stars, flying through the sky over the Targa" (435). Her celestial revelation adds a universalist dimension to her particular vision, a moment of magical realism in Matt Cohen's invention of a medieval world filled with apocalypse and apotheosis. "She was falling slowly through the sky, a naked woman floating among the planets, Vil-adestes' candle in hand, gliding slow and serene through the warm white river of stars. For one last moment she had the whole view: then she plunged into Avram's arms again, their own small heaven of skin and warmth, the past snipped away like a cluster of stray threads with nothing to join." *The Spanish Doctor* sutures a split univer-se, ranging between milky way and nursing breast, heaven and hell, whole views of history and the momentary madness of apocalyptic fragmentation.

Where *The Spanish Doctor* chronicles medieval extraterritoriality, *Nadine* breaks chronological sequences and aims for extraterrestrial postmodernism. The epigraph to *Nadine* acts as a transition between these two novels and between medieval and modern worlds: "Sup-pose the universe has a code. Suppose the maps we make of the sky are the maps of our own psyche, and the constellations in fact the countries of the heart." From anatomy to astronomy, from Avram Halevi's "Guide to the Unknown Country of Man" to D.B. Miller's *Shooting Stars*, and from Gabriela Santangel's free fall to Nadine San-tangel's freer narrative, Matt Cohen leaps from the Inquisition to the Holocaust, mapping and encoding a psychic diaspora. While the highly dramatic, fast-paced plot of *The Spanish Doctor* lends itself to the creation of a Hollywood epic, *Nadine* is far more fragmented and internalized, trailing off from book I to book II in Toronto, and losing most interest in the British political events in book III. In both novels Cohen has taken certain risks: in the former, he sacrifices complexity to moving plot and heroic protagonist; in the latter he subdues heroic impulses, but in his quest for complexity, he loses some dramatic tension, and the reader can only hope for a balance in the best parts of the two novels.

Nadine begins in the present tense with the first-person narration of the eponymous Nadine Santangel, who reconstructs her childhood in Paris forty years earlier just as surgeons reconstructed her body after an explosion in Jerusalem all but destroyed it. Cinematic ima-gery throughout the novel adds to this palimpsest of present over past, of flesh grafted on to the original: "I find myself reconstructing my favourite movie — the one about me."[6] If she moves through a movie on the streets of Paris, she writes stories to herself inside her apartment; Nadine, however, is not simply narcissistic, for a larger pattern imposes itself on her life. She has been blown apart in order to come together — a recurrent theme in Cohen's fiction; her "soul has torn free and is flying through the universe like a runaway star"

(6) or like Gabriela Santangel in Cohen's cosmic intertext. Nadine is her self and her fiction, recreated from letters, documents, photographs, underground ghosts, and a lost planet of hopes; she declares herself a woman, a scientist, a Jew born in France and now a citizen of Canada. Torn apart by an explosion of memory, she is inhabited by another self, her soul mate Miller: "For most of our lives we were like twin stars, revolving around each other, sometimes finding our selves dimmed and obscured by our closeness, but at our best and most rare moments, casting our light in harmony" (8). But the horoscopes of history deny Jewish gemini any harmony of the spheres, replacing it instead with broken globes, a diasporic discord between old and new hemispheres.

Tenses shift in the flashback to 1940 as we learn of the fate of Nadine's parents and her own escape from Paris because her birth went unrecorded. Orphaned by anti-semitism, Cohen's heroes and heroines may require a doppelgänger of the opposite sex for completion of animus and anima. Nadine interrupts the narrative: "At this point the story I like to tell myself, the story of how I survived the war, becomes fragmented and disconnected" (37). Just as her body has been twisted out of shape, so her memories are distorted through *brisure* and the gesture of a ring passed on to her from her mother's soul. The reader of *Nadine* decodes its message.

After the war Nadine comes to Toronto where she meets Miller. Together they combine to form one whole person: "I am always the one to dive into inner space, the land of memories and speculation. Miller was the opposite. One day, he would say, outer space will be our home" (52). Cohen's disinherited mind tries to patriate or domesticate his astronomical ambitions, but *Nadine* does not measure up to Bellow's *Mr. Sammler's Planet* or Cynthia Ozick's *The Cannibal Galaxy*. Against a backdrop of the Holocaust — Europe's "theatre of disappearance" (76) in which Jews tried to remain invisible — *Nadine* posits Miller's comet, a bright light in the mystery of space. Both Nadine and Miller are students of Professor Piakowski, an astronomer at the University of Toronto who fled Poland and France. In his addiction to opium, Piakowski resembles Avram Halevi's teacher Ben Ishaq who expresses his love for the infinite (the title, incidentally, of one of Cohen's short stories) through hashish and the medical power of herbs. In measuring the bending of light as it passes by heavy stars, Piakowski repeats Einstein's experiment and claims an illustrious lineage for himself. "For just as Piakowski would speak of his genetic grandfather, the Count, he also made it clear that he occupied the same Olympian intellectual peak as Einstein, Plato and, very oddly, Marcel Proust. Proust was his eccentricity" (97). Cohen's remembrance of things past cracks a grotesque genetic code and Miller's universal code, but is Piakowski's planet of love and drugs the means for digging into the centre of a nightmare?

While Miller discovers his comet, Piakowski explains that these seemingly homeless, wandering rocks actually have two homes: "One is the sun, the other a mathematically determined point somewhere in outer space. Comets are like hearts ... alternately attracted to heat and nothingness" (210). These cardiac arrests lie frozen between the particular warmth of families and the universal loss of *le néant*. Metaphysical conceits work well because of their brevity and wit, but Cohen's extended metaphors do not strengthen the fabric of *Nadine's* fiction over hundreds of pages. "Zodiac. Zo-di-ac. A strange word. And if zodiac sounds as foreign to you as it once did to me, imagine that broad highway across the southern sky shared by the sun, the moon, the planets" (236). As a statement of post-Holocaust estrangement or lyrical esctasy, Cohen's prose blatantly fails; his lost planet or paradise may symbolize lost homes and hopes, but it also runs the risk of loss in interest, for the reader will not be transported by myopic scopes.

Matt Cohen's shooting souls are convincing when their feet touch the ground: "Feet tell the story," advises Joseph Benares's landlady and, by extension, landed immigrants.[7] Disinherited and expatriated brows may reach the heavens, but life on this planet involves stiff-necked immersion in the swamp of the past, present, and future. In his "Salem" novels Matt Cohen succeeds in capturing a regional agrarian society; in his Jeru-salem novels he falls short of his universalist intentions. By combining two particular kinds of vision — Jewish and Canadian — he may yet succeed in a fulfilment or wholeness implied in the Hebrew meaning of Salem, but denied by the condition of exile.

From *The Colours of War* to the shattering explosions in *Nadine*, Cohen continues a Jewish-Canadian tradition of dual fragmentation, the double loss of orphans and refugees. In *The Second Scroll* one of Melech Davidson's aliases is Luis de Santangel, one of thirty-six saintly incognitos — "endless, tantalizingly familiar, yet forever elusive."[8] The Santangels, with their history of martyrdom culminating in Nadine's disfiguration in Jerusalem, share an ancestry with Uncle Melech who is similarly martyred in Israel. Their disfiguration contributes to a tantalizing invisibility, elusiveness, and familiarity in Canadian literature. By retracing blurred genealogical lines, by deviating from and returning to home and tradition, Matt Cohen remembers his grandfathers.

Conclusion

Towards the end of his writing career, Klein wrote "In Praise of the Diaspora" (1953), a long speech he never delivered. In this eulogy, Klein personifies the Diaspora as "Uncle Galuth," an affectionate kinsman recalling that other paradigmatic wanderer, Uncle Melech Davidson. Ever the rhetorician and dialectician in his silent speech, Klein remains ambiguous on his position regarding Zion and Diaspora: initially, he champions the former to discredit the latter, but soon shifts his praise to trace the rich and varied history of the Jews during the past two millenia. His talmudic defense of equivocation is aimed not at perfect comprehension, but at approximate human understanding between minds and attitudes: "Seldom, if ever, is the truth one-sided. Truth, oftenest, is a composite, a series of gradations, a harmony in which *yea* and *nay* echo one another."[1] An exponent of multiple meanings, a harmonizer of negatives, and an echoer of Buber's "I-Thou" relationship, Klein places himself in the tradition of ben Bag Bag who turned the texts of Holy Writ unceasingly, as if decentring meanings were somehow linked to a diasporic destiny — a lesson well absorbed by modern Jewish writers. The Diaspora's message, according to Klein, is that recreation is the consequence of walking abroad — that long trek in *The Second Scroll* which has to be turned and turned for its unending messages.

In this continuing process of walking abroad, the Jews encounter a multiplicity of barriers such as Sambation — an imaginary, cabbalistic river that fascinated Klein. According to legend, some of the ten "lost tribes" of Israel were exiled beyond Sambation, the raging river which is calm only on the Sabbath when crossing would be possible but prohibited by law — a Kafkaesque or catch-22 dilemma. Exiled from his own religion and ultimately from his own writing, this first Jewish poet of English was inevitably drawn to the hidden vortices of

Sambation — the dividing line between rage and sanity, turmoil and silence — for Klein died as a result of being a poet, in the spirit of Kafka and Walter Benjamin. Aside from these biographical and psychological speculations about Jews and poets, Sambation symbolizes the challenging boundaries of *différance*: a dividing line between centre and circumference, Zion and Diaspora, origin and margin, presence and absence, sacred and profane, accomplishment and deferment, tradition and adventure, promised land and desert. This fabled river, like Klein's fabled city, exists in space's vapours and time's haze. A chiasmus for qualified meanings, this border accentuates the ambiguities of the Diaspora. Neither demonic Styx nor decisive Rubicon, Sambation flows endlessly with hidden undercurrents; its Canadian tributaries are the St Lawrence, and further west, Ludwig's, Waddington's, and Wiseman's Assiniboine, Mandel's Souris, and Kreisel's Saskatchewan.

Initially, writing and an ironic sense enabled Klein to cross his Sambation, words were his bridges to the beyond. His 1949 "Notebook of a Journey," the skeleton of *The Second Scroll*, demonstrates the tensions between Montreal's ghetto regionalism and the universalism of a Diaspora, between parochial religion and modern skepticism. Klein's childlike excitement at leaving home for another kind of home in Israel pervades every entry in his notebook. Acquiring the necessary visas for his journey, he defines utopia as "a visaless world. Everyman can go everywhere anytime."[2] Utopia is a kind of voluntary borderless diaspora where freedom of movement and interpretation challenges the limits of space and time; Klein's vision comes as a reaction to the Nazis' dystopia earlier in the decade when his fellow Jews were nowhere granted refuge. He juxtaposes this paradoxical utopia, or pervasive no-place, with an ironic interpretation of the Israeli consulate in Montreal's no-man's land: "What more natural than that in a city in which saints meet at every street-corner there should also be a parcel of Holy Land."[3] Klein's irony misallies Roman Catholic meeting places with a Jewish almost meeting where margins and centres shift, where St Urbain is endowed with a ghetto's savvy or a Jewboy's pavement dreams. Poets retrieve cities of loss from Montreal to Jerusalem via an erased Vilna: "a surrogate city in French Canada, with its Catholic churches, its river and mountain, its babble of tongues, somehow intimated the loss of a birthplace I never knew. There was even an Old City, though it lacked a wall."[4] Accustomed to bilingualism, trilingualism, or multilingualism, Montreal's Jewish writers, with their matter of cities and mind of ghettos, salvage the ruins and revive nineteenth-century Galician or Rumanian ghosts even as they invent new Canadian identities. Straddling that absent wall, they mediate various solitudes before transcending downward or upward to a buried past.

Robert Kroetsch speculates that "Canadian writing takes place between the vastness of (closed) cosmologies and the fragments found in the (open) field of the archaeological site. It is a literature of dangerous middles."[5] Dangerous middlemen of Jewish-Canadian literature mediate between cosmologies and archaeology, open prairie and enclosed ghettoscape, two or more solitudes. Dreaming pavement into Bible-land may proceed by two different routes: digging downwards and backwards through layers of the past, or transcending through astronomy upwards and forwards towards a messianic future. In this light, Proust's portrait of the Jew as prophet and bounder may be expanded: above ground, prophet, astronomer, and *luftmensch* project their high-brow vision toward heaven; below, the *pusherke* struggles against becoming a cloacal *schlemiel*, the archaeologist of the frivolous. Klein's poet articulates heaven and the seven-circled air, zooms to zenith, and climbs another planet; or, the lost poet, depressed to nadir, is a relict at the bottom of the sea. Klein's rocking chair of the Diaspora oscillates between these polarities, from sunken pendulum to national bird, from tradition to future plans. His *luftmensch* creates an "Air-Map" to chart the "world's crossroads" from the St Lawrence to the layers of Mount Royal which contain the "history of mankind." "One would say the hidden stars were bells / dangling between the shafts of the Zodiac."[6] One would say that Jewish-Canadian writers were men and women dangling between archaeological fragments and Zodiac shafts.

Phyllis Gotlieb, another ironic astronomer of Zohar and zodiac, understates instead of overreaches in her yeshiva poem, "A Commentary," from *Ordinary, Moving*, which ends in negation of a Hotspur-Glendower boast:

the day that I was born
no star shook itself
no comet vectored the heavens
the earth turned once on its axis.[7]

With Gotlieb's "ordinary moving," breaking the circle in modern Jewish poetry deflates celestial cycles to a more domesticated mythology: an ironic tension between cannibal galaxies and a tiny clear image at the front end of a telescope. Cross-eyed optics fill and invert a poetics of absence in Gotlieb's ironic "Nothing":

oh it's a nudnik nothing night a sniveller a snuffer
of joie de vivre you could turn my
dissenting decentralized reticular structure to a
rebus a ratchet a rocket a tower of babel a ring
around a rosy upsydaisy arsyversy.[8]

In the extraordinary nomadism of *Ordinary, Moving*, she decentres
Toronto through her retina towards a diasporic constellation. Like
other dissenters, she stubbornly takes apart resistant structures; and
her lowered brow retreats from these heights to alight on a ghetto
wall of graffiti:

Rabbi, Inquisitor, mapmaker, bricklayer
what did you sing in the street?
what did you write on the wall?[9]

This wall is a vertical text extending above archaeological pavement
toward astronomical heights, separating the ghetto's individualism
from the surrounding universe, and almost meeting between and
beyond vertical and horizontal boundaries. Only by inscribing on
divisive walls can the triply displaced Jew, Canadian, and poet, gain
access to an enriched diaspora and the ironies of a ghettoized cosmos.

Through improved binoculars Irving Layton demands that the
muse polevault over Montreal's atavistic walls, to shatter plinths, and
to unscramble galactic space as well as the fertile muck and cold
green element. Waiting for her Messiah, Miriam Waddington travels
through her "dream telescope" through a "dangling world" where
she celebrates little fringes and frayed edges, in-between spaces.
Semitic and semiotic, Hebraic and Hellenic, Eli Mandel excavates the
prairie landscape to return to origins. Alien, schizoid, "Crusoe"
searches for the "snail's trace: / doubtful words."[10] Displaced, incongruous, the archaeologist digs his poetry out of prairie or ghetto;
deferred between origin and repetition, he belongs to "another
time," dreaming backwards, doubling from "Notes from the Underground" to "Galaxy." Archaeologist and astronomer return to Saskatchewan origins where signs cut in prairie rock recall the etched
Mosaic tablets:

the Hebrew alphabet
Invictus the first three
lines of Genesis
the unremembered man who stole
children from an empty town and

Latin   heroes in the hills and
glyphs uncles cousins step-
grandfather's son and sisters
whatever has been hidden here
remains of speech

            the town lives
in its syntax we are ghosts
look on the road beyond
mesas and moonscape
hoodoos signs   cut in rock
graffiti   gods
an indescribable border. [11]

Postmodern markers measure the figures in the Diaspora's ground: indescribable borders, empty spaces, dangerous middles, glyphs, graffiti, graphs, grafts, and metaleptic maps for the poet's extended family.

Out of the prophetic tradition and Klein's polished lens, Layton's improved binoculars and Richler's and Cohen's wrong-ended telescopes aim their satiric vision at the immorality of Jews and Gentiles alike in modern society. As much as they wish to remain above prairie ground, Jack Ludwig and Adele Wiseman welcome "revolutionary archaeologists" to uncover Winnipeg's past. They celebrate confusions between archaeology and astronomy, for they ride an elevator in their "heebie-jeebie" world, one minute shaking hands with the man in the moon, the next matching sorrow with Dostoyevsky's undergroud man. These wanderers carry their nomadic texts with them through a visaless diaspora; their archi-texts excavate Montreal, Ottawa, Winnipeg, and Edmonton to become intertexts with European precedents. Kafka may reverse this sense of archaeology in his ironic metamorphosis of evolution, but Jewish writers are trapped in ooze, boggy shelter, fertile muck, or *nostalgie de la boue*: "their hind legs were bogged down in their father's Judaism and their front legs could find no new ground. The resulting despair was their inspiration." [12] Unable to settle permanently, Jewish-Canadian quadrupeds with their fourfold slanted vision remain unsettled temporarily.

Anarchic breezes from Kafka's cabbalistic background provide some of that desperate inspiration which simultaneously disfigures representation and levels Canadian landscape and culture. As the winds of unorthodoxy sweep down from Mount Royal (Klein's spirit's mother and Laurentian cord), they fan the flames of Melech Davidson's immolation and end up as a whirlwind, for Klein's messianic harbinger introduces secular Hassidism to Canadian literature. These transatlantic breezes also fan the fire that reveals Melech Adler's "true" photographs and his son's "false" saving of the Torah scrolls; as well, they propel Isaac blindly toward Winnipeg's burning synagogue where he saves the Torah but loses his life. Buffeting characters in opposing directions, these storms create blurred vision as in Melech's multiple exposure where the single camera view is no longer possible. Adele Wiseman, Jack Ludwig, Mordecai Richler, Leonard and Matt Cohen combine cinematic techniques with cabbalistic breezes in their fiction to distort any clear representation of reality. Out-of-focus narrative lenses convey their author's sense of alienation in the Canadian landscape. Monique Bosco's mirrors distort while tragic winds turn back the face of Lot's wife. Transatlantic winds from Ottawa to the British Isles ripple Norman Levine's tightrope as Canadian waves wash up on the empty Cornish coast. That same breeze that blows in both directions across the Atlantic impels Jacob Grossman to return to Vienna to misread his family history; similarly, it drives Theodore Stappler across the Canadian prairies towards an arctic mystery that is Henry Kreisel's blank, Hassidic text.

Eli Mandel, anarchist-poet with "black bursts of unmeaning,"[13] catches this spirit which causes his poem to flicker and drift from Auschwitz across the prairies. He doubles back to absent origins: "a book closing / a closed white book"[14] and "we cannot read the ancient script."[15] Waiting for her Messiah at the end of time, Phyllis Gotlieb returns to an earlier Hassidic time when colourful ancestral towns unite in an aniconic blur: ":ghostmarch in the noon of night / from pane to pane black brown pink white."[16] And in another one of her cross-eyed juxtapositions she concludes, "my ghost directories are / yellowpage clear through, the / crossroads of the past / are one-way thoroughfares."[17] These blind alleys become two-way avenues through history, and create a double crossroad through precursed ghost directories. Walter Benjamin captures the essence of these negatives in dialectics and representation when he pictures the angel of history:

His face is turned toward the past. Where we perceive a chain of events, he sees one single catastrophe which keeps piling wreckage upon wreckage and hurls it in front of his feet. The angel would like to stay, awaken the dead, and make whole what had been smashed. But a storm is blowing from Paradise; it has got caught in his wings with such violence that the angel can no longer close them. This storm irresistibly propels him into the future to which his back is turned, while the pile of debris before him grows skyward. This storm is what we call progress."[18]

Klein could not weather this storm, but later Jewish-Canadian writers have wrestled with their necessary, if incomplete, angel.

If secularized forms of Hassidic tales permeate modern Jewish literature, so too does humanism, another legacy from Buber's philosophy. With his characteristic blend of truth and hyperbole, Leslie Fiedler describes Buber's influence on Jewish culture in North America: "Certainly, we live at a moment when, everywhere in the realm of prose, Jewish writers have discovered their Jewishness to be an eminently marketable commodity, their much vaunted alienation to be their passport into the heart of Gentile American culture. It is, indeed, their quite justified claim to have been *first* to occupy the Lost Desert at the center of the Great American Oasis (toward which everyone now races, Coca-Cola in one hand, Martin Buber in the other)."[19] As part of his two-fold quest in *The Second Scroll*, Klein's narrator does indeed juggle his North American bottle of pragmatism and his Jewish book of Hassidism, for Klein was the first to occupy Canada's lost desert. Montreal's alienated poet also held in hand the poetry of Bialik and the fiction of Mendele, Peretz, and Sholom Aleichem whose ironies about Russian persecution he transferred to life in the New World. Neither quite European nor quite American, his Jewish-Canadian subculture invented its own stories and rhythms which recount ironic losses from biblical times to the present.

Like secular Hassidism, Hebrew and Yiddish humanism influenced Jewish-Canadian poets and novelists after Klein. In poetry this liberalism takes a variety of forms from Irving Layton's satiric, prophetic denunciation of brutality and materialism to Leonard Cohen's tortured black romanticism which venerates Hebrew holiness and attacks crass manifestations of Jewishness. A veneration of ancient ideals goes hand in hand with a condemnation of fallen, modern reality; and into that historic gap, the Jewish satirist vents his rage. Miriam Waddington forges her compassion out of a destroyed Russian past and an empty Manitoba present while Phyllis Gotlieb's verse takes the form of an absurd sing-song nursery rhyme that links her disappeared European heritage with a child's freedom and celebrates an open, optimistic future. Eli Mandel's humanism manifests itself in a quest for prairie origins, family romance, and the road back to Kiev. His doubling of ancient Indian petroglyphs and Hebraic inscriptions humanizes myth and landscape. All of these portraits of the Jewish poet as Canadian landscape reveal their empathy for downtrodden third solitudes.

In fiction, Jacob Grossman, the impoverished rich man, grows out of Mendele's, Peretz's, and Sholom Aleichem's tradition of Yiddish paupers who are incapable of helping their families in the face of imminent disaster. Kreisel's immigrant socialism is shared by other Jewish-Canadian novelists. Norman Levine's Ottawa stories depict ghetto peddlers descended from Sholom Aleichem's fiction, while his later stories of life in rural England portray the hardships and poverty of an isolated artist sensitive to naturalism. Similarly, Jack Ludwig's peddler Bibul emerges from Winnipeg's ghetto, a Canadian version of an East European *shtetl*, while his other protagonists attempt to enter the American mainstream and drag along their nostalgia for a Jewish past. Adele Wiseman celebrates that same ghetto in Winnipeg, so full of irony and nostalgia for the past of Mendele, Peretz, and Sholom Aleichem where families of Jewish immigrants struggle to maintain their integrity in a hostile world. Mythic resonances from the Bible to East European life pervade Winnipeg's *shtetl* where families huddle together against an alien culture and the vastness of the prairies, an openness in nature almost without precedent in their diasporic heritage. *Yiddishkeit* in an enclosed ghetto had provided no training ground for boundless horizons. In that mysterious frontier landscape of Western Canada, these authors and their characters try to find a meaning that may somehow be related to their earlier transatlantic history so removed from nature.

On Mount Royal and in the Laurentians, Montreal's Jewish writers experience nature as a retreat from urban oppression and as a mythic, displaced Mount Sinai, but their main focus resides in the warmth and conflicts within the family. Underneath Richler's, Cohen's, and Layton's scatological satire lies a fierce moralism that exposes the hypocrisies of a conservative WASP establishment as well as the foibles of a *nouveau riche* Jewish community that has abandoned its spiritual roots in favour of an illusory security within the Canadian mainstream. Monique Bosco and Naim Kattan, separated from both English and French mainstreams, see themselves as third solitudes, reaching out to connect cultures from a lost semitic world. Montreal and Winnipeg take their place alongside New York and Chicago in offering a unique perspective for Jewish experience in North America.

Writing for their Messiah, waiting in lines, in letters, on walls, on tables, and over borders, Jewish-Canadian writers defer meaning even as they blow on imagination's trumpet. Surrounded by English and French in Montreal, and a frozen desert on the prairies, they mediate and transcend: beneath — the archaeological dig, sifting through evidence, hidden sources, cracked pots, and scrolls; between — the anthropological mind among nations, categorizing totems and taboos; beyond — the astronomical panopticon, surveying transcendence. Haunted by second scrolls and selves — doubles, *dybbuks*, doppelgängers, and alter egos — the Freudian ego exorcises these demons through writing about betrayals, tight-rope walkers, confusions, crackpots, runners, favourite games, Lot's wives, and reprisals. Early to antiquity and late to modernism, wayfarers in words tarry the night, listening for messianic footsteps on the other side of the atavistic wall where Rabbi Tarphon inscribes the closing words: "It is not required of you that you complete the work, but neither are you free to desist from it."[20]

Glossary

Aggadah Rabbinic Lore, legend, narrative; in general, the non-legal material of the Talmud in contrast to the legal material, or *halacha*.

Baalei teshuvah Those who repent and return to the fold.

Cabbala, kabbala Jewish mystical literature.

Cadi Arabic judge.

Cheder Room of the Hebrew or Jewish school.

Chetiv Written law in the Torah or Pentateuch.

Dybbuk, dibbuk From Jewish folklore. A demon or departed soul that takes possession of the living and must be exorcised.

Freilach A happy dance at a wedding or Hassidic gathering.

Galut Diaspora, dispersion, exile from Zion.

Gelt Money.

Gematria Rabbinic method of interpretation based on computing numerical values of words.

Gilgul mecholot Apocalyptic concept associated with resurrection and the rolling of the body and soul after death.

Golem Legendary creature made from clay with a strong body and no soul, used by its maker to take revenge on enemies.

Hakafos Ritual parade in synagogue during which the Torah is carried around the congregation.

Haskala The Enlightenment.

Hassidism, Chassidism A religious movement founded by the Ba'al Shem Tov in the eighteenth century, and characterized by a mystical-emotional view of Judaism in contrast to the rationalism of the Enlightenment.

Keri Oral law of Rabbinic interpretation and amplification.

Kleine mentscheleh Small, humble person.

Lamed vavnek One of the thirty-six saintly, unknown souls for whom alone God allows the world to continue.

Luftmensh Literally, a person of the air; one who pays little attention to material events.

Megillah Scroll.

Melech King.

Mellah Casablanca's squalid ghetto.

Mensch Literally, a man; one who acts in a decent manner.

Menschlechkeit Code of decent behaviour.

Midrash Interpretative study of the Bible.

Pentateuch The Five Books of Moses.

Pilpul Dialectic, question-and-answer method of argumentation used for talmudic interpretation.

Pintele yid An impoverished Jew, characterized by humility.

Pusherke Aggressive, pushy person.

Schlemiel Simple character who constantly stumbles.

Schlimazl Character who cannot escape bad luck.

Schnorrer Beggar.

Shickseh Pejorative Yiddish term for a non-Jewish woman.

Taiku A stalemate, or irresolution, of argument in talmudic discourse; the point at which argument can go no further. Similar to the Greek term *aporia*. In modern Hebrew, a *taiku* is a tied score.

Talis, talesim (pl) Prayer shawl, traditionally worn by adult men only.

Talmud Compilation of the oral parts of the Torah, including *Mishnah, Gemara, Baba Kama, Baba Bathra*.

Techiyat hamaitim Resurrection, or Return of the Dead. Similar to *apophrades*.

Tishbite Elijah the prophet.

Torah The entire body of Jewish religious teaching; the *Pentateuch* is the basic, central text in the Torah which also includes classic commentaries on this basic text.

Yeshiva House of higher, religious study, usually in preparation for the rabbinate.

Zohar The Book of Light, composed in Spain in the thirteenth century. One of the most important texts of Jewish mysticism.

Notes

INTRODUCTION

1 Fiedler, "Some Notes on the Jewish Novel in English," in Sheps, ed., *Mordecai Richler*, 101. Fiedler echoes Edmund Wilson's remarks to the effect that the background of Canadian stories seems alien to England and the United States, but not strange enough to exercise the spell of the truly exotic. See Edmund Wilson, *O Canada*, 10, 37, 41; see also Gerson, "Some Patterns of Exile in Jewish Writing of the Commonwealth," 104; Nadel, *Jewish Writers in North America*, xviii; Shechner, "Jewish Writers," in Hoffman, ed., *The Harvard Guide to American Writing*, 191ff.

2 Lewisohn, "Forward," to Klein's *Hath Not a Jew* reprinted in Klein, *Collected Poems*, 350.

3 Quoted in Caplan, *Like One that Dreamed*, 113.

4 Ibid., 114.

5 Richler, "Their Canada and Mine," in Sinclair and Wolfe, eds., *The Spice Box*, 235. Several books on the New York Intellectuals have recently appeared and all of them overlap. For the most thorough history see Alexander Bloom, *Prodigal Sons*. Se also Howe, *World of Our Fathers*, 588.

6 Kreisel, "Chassidic Song," *The Almost Meeting and Other Stories*, 35.

7 See Leonard Cohen, "Last Dance at the Four Penny," *Selected Poems 1956–1968*, 69; Mandel, "Snake Charmers," *Stony Plain*, 32; Gotlieb, *Ordinary, Moving*, 1–8; and Gotlieb, "Hassidic Influences in the Work of A.M. Klein," in Mayne, ed., *The A.M. Klein Symposium*, 47–64.

8 Layton, *The Pole-Vaulter*, 28.

9 Layton, *Collected Poems*, 330.

10 Waddington, *Say Yes*, 59.

11 Klein, *Collected Poems*, 234.

12 Kreisel, *The Almost Meeting*, 17.

13 Ibid., 21.

14 See Spiro, *Tapestry and Designs*, 3–6; Fischer, *In Search of Jerusalem*, especially 2–3, 207, for Klein's relationship to Spinoza, Hassidism, and Cabbala.

15 Quoted in Caplan, *Like One That Dreamed*, 197. See also Pollock, "From 'Pulver' to 'Portrait': A.M. Klein and the Dialectic."

16 Auerbach, *Mimesis*, 1–20.

17 Adapted from Kafka, *The Basic Kafka*, 238.

18 See Jay, *Adorno*, 15, 19–21; Jay, *The Dialectical Imagination*, 34, 54, 182, 260–3; and Buck-Morss, *The Origin of Negative Dialectics*, 186–7.

19 Hartman, *Criticism in the Wilderness*, 102. See also Arendt, "Introduction" in Benjamin, *Illuminations*, 10–15; Chametsky, *Our Decentralized Literature*, for comparisons of mediated and unmediated Jewish points of view; Perlina, "Mikhail Bakhtin and Martin Buber," 13–28. For "heretic hermeneutics" see Handelman, *The Slayers of Moses*.

20 Rabinbach and Zipes, "Lessons of the Holocaust," 3. See also Scholem, *The Messianic Idea in Judaism*, 19–21, 304–13; and Biale, *Gershom Scholem*, 11–12.

21 Hartman, "On the Jewish Imagination," 213.

22 Buber, *Meetings*, 18.

23 Hartman, *Criticism in the Wilderness*, 78.

24 Diamond, "The State of Being Jewish," 2.

25 Klein, "In Praise of Diaspora," *Beyond Sambation*, 473. See also Derrida, *Writing and Difference*.

26 Kreisel, *Another Country*, 165–6.

27 Kroetsch, "Beyond Nationalism: A Prologue," xi. See also Kroetsch, "Canadian Writings: No Name is My Name," in Staines, ed., *The Forty-ninth and Other Parallels*, 122–3.

28 Frye, "Conclusion," in Klinck, ed., *Literary History of Canada*, 829.

29 Derrida, *Glas*, 268b–9b; quoted in Handelman, *The Slayers of Moses*, 165.

30 Klein, *The Second Scroll*, 20.

31 Leonard Cohen, *Selected Poems*, 82–3.

32 Kafka, *Parables and Paradoxes*, 92.

33 Freud, *Complete Psychological Works*, 17; 219–52.

34 Quoted in Scholem, *On Jews and Judaism in Crisis*, 82.

35 Klein, *The Rocking Chair and Other Poems*, 12.

36 Woodcock, *Mordecai Richler*, 23–4.

37 Richler, *Sons of a Smaller Hero*, 14.

38 Layton, "Preface," *Collected Poems*.

39 Waddington, *Driving Home*, 164.

40 Ibid., 149.

41 Waddington, "Fortunes," ibid., 121.

42 Richler, *Joshua Then and Now*, 190–1.

CHAPTER ONE

1 Quoted in Caplan, *Like One That Dreamed*, 172.
2 Quoted in Mayne, ed., *The A.M. Klein Symposium*, 13.
3 Klein, *The Second Scroll*, 28. References which follow in the text are to this edition.
4 Derrida, *Dissemination*, 345.
5 Waddington, *A.M. Klein*, 100.
6 See Marshall, "Theorems Made Flesh: Klein's Poetic Universe," 46–7.
7 Ross, *Canadian Forum*, 234.
8 Buck Morss, *The Origin of Negative Dialectics*, 186.
9 Pacey, *Ten Canadian Poets*, 286.
10 On metalepsis and transumption see Harold Bloom, *The Breaking of the Vessels*. On Klein's ethical and sociopolitical position see Steinberg, "The Conscience of Art: A.M. Klein on Poets and Poetry," in W.H. New, ed., *A Political Art*, 82–93.

CHAPTER TWO

1 Quoted in Steiner, *Language and Silence*, 75. See also Jay, *Adorno*, 19.
2 Alvarez, "The Literature of the Holocaust," *Beyond All This Fiddle*, 26.
3 Mandel, "Auschwitz: Poetry of Alienation," 217.
4 For a discussion of Levinas' position see Handelman, *The Slayers of Moses*, 170–5.
5 Klein's review of Layton's early poetry appears in Mayne, ed., *Irving Layton*, 25.
6 Ibid., 20.
7 Derrida, *Writing and Difference*, 108.
8 Layton, "Ex-Nazi," *Collected Poems*, 54.
9 Layton, "Das Wahre Ich," ibid., 292.
10 Layton, "Rhine Boat Trip," ibid., 389.
11 Layton, "The Shadow," *The Pole Vaulter*, 18–20.
12 Leonard Cohen, *Flowers for Hitler*, i.
13 Leonard Cohen, "Lines From My Grandfather's Journal," *Selected Poems*, 82.
14 Quoted in Rosenfeld, *A Double Dying*, 21.
15 Leonard Cohen, *Flowers for Hitler*, 28–9.
16 Woodcock, "The Song of the Sirens: Reflections on Leonard Cohen," *Odysseus Ever Returning*, 102. Djwa also questions the integrity of Cohen's vision in "Leonard Cohen: Black Romantic," 32–42.
17 Leonard Cohen, "It Uses Us!" *Flowers for Hitler*, 31.
18 Leonard Cohen, "The Invisible Trouble," ibid., 39.

19 Leonard Cohen, "Hitler the Brain-Mole," ibid., 43.
20 Leonard Cohen, "Hitler," ibid., 125.
21 Mandel, "On the 25th Anniversary of the Liberation of Auschwitz," *Stony Plain*, 66.
22 Ibid., 63.
23 Compare Milton Wilson's use of the phrase in Milton Wilson, "Recent Canadian Verse," 271.
24 Mandel, "Auschwitz: Poetry of Alienation," 217.
25 Langer, *The Holocaust and the Literary Imagination*, 3.
26 Klein, "And in that Drowning Instant," *The Second Scroll*, 141.
27 See Lang, "Writing-the-Holocaust: Jabès and the Measure of History," in Gould, ed., *The Sin of the Book*, 195–6.
28 Neher, *The Exile of the Word*, 142.
29 Ibid., 239.

CHAPTER THREE

1 Kreisel, "Homecoming," *The Almost Meeting*, 69.
2 Kreisel, *The Rich Man*, 10. References which follow in the text are to this edition.
3 Kreisel, *The Betrayal*, 125. References which follow in the text are to this edition.
4 See Kreisel, "The Prairie: A State of Mind," in Mandel, ed., *Contexts of Canadian Criticism*, 254–66. See also Lecker, "States of Mind: Henry Kreisel's Novels," 82–93.

CHAPTER FOUR

1 Levine, *The Tight-Rope Walker*. References to Levine's poetry which follow in the text are to this edition.
2 Levine, *Selected Stories*, 107. For my discussion of Levine's Jewish regionalism I rely on two short stories which serve as companion pieces, "A Father" and "In Lower Town." References to these short stories which appear in the text are taken from this edition, but the stories have been reprinted in *Champagne Barn*.
3 Levine, "The Playground," *One Way Ticket*, 18. References which follow in the text are to this edition.
4 *From a Seaside Town* has been reissued as *She'll Only Drag You Down*. References which follow in the text are to this edition.
5 For Levine's reaction to the Holocaust see Levine, *Canada Made Me*, 13, 40, 232.
6 Though his style in no way resembles Bellow's, Levine may have been influenced by *Dangling Man* whose protagonist Joseph, a Canadian, re-

signs his job at the Inter-American Travel Bureau to await induction into the American Army. Waiting for meaning, both Josephs are dangling men or tight-rope walkers, belatedly imitating Kafka's Joseph K. In sparse style and sense of exile Levine also copies Camus' Joseph Grand in *The Plague*.

7 For the philosophical and phenomenological underpinnings of the Jew as letter writer, and as the travel writer with his postcards, see Derrida, *La carte postale*.

CHAPTER FIVE

1 Ludwig, *Confusions*, viii. References which follow in the text are to this edition.

2 Shechner, "Saul Bellow and Ghetto Cosmopolitanism," 35.

3 Ludwig, "Requiem for Bibul," in Lucas, ed., *Great Canadian Short Stories*, 219. References to this short story which follow in the text are to this edition. For a discussion of Ludwig's early fiction see Stonehewer, "Anatomy of Confusion: Jack Ludwig's Evolution," 34–42.

4 Roth, *Reading Myself and Others*, 82–3.

5 Ludwig, *Above Ground*, 3. References which follow in the text are to this edition.

6 Ludwig, "You Always go Home Again," 108. See also the interview in Cameron, ed., *Conversations with Canadian Novelists*, 119.

7 See Culler, *On Deconstruction*, 140.

8 Harold Bloom, "Introduction," in Revault d'Allones, *Musical Variations on Jewish Thought*, 13.

9 Ludwig, *A Woman of Her Age*, 184.

10 Ludwig, "You Always Go Home Again," 109. See also Brown, "The Canadian Eve." For affinities to Isaac Babel and Joyce see his "Winnipeggers: Before and After Dubliners," in W. H. New, ed., *A Political Art*, 3–14.

CHAPTER SIX

1 Wiseman, "A Brief Anatomy of an Honest Attempt," 102.

2 Wiseman, *Old Woman at Play*, 54.

3 Mandelstam, *The Complete Critical Prose and Letters*, 252.

4 Ibid., 261.

5 Wiseman, *The Sacrifice*, 3. References which follow in the text are to this edition.

6 Derrida, *Writing and Difference*, 93.

7 Harold Bloom, *Kabbalah and Criticism*, i.

8 Wiseman, *Crackpot*, 5. References which follow in the text are to this edition.

9 See Handelman, *The Slayers of Moses*, 141; and Baumgarten, *City Scriptures*, 132.

10 Klein, "Portrait of the Poet as Landscape," *The Rocking Chair and Other Poems*, 51–2.

CHAPTER SEVEN

1 Klein, *Collected Poems*, 130.

2 See Djwa, "Leonard Cohen: Black Romantic," 32–42.

3 Leonard Cohen, *The Favourite Game*, 14. References which follow in the text are to this edition.

4 See Derrida, *Of Grammatology*, 46–7, for a discussion of the metaphysics of "trace."

5 The best discussion of *The Favourite Game* appears in Scobie, *Leonard Cohen*, 73–96. I have built upon Scobie's analysis of sympathy and distance, the lover and the artist in Breavman's character, by demonstrating its poststructuralist affinities. Morley, *The Immoral Moralists*, also contains interesting material on Cohen's quest for truth and Breavman's role as outsider. The novel's lyricism is examined in Ondaatje, *Leonard Cohen*.

6 See Revault d'Allones, *Musical Variations on Jewish Thought*.

7 See Derrida, *Dissemination*, for a relevant discussion of *pharmakos, pharmakon*, and *pharmakeus* — all roles played by Breavman. My discussion of linear imagery is indebted to Miller, "Ariadne's Thread: Repetition and the Narrative Line." For another discussion of blanks, black and white see Harold Bloom, *The Breaking of Vessels*, 75–107.

8 Leonard Cohen may have been influenced by Schwartz, "In Dreams Begins Responsibilities." For a discussion of the role of film in Schwartz and Benjamin, see Elisa New, "Reconsidering Delmore Schwartz." One can extend her remarks to the cinematic effects of *The Favourite Game* and *Crackpot*.

9 Klein, "Indian Reservation: Caughnawaga," *Collected Poems*, 304.

10 Leonard Cohen, *Beautiful Losers*, 17. References which follow in the text are to this edition. In addition to Scobie's discussion of the novel, see Hutcheon, "*Beautiful Losers*: All the Polarities," in Woodcock, ed., *The Canadian Novel in the Twentieth Century*, 298–311.

11 Derrida, "Shibboleth," in Hartman and Budick, eds., *Midrash and Literature*, 341.

CHAPTER EIGHT

1 Kriegel, *Les Juifs et le monde moderne*, 61.

2 Richler, *The Acrobats*, 25. References which follow in the text are to this edition.

3 Richler, *Son of a Smaller Hero*, 55. References which follow in the text are to this edition.

4 Richler, *The Apprenticeship of Duddy Kravitz*, 91. References which follow in the text are to this edition.

5 Culler, *On Deconstruction*, 149.

6 See Ferns, "Sympathy and Judgement in Mordecai Richler's *The Apprenticeship of Duddy Kravitz*." The reader's choice, offered by Ferns, between sympathy for and condemnation of Duddy Kravitz may be denied if one follows recent trends in reader-response criticism, for, as Stanley Fish has demonstrated in the case of *Paradise Lost*, the reader of *Duddy Kravitz* may be surprised by Duddy's sins because the reader has also fallen. Since every character in the novel is the object of Richler's satire, the reader has no one with whom to identify — hence he must regard himself also as one of Richler's targets. Part 2 ends with Duddy asking Yvette, "What's your opinion of Duddy now?", a question also directed to the reader. But the answer may not be forthcoming since the reader must judge himself before passing judgment on a fictional character who is a false reader of *How to Increase Your Word Power* and *God's Little Acre*.

7 My observations occasionally intersect with Ower's in "Sociology, Psychology, and Satire, in *The Apprenticeship of Duddy Kravitz*," however our critical strategies fundamentally diverge. For example, where Ower takes liberties in invoking Pound's "intravaginal warmth" to interpret Simcha's shoe repair shop, I would include Simcha's occupation within the pattern of mobility. Simcha's vocation may also be seen as a substitute for the repair of walking or running; moreover, his stature in the community rises when he heals the broken leg of Blondin the blacksmith who had been kicked by a horse. Henceforth, whenever there was an accident in the neighbourhood Simcha was sent for. Unfortunately, Lennie fails to inherit his grandfather's medical talents.

8 For a stimulating discussion of the role of cliché in culture and society see McLuhan, *From Cliché to Archetype*. See also Girard, *Deceit, Desire, and the Novel*, 7, 15, for a discussion of the *vaniteux* and triangular desire which lends itself to a further understanding of Duddy's character. Indeed, where Richler's first three novels focus on the characters from a predominantly Existentialist point of view where guilt may be assigned to an individual, from *Duddy Kravitz* onwards the novels become increasingly Freudian.

9 Richler, *St. Urbain's Horseman*, 180. References which follow in the text are to this edition.

10 *Kikeleh* (Yiddish for a small cookie) is collocated with Kik Cola, while it also forms the diminutive of the anti-semitic, pejorative "kike."

11 My interpretation accords with Sheps' sense of "vicarious" in "Waiting for Joey: The Theme of the Vicarious in *St. Urbain's Horseman*." My refer-

ences to Harold Bloom's "anxiety of influence" extend Pollock's view of Auden as judge to include other literary predecessors. See Pollock, "The Trial of Jake Hersh."

12 Richler, *Joshua Then and Now*, 364.

CHAPTER NINE

1 Bosco, *Schabbat 70–77*, 95.

2 Lévesque et McDonald, eds., *L'Oreille de l'Autre*, 198, 203.

3 Marcotte, *Une Littérature qui se fait*, 62–76; Escomel, "Monique Bosco ou le miroir brisé," 90–7. For a discussion of Jewish vertigo and the messianic, see Stoehr, "Paul Goodman and the New York Jews," 61.

4 Bosco, *Un Amour maladroit*, 7. References which follow in the text are to this edition.

5 Giguère, *Le Temps des jeux*, 9.

6 Bosco, *La Femme de Loth*. References which follow in the text are to this edition.

7 Escomel, "Monique Bosco ou le miroir brisé," 93.

8 Bosco, *Charles Lévy, m.d.*, 14. References which follow in the text are to this edition.

9 Bosco, *Jericho*, 45.

10 Waddington, *Driving Home*, 41.

11 Derrida, *Spurs*, 69.

12 Waddington, "Exile: A Woman and a Stranger Living out the Canadian Paradox," 41.

13 Waddington, *The Price of Gold*, 7, 111.

14 Waddington, *A.M. Klein*, 130–1.

15 Quoted in the epigraph to Robin's *La Québécoite*.

CHAPTER TEN

1 Kattan, "A.M. Klein: Modernité et Loyauté," 22–3. This link between Irish and Jewish innovation in Western culture has also been noted in Borges, "The Argentine Writer and Tradition," 184.

2 Derrida, *Writing and Difference*, 66.

3 Kattan, *La mémoire et la promesse*, 23.

4 Caws, *The Eye in the Text*, 15.

5 Kattan, *Reality and Theatre*, 4.

6 Kattan, *Farewell, Babylon*, 33. References which follow in the text are to this edition. For Kattan's own interpretation of his work, see the interview in *Voix et images*.

7 For a discussion of "river" and "sand" symbols see Canetti, *Crowds and Power*, 83–4, 86–7. For the semiotics of boundaries, border regions, and "rivage" see Ubersfeld, "The Space of *Phèdre*," 203–6.

8 Kattan, "L'Islam, Le Judaïsme et l'Occident," in Olender, ed., *Le Racisme. Mythes et sciences*, 404.
9 Kattan, *Dans le désert*, 11. References which follow in the text are to this edition.
10 Kattan, *La Traversée*, 19. References which follow in the text are to this edition.
11 Kattan, *Le Rivage*.
12 Kattan, *Le Sable de l'île*, 7. References which follow in the text are to this edition.
13 Kattan, *La reprise*, 62. References which follow in the text are to this edition.

CHAPTER ELEVEN

1 Matt Cohen, *The Colours of War*, 49. References which follow in the text are to this edition.
2 Matt Cohen, *Columbus and the Fat Lady and Other Stories*, 13. References to "The Watchmaker" which follow in the text are to this edition.
3 Matt Cohen, *Night Flights*, 122. References to "The Universal Miracle" and "Vogel" which follow in the text are to this edition.
4 Matt Cohen, *Café Le Dog*, 80. References to "The Sins of Tomas Benares" and "Sentimental Meetings" which follow in the text are to this edition.
5 Matt Cohen, *The Spanish Doctor*, 35. References which follow in the text are to this edition.
6 Matt Cohen, *Nadine*, 3. References which follow in the text are to this edition. For a detailed discussion of Cohen's other fiction, see Kertzer, "Time and Its Victims: The Writing of Matt Cohen."
7 Matt Cohen, *Café Le Dog*, 124.
8 Klein, *The Second Scroll*, 76.

CONCLUSION

1 Klein, *Beyond Sambation*, 467.
2 Ibid., 342.
3 Ibid.
4 Roskies, *Against the Apocalypse*, 2.
5 Kroetsch, "Beyond Nationalism," xi.
6 Klein, "Winter Night: Mount Royal," *Rocking Chair*, 32.
7 Gotlieb, *Ordinary, Moving*, 8.
8 Ibid., 41.
9 Ibid., 58.
10 Mandel, *Crusoe*, 2.
11 Mandel, *Out of Place*, 14.

12 Kafka, *Briefe 1902-1924*, 337. See Robert, *From Oedipus to Moses*, 9; and Taranovsky, *Essays on Mandelstam*, 53–5.
13 Mandel, *Crusoe*, 84.
14 Mandel, "Ottawa October 70," *Stony Plain*, 89.
15 Mandel, "On Cultural Revolution," ibid., 77.
16 Gotlieb, *Ordinary, Moving*, 7.
17 Ibid., 12.
18 Benjamin, *Illuminations*, 257–8.
19 Fiedler, *Waiting for the End*, 65. See also Howe, *Celebrations and Attacks*, 11–26.
20 Quoted in Harold Bloom, "The Masks of the Normative," 23.

Bibliography

Alter, Robert. *Defenses of the Imagination: Jewish Writers and Modern Historical Crisis*. Philadelphia: Jewish Publication Society 1977.

Alvarez, A. *Beyond All This Fiddle: Essays 1955–1967*. London: Allen Lane 1968.

Auerbach, Erich. *Mimesis: The Representation of Reality in Western Literature*. Trans. Willard Trask. New York: Anchor 1957.

Babel, Isaac. *The Collected Stories*. Introduction by Lionel Trilling. New York: Meridian 1960.

Baumgarten, Murray. *City Scriptures: Modern Jewish Writing*. Cambridge, Mass.: Harvard University Press 1982.

Benjamin, Walter. *Illuminations*, edited and with an introduction by Hannah Arendt. Trans. Harry Zohn. New York: Schocken 1969.

Biale, David. *Gershom Scholem: Kabbalah and Counter-History*. Cambridge, Mass.: Harvard University Press 1979.

Bloom, Alexander. *Prodigal Sons: The New York Intellectuals and Their World*. New York: Oxford University Press 1986.

Bloom, Harold. *Agon: Towards a Theory of Revisionism*. New York: Oxford University Press 1982.

— *The Anxiety of Influence: A Theory of Poetry*. New York: Oxford University Press 1973.

— *The Breaking of the Vessels*. Chicago: The University of Chicago Press 1982.

— *Kabbalah and Criticism*. New York: Seabury 1975.

— "The Masks of the Normative," *Orim* 1, 1 (1985): 9–24.

Borges, Jorge Luis. *Labyrinths: Selected Stories and Other Writings*. New York: New Directions 1964.

Bosco, Monique. *Un Amour maladroit*. Paris: Gallimard 1961.

— *Charles Lévy, m.d.* Montréal: Quinze 1977.

— *La Femme de Loth*. Montréal: Éditions HMH 1970.

— *Jéricho*. Montréal: Hurtubise HMH 1971.

— *Schabbat 70–77*. Montréal: Quinze 1978.

Brown, Russell. "The Canadian Eve," *Journal of Canadian Fiction* 3, 3 (1974): 89–93.

Buber, Martin. *Meetings*. Edited by Maurice Friedman. LaSalle, Ill.: Open Court 1973.

Buck-Morss, Susan. *The Origin of Negative Dialectics: Theodor W. Adorno, Walter Benjamin, and the Frankfurt Institute*. London: Harvester 1977.

Cameron, Donald, ed. *Conversations with Canadian Novelists*. Toronto: Macmillan 1973.

Canetti, Elias. *Crowds and Power*. New York: Seabury 1978.

Caplan, Usher. *Like One That Dreamed: A Portrait of A.M. Klein*. Toronto: McGraw-Hill Ryerson 1982.

Caws, Mary Ann. *The Eye in the Text: Essays in Perception, Mannerist to Modern*. Princeton: Princeton University Press 1981.

Chametzky, Jules. *Our Decentralized Literature: Cultural Mediations in Selected Jewish and Southern Writers*. Amherst: The University of Massachusetts Press 1986.

Cohen, Albert. *Le livre de ma mère*. Paris: Gallimard 1954.

Cohen, Leonard. *Beautiful Losers*. Toronto: McClelland and Stewart 1966.

— *The Favourite Game*. Toronto: McClelland and Stewart 1970.

— *Flowers for Hitler*. Toronto: McClelland and Stewart 1964.

— *Selected Poems 1956–1968*. Toronto: McClelland and Stewart 1968.

Cohen, Matt. *Café Le Dog*. Markham, Ont.: Penguin 1985.

— *The Colours of War*. Toronto: McClelland and Stewart 1977.

— *Columbus and the Fat Lady and Other Stories*. Toronto: Anansi 1972.

— *The Expatriate*. Toronto: General 1982.

— *Nadine*. Toronto: Viking 1986.

— *Night Flights*. Toronto: Doubleday 1978.

— *The Spanish Doctor*. Markham, Ont.: Penguin 1985.

Cuddihy, John Murray. *The Ordeal of Civility: Freud, Marx, Lévi-Strauss, and the Jewish Struggle with Modernity*. New York: Basic 1974.

Culler, Jonathan. *On Deconstruction: Theory and Criticism after Structuralism*. Ithaca: Cornell University Press 1982.

Derrida, Jacques. *La Carte postale*. Paris: Flammarion 1980.

— *Dissemination*. Trans. Barbara Johnson. Chicago: University of Chicago Press 1981.

— *Glas*. Paris: Galilée 1974.

— *Of Grammatology*. Trans. G.C. Spivak. Baltimore: Johns Hopkins University Press 1976.

— *Spurs: Nietzsche's Styles*. Trans. Barbara Harlow. Chicago: University of Chicago Press 1978.

— *Writing and Difference*. Trans. Alan Bass. Chicago: University of Chicago Press 1978.

Diamond, Stanley. "The State of Being Jewish," *Dialectical Anthropology* 8, 1 and 2 (1983): 1–12.

Djwa, Sandra. "Leonard Cohen: Black Romantic," *Canadian Literature* 34 (1967): 32–42.

Escomel, Gloria. "Monique Bosco ou le miroir brisé," *La Nouvelle Barre du jour*, 65 (1978): 90–7.

Ferns, John. "Sympathy and Judgement in Mordecai Richler's *The Apprenticeship of Duddy Kravitz*," *Journal of Canadian Fiction* 3, 1 (1974): 77–82.

Fiedler, Leslie. *Waiting for the End*. New York: Dell 1965.

Fischer, G.K. *In Search of Jerusalem: Religion and Ethics in The Writings of A.M. Klein*. Montreal: McGill-Queen's University Press 1975.

Freud, Sigmund. *The Complete Psychological Works of Sigmund Freud*. Edited by James Strachey. 24 vols. London: Hogarth 1917–19.

Gerson, Carole. "Some Patterns of Exile in Jewish Writing of the Commonwealth." *Ariel* 13, no. 4 (1982): 103–14.

Giguère, Diane. *Le Temps des jeux*. Montréal: Le Cercle du Livre de France 1961.

Girard, René. *Deceit, Desire, and the Novel*. Baltimore: Johns Hopkins University Press 1965.

Gotlieb, Phyllis. *Ordinary, Moving*. Toronto: Oxford University Press 1969.

Gould, Eric, ed. *The Sin of the Book: Edmond Jabès*. Lincoln: University of Nebraska Press 1985.

Handelman, Susan. *The Slayers of Moses: The Emergence of Rabbinic Interpretation in Modern Literary Theory*. Albany: State University of New York Press 1982.

Hartman, Geoffrey. *Criticism in the Wilderness: The Study of Literature Today*. New Haven, Conn.: Yale University Press 1980.

— "On the Jewish Imagination." *Prooftexts* 5, 3 (1985): 203–21.

—, ed. *Midrash and Literature*. New Haven, Conn.: Yale University Press 1986.

Hoffman, Daniel, ed. *Harvard Guide to Contemporary American Writing*. Cambridge, Mass.: Harvard University Press 1979.

Howe, Irving. *Celebrations and Attacks*. New York: Harcourt Brace Jovanovich 1979.

— *World of Our Fathers*. New York: Harcourt Brace Jovanovich 1976.

Jabès, Edmond. *The Book of Questions*. Trans. Rosmarie Waldrop. Middletown, Conn.: Wesleyan University Press 1976.

Jay, Martin. *Adorno*. Cambridge, Mass.: Harvard University Press 1984.

— *The Dialectical Imagination: A History of the Frankfurt School and the Institute of Social Research 1923–50*. Boston: Little, Brown 1973.

Kafka, Franz. *The Basic Kafka*. Introduction by Erich Heller. New York: Washington Square 1979.

— *Briefe 1902–1924*. New York: Schocken 1961.

— *Parables and Paradoxes*. New York: Schocken 1961.

Kattan, Naim. "A.M. Klein: Modernité et Loyauté." *Journal of Canadian Studies* 19, 2 (1984): 22–6.

— *Dans le désert*. Montréal: Leméac 1974.

— *Farewell, Babylon*. Trans. Sheila Fischman. Toronto: McClelland and Stewart 1976.

— *La mémoire et la promesse*. Montréal: Hurtubise HMH 1978.

— *Reality and Theatre*. Trans. Alan Brown. Toronto: Anansi 1972.

— *La reprise*. Montréal: HMH 1985.

— *Le Rivage*. Montréal: HMH 1979.

— *Le Sable de l'île*. Paris: Gallimard 1981.

— *La Traversée*. Montréal: HMH 1976.

Kertzer, J.M. "Time and Its Victims: The Writing of Matt Cohen." *Essays on Canadian Writing* 17 (1980): 93–101.

Klein, A.M. *Beyond Sambation: Selected Essays and Editorials 1928–1955*. Edited by M.W. Steinberg and Usher Caplan. Toronto: University of Toronto Press 1982.

— *The Collected Poems of A.M. Klein*. Compiled and with an introduction by Miriam Waddington. Toronto: McGraw-Hill Ryerson 1974.

— *The Rocking Chair and Other Poems*. Toronto: Ryerson 1948.

— *The Second Scroll*. Toronto: McClelland and Stewart 1966.

Klinck, Carl, ed. *Literary History of Canada*. Toronto: University of Toronto Press 1965.

Kreisel, Henry. *The Almost Meeting and Other Stories*. Edmonton: NeWest 1981.

— *Another Country*. Edited by Shirley Neuman. Edmonton: NeWest 1985.

— *The Betrayal*. Toronto: McClelland and Stewart 1971.

— *The Rich Man*. Toronto: McClelland and Stewart 1961.

Kriegel, Annie. *Les Juifs et le monde moderne*. Paris: Seuil 1977.

Kroetsch, Robert. "Beyond Nationalism: A Prologue." *Mosaic* 14, 2 (1981): v–xi.

Langer, Lawrence. *The Holocaust and the Literary Imagination*. New Haven, Conn.: Yale University Press 1975.

Layton, Irving. *The Collected Poems of Irving Layton*. Toronto: McClelland and Stewart 1971.

— *The Pole-Vaulter*. Toronto: McClelland and Stewart 1974.

Lecker, Robert. "States of Mind: Henry Kreisel's Novels." *Canadian Literature* 77 (1978): 82–93.

Lévesque, Claude et Christie McDonald, eds. *L'Oreille de l'Autre: Textes et débats avec Jacques Derrida*. Montréal: VLB 1982.

Levine, Norman. *Canada Made Me*. London: Putnam 1958.

— *Champagne Barn*. Harmondsworth: Penguin Books 1984.

— *One Way Ticket*. London: McClelland and Stewart 1961.

— *Selected Stories*. Ottawa: Oberon 1975.

— *She'll Only Drag You Down*. Toronto: Paperjacks 1975.

— *The Tight-Rope Walker*. London: Totem 1950.

Lucas, Alec, ed. *Great Canadian Short Stories*. New York: Dell 1971.

Ludwig, Jack. *Above Ground*. Toronto: McClelland and Stewart 1974.

— *Confusions*. Toronto: McClelland and Stewart 1967.

— *A Woman of Her Age*. Toronto: McClelland and Stewart 1973.

— "You Always Go Home Again." *Mosaic* 3, 3 (1970): 107–11.

Mandel, Eli. "Auschwitz: Poetry of Alienation." *Canadian Literature* 100 (1984): 213–18.

— ed. *Contexts of Canadian Criticism*. Chicago: University of Chicago Press 1978.

— *Crusoe: Poems Selected and New*. Toronto: Anansi 1973.

— *Out of Place*. Don Mills, Ont.: Musson 1977.

— *Stony Plain*. Erin, Ont.: Porcépic 1973.

Mandelstam, Osip. *The Complete Critical Prose and Letters*. Edited by Jane Gary Harris. Ann Arbor: Ardis 1978.

Marcotte, Gilles. *Une Littérature qui se fait*. Montréal: HMH 1968.

Marshall, Tom, ed. *A.M. Klein*. Toronto: Ryerson 1970.

— "Theorems Made Flesh: Klein's Poetic Universe," *Canadian Literature* 25 (1965).

Mayne, Seymour, ed. *The A.M. Klein Symposium*. Ottawa: University of Ottawa Press 1975.

— ed. *Irving Layton: The Poet and His Critics*. Toronto: McGraw-Hill Ryerson 1978.

McLuhan, Marshall. *From Cliché to Archetype*. New York: Viking 1970.

Miller, J. Hillis. "Ariadne's Thread: Repetition and the Narrative Line." *Critical Inquiry*, 3, 1 (1976): 58–77.

Morley, Patricia. *The Immoral Moralists*. Toronto: Clarke Irwin 1972.

Nadel, Ira. *Jewish Writers of North America*. Detroit: Gale 1981.

Neher, André. *The Exile of the Word: From the Silence of the Bible to the Silence of Auschwitz*. Trans. David Maisel. Philadelphia: Jewish Publication Society 1981.

New, Elisa. "Reconsidering Delmore Schwartz." *Prooftexts* 5 (1985): 252–5.

New, W.H., ed. *A Political Art: Essays and Images in Honour of George Woodcock*. Vancouver: University of British Columbia Press 1978.

Olender, Maurice, ed. *Le Racisme. Mythes et sciences*. Brussels: Éditions Complexe 1981.

Ondaatje, Michael. *Leonard Cohen*. Toronto: McClelland and Stewart 1970.

Ower, John. "Sociology, Psychology, and Satire in *The Apprenticeship of Duddy Kravitz*." *Modern Fiction Studies* 22 (1976): 413–28.

Ozick, Cynthia. *Art and Ardor*. New York: Knopf 1983.

Pacey, Desmond. *Ten Canadian Poets*. Toronto: Ryerson 1958.

Perlina, Nina. "Mikhail Bakhtin and Martin Buber: Problems of Dialogic

Imagination." *Studies in Twentieth-Century Literature* 9, 1 (1984): 13–28.

Pollock, Zailig. "The Trial of Jake Hersh." *Journal of Canadian Fiction* 22 (1978): 93–105.

— "From 'Pulver' to 'Portrait': A.M. Klein and the Dialectic," unpublished paper delivered at MLA. New York 1984.

Rabinbach, Anson and Zipes, Jack. "Lessons of the Holocaust." *New German Critique* 19 (1980): 3–7.

Revault d'Allonnes, Olivier. *Musical Variations on Jewish Thought*. Introduction by Harold Bloom. Trans. Judith Greenberg. New York: George Braziller 1984.

Richler, Mordecai. *The Acrobats*. London: André Deutsch 1954.

— *The Apprenticeship of Duddy Kravitz*. Toronto: McClelland and Stewart 1969.

— *Joshua Then and Now*. Toronto: McClelland and Stewart 1980.

— *Son of a Smaller Hero*. Toronto: McClelland and Stewart 1977.

— *St. Urbain's Horseman*. Toronto: McClelland and Stewart 1976.

Robert, Marthe. *As Lonely as Franz Kafka*. Trans. Ralph Manheim. New York: Schocken 1986.

— *From Oedipus to Moses: Freud's Jewish Identity*. Trans. Ralph Manheim. Garden City, N.Y.: Doubleday 1976.

Robin, Régine. *La Québécoite*. Montréal: Québec/Amérique 1983.

Rosenfeld, Alvin. *A Double Dying: Reflections on Holocaust Literature*. Bloomington: Indiana University Press 1980.

Roskies, David. *Against the Apocalypse: Responses to Catastrophe in Modern Jewish Culture*. Cambridge, Mass.: Harvard University Press 1984.

Ross, Malcolm. *Canadian Forum* (January 1952): 234.

Roth, Philip. *Reading Myself and Others*. New York: Penguin 1985.

Scholem, Gershom. *On Jews and Judaism in Crisis*. New York: Schocken 1978.

— *The Messianic Idea in Judaism*. New York: Schocken 1971.

Schwartz, Delmore. *In Dreams Begin Responsibilities*. Norfolk, Conn.: New Directions 1938.

Scobie, Stephen. *Leonard Cohen*. Vancouver: Douglas and McIntyre 1978.

Shechner, Mark. "Saul Bellow and Ghetto Cosmopolitanism." *Modern Jewish Studies Annual* 2 (1978): 33–44.

Sheps, G. David, ed. *Mordecai Richler*. Toronto: McGraw-Hill 1971.

— "Waiting for Joey: The Theme of the Vicarious in *St. Urbain's Horseman*." *Journal of Canadian Fiction* 3, 1 (1974): 83–92.

Sinclair, Gerri and Wolfe, Morris, eds. *The Spice Box: An Anthology of Jewish Canadian Writing*. Toronto: Lester & Orpen Dennys 1981.

Spiro, Solomon. *Tapestry for Designs: Judaic Allusions in The Second Scroll and in the Collected Poems of A.M. Klein*. Vancouver: University of British Columbia Press 1984.

Staines, David, ed. *The Forty-ninth and Other Parallels: Contemporary Canadian Perspectives*. Amherst: University of Massachusetts Press 1986.

Steiner, George. *Language and Silence*. Harmondsworth: Penguin 1969.

Stoehr, Taylor. "Paul Goodman and the New York Jews." *Salmagundi* 66 (1985): 50–103.

Stonehewer, Lila. "Anatomy of Confusion: Jack Ludwig's Evolution." *Canadian Literature* 29 (1966): 34–42.

Taranovsky, Kiril. *Essays on Mandelstam*. Cambridge, Mass.: Harvard University Press 1976.

Ubersfeld, Anne. "The Shape of *Phèdre*." *Poetics Today* 2, 3 (1981): 201–10.

Voix et images 11, 1 (1985): 15–26.

Waddington, Miriam. *A.M. Klein*. Toronto: Copp Clark 1970.

— *Driving Home*. Toronto: Oxford University Press 1972.

— "Exile: A Woman and a Stranger Living out the Canadian Paradox." *Maclean's* 87 (March 1974): 40–43.

— *The Price of Gold*. Toronto: Oxford University Press 1976.

— *Say Yes*. Toronto: Oxford University Press 1969.

Wilson, Edmund. *O Canada*. New York: Farrar, Straus, & Giroux 1965.

Wilson, Milton. "Recent Canadian Verse." *Queen's Quarterly* 66 (1959): 269–73.

Wiseman, Adele. "A Brief Anatomy of an Honest Attempt at a Pithy Statement about the Impact of the Manitoba Environment on My Development as an Artist." *Mosaic* 3, 3 (1970): 98–106.

— *Crackpot*. Toronto: McClelland and Stewart 1974.

— *Old Woman at Play*. Toronto: Clarke, Irwin 1978.

— *The Sacrifice*. Toronto: Macmillan 1968.

Woodcock, George, ed. *The Canadian Novel in the Twentieth Century*. Toronto: McClelland and Stewart 1975.

— *Mordecai Richler*. Toronto: McClelland and Stewart 1966.

— *Odysseus Ever Returning: Essays on Canadian Writers and Writings*. Toronto: McClelland and Stewart 1970.

Index